THE
REFERENCE
SHELF

REPRESENTATIVE

AMERICAN SPEECHES,

1993–1994

Edited by OWEN PETERSON
Professor, Department of Speech Communication
Louisiana State University

THE REFERENCE SHELF

Volume 66 Number 6

THE H. W. WILSON COMPANY

New York   1994

THE REFERENCE SHELF

The books in this series contain reprints of articles, excerpts from books, and addresses on current issues and social trends in the United States and other countries. There are six separately bound numbers in each volume, all of which are generally published in the same calendar year. One number is a collection of recent speeches; each of the others is devoted to a single subject and gives background information and discussion from various points of view, concluding with a comprehensive bibliography that contains books and pamphlets and abstracts of additional articles on the subject. Books in the series may be purchased individually or on subscription.

The Library of Congress has cataloged this serial title as follows:

Representative American speeches. 1937/38–
    New York, H. W. Wilson Co.
    v. 21 cm.—(The Reference shelf)
    Annual.
    Indexes:
        Author index: 1937/38–1959/60, with 1959/60;
        1960/61–1969/70, with 1969/70; 1970/71–1979/80,
        with 1979/80; 1980/81–1989/90, with 1990.
    Editors: 1937/38–1958/59, A. C. Baird.—1959/60—1969/70, L.
    Thonssen.—1970/71–1979/80, W. W. Braden.—1980/81— O.
    Peterson.
    ISSN 0197-6923 Representative American speeches.
        1. Speeches, addresses, etc., American. 2. Speeches, addresses, etc.
    I. Baird, Albert Craig, 1883–1979 ed. II. Thonssen,
    Lester, 1904– ed. III. Braden, Waldo Warder, 1911–1991 ed.
    IV. Peterson, Owen, 1924– ed. V. Series.
PS668.B3   815.5082   38-27962
                                                        MARC-S
Library of Congress [8503r85]rev4

Printed in the United States of America

CONTENTS

V. ARTS AND THE HUMANITIES

VI. INTERNATIONAL POLICY DECISIONS

PREFACE

Following the inauguration of Bill Clinton as forty-second President of the United States on January 20, 1993, the media, anticipating the interest of the public, paid very close attention to the actions and utterances of the new-elected president and his administration. They also gave almost as much attention to his wife, Hillary Rodham Clinton, a new kind of "activist" first lady.

Early skirmishes over presidential appointees to the Supreme Court and high-level government jobs temporarily distracted public attention from the issues that had led to Clinton's election. In time, however, public debate returned to the problems of health care, violence, crime, the economy, poverty, education, drugs, and racism. Both the President and Mrs. Clinton were extremely active in taking their messages to the public in speeches and town meetings throughout the country.

Out of the White House for the first time in twelve years, the Republicans sought to regroup. While some began to campaign actively for the party's presidential nomination in 1996, others became increasingly concerned with what they perceived as the efforts of the Religious Right to gain control of the Republican party through grass-root efforts—often successful—to elect their candidates to office.

Much of the public address that is most influential in shaping opinion never makes the headlines. It occurs in towns and communities and addresses local concerns and problems.

I am indebted to many people for their help in preparing this collection of speeches. I am especially appreciative of the research contributions of Claire Hopson who provided valuable information about the speeches, speakers, audiences, and occasions. Alison Rodriguez has been very helpful in obtaining information and in typing manuscripts, introductions, and biographical sketches. Both Ginger Conrad and Lisa Landry again have been helpful in putting together this volume. My Louisiana State University colleagues and students, Stephen Braden, Stephen Cooper, Gresdna Doty, Michael Eidenmuller, and James Traynham, have also provided helpful suggestions and insights. In addition, I wish to acknowledge the support of my department chairman, Dr. Andrew King.

Others who assisted in various ways in the preparation of this volume are Melissa M. Bender, Senator David Boren, David Carle, Erika Gabrielsen, Kathleen Hilbum, Mike Hill, Gary Krull, Mary Margaret Roberts, Tricia Robin, Barbara Sakamoto, Heather Sarni, Robert Schmuhl, Anne Sesler, Senator Paul Simon, and F. William Smullen III.

OWEN PETERSON

Baton Rouge, Louisiana
June 10, 1994

STATE OF THE UNION ADDRESS[1]
WILLIAM J. CLINTON[2]

One of the most important speeches a President delivers is the annual State of the Union Address in which, traditionally, he reviews the accomplishments of his administration, sets forth major problems requiring action, and proposes legislation. At one time, presidents merely wrote their State of the Union Addresses and sent them to the Congress; only later did presidents actually appear before Congress to read the speech; in recent years the President's address to the Congress has been telecast live nationally.

President William J. Clinton had delivered what could be called a State of the Union Address on February 17, 1993, but since he had been sworn into office only a month before, his speech consisted largely of goals and aspirations. (See *Representative American Speeches, 1992–1993* pp. 24–35 for this address.)

On January 25, 1994, President Clinton appeared before another joint session of Congress to deliver his second (but first formal) State of the Union Address in a nationally televised broadcast. In the year since his inauguration, he had encountered both defeats and victories in his legislative proposals and nominations.

President Clinton entered the House chamber to rousing applause at 9:10 p.m., grabbing hands and patting backs as he made his way to the podium. As has become customary in recent state of the Union addresses, his speech was interrupted frequently by applause, often partisan and predictable.

Response to the speech was generally favorable. Alan Brinkley writing in the *New York Times* (Jan. 26, 1994) observed:

The President was in other words, trying to do more on Tuesday night than boast of his accomplishments and jump-start his health care plan. He did those things effectively, but he was also trying to reclaim from the

[1]Delivered before joint session of congress in the chamber of the United States House of Representatives, Washington, D.C., January 25, 1994, 9:10 p.m.
[2]For biographical note, see Appendix.

Right a moral language that liberals have in recent years largely abdicated. . . No recent president has been better than Bill Clinton at explaining policies."

Anna Quindlen, also in the *New York Times* (Feb. 2, 1994)
wrote: "Bill Clinton gives a good speech. There is in him a bit of
the preacher, some of the earnest high school orator, a little carni-
val barker, and some door-to-door salesman." She concluded that
this formula seemed to work, explaining that before the State of
the Union speech a Gallup poll gave the President a 67% approval
rating, while afterward the percentage rose to 85%.

President Clinton's speech: Mr. Speaker, Mr. President, members of
the 103d Congress, my fellow Americans: I'm not at all sure what
speech is in the Teleprompter tonight, but I hope we can talk
about the state of the Union.

I ask you to begin by recalling the memory of the giant who
presided over this chamber with such force and grace. Tip O'Neill
liked to call himself a man of the House, and he surely was that.
But even more, he was a man of the people, a bricklayer's son who
helped to build the great American middle class. Tip O'Neill
never forgot who he was, where he came from or who sent him
here. Tonight he's smiling down on us for the first time from the
Lord's gallery. But in his honor may we, too, always remember
who we are, where we come from and who sent us here.

If we do that, we will return over and over again to the principle that if we simply give ordinary people equal opportunity,
quality education and a fair shot at the American dream, they will
do extraordinary things.

We gather tonight in a world of changes so profound and
rapid that all nations are tested. Our American heritage has always been to master such change, to use it to expand opportunity
at home and our leadership abroad. But for too long and in too
many ways, that heritage was abandoned, and our country
drifted.

For 30 years, family life in America has been breaking down.
For 20 years, the wages of working people have been stagnant or
declining. For the 12 years of trickle-down economics, we built a
false prosperity on a hollow basis. Our national debt quadrupled.
From 1989 to 1992 we experienced the slowest growth in a half-
century.

For too many families, even when both parents were working,
the American dream has been slipping away.

In 1992, the American people demanded that we change.

A year ago, I asked all of you to join me in accepting responsibility for the future of our country. Well, we did. We replaced drift and deadlock with renewal and reform.

And I want to thank every one of you here who heard the American people, who broke gridlock, who gave them the most successful teamwork between a President and a Congress in 30 years.

This Congress produced a budget that cut the deficit by half a trillion dollars, cut spending and raised income taxes on only the wealthiest Americans. This Congress produced tax relief for millions of low-income workers to reward work over welfare. It produced Nafta. It produced the Brady Bill, now the Brady Law.

And thank you, Jim Brady, for being here, and God bless you, sir.

This Congress produced tax cuts to reduce the taxes of 9 out of 10 small businesses, who used the money to invest more and create more jobs. It produced more research and treatment for AIDS, more childhood immunizations, more support for women's health research, more affordable college loans for the middle class, a new national service program for those who want to give something back to their country and their communities for higher education, a dramatic increase in high-tech investments to move us from a defense to a domestic high-tech economy.

This Congress produced a new law, the motor voter bill, to help millions of people register to vote. It produced family and medical leave.

All passed, all signed into law with not one single veto.

These accomplishments were all commitments I made when I sought this office, and in fairness they all had to be passed by you and this Congress. But I am persuaded that the real credit belongs to the people who sent us here, who pay our salaries, who hold our feet to the fire.

But what we do here is really beginning to change lives. Let me just give you one example. I will never forget what the family and medical leave law meant to just one father I met early one Sunday morning in the White House.

It was unusual to see a family there touring early Sunday morning, but he had his wife and his three children there, one of them in a wheelchair. I came up, and after we had our picture taken and had a little visit, I was walking off, and that man grabbed me by the arm and he said,

"Mr. President, let me tell you something. My little girl here is desperately ill. She's probably not going to make it. But because of the family leave law I was able to take time off to spend with her, the most important time I ever spent in my life without losing my job and hurting the rest of my family. It means more to me than I will ever be able to say. Don't you people up here ever think what you do doesn't make a difference. It does."

Though we are making a difference, our work has just begun. Many Americans still haven't felt the impact of what we've done. The recovery still hasn't touched every community or created enough jobs. Incomes are still stagnant. There's still too much violence and not enough hope in too many places. Abroad, the young democracies we are strongly supporting still face very difficult times and look to us for leadership.

And so tonight, let us resolve to continue the journey of renewal, to create more and better jobs, to guarantee health security for all, to reward welfare work over welfare, to promote democracy abroad and to begin to reclaim our streets from violent crime and drugs and gangs, to renew our own American community.

Last year, we began to put our house in order by tackling the budget deficit that was driving us toward bankruptcy. We cut $255 billion in spending including entitlements and over 340 separate budget items. We froze domestic spending and used honest budget numbers.

Led by the Vice President, we launched a campaign to reinvent government. We cut staff, cut perks, even trimmed the fleet of Federal limousines. After years of leaders whose rhetoric attacked bureaucracy but whose actions expanded it, we will actually reduce it by 252,000 people over the next five years. By the time we have finished, the Federal bureaucracy will be at its lowest point in 30 years.

Because the deficit was so large and because they benefited from tax cuts in the 1980's, we did ask the wealthiest Americans to pay more to reduce the deficit. So on April the 15th, the American people will discover the truth about what we did last year on taxes. Only the top—yeah, listen—the top 1.2 percent of Americans, as I said all along, will pay higher income tax rates. Let me repeat, only the wealthiest 1.2 percent of Americans will face higher income tax rates and no one else will and that is the truth.

Of course, there were, as there always are in politics, naysayers who said this plan wouldn't work, but they were wrong.

In one year, with Nafta, with GATT, with our efforts in Asia and the national export strategy, we did more to open world markets to American products than at any time in the last two generations. That means more jobs and rising living standards for the American people, low deficits, low inflation, low interest rates, low trade barriers and high investments. These are the building blocks of our recovery.

But if we want to take full advantage of the opportunities before us in the global economy, you all know we must do more.

As we reduce defense spending, I ask Congress to invest more in the technologies of tomorrow. Defense conversion will keep us strong militarily and create jobs for our people here at home.

As we protect our environment, we must invest in the environmental technologies of the future, which will create jobs. This year, we will fight for a revitalized Clean Water Act and a Safe Drinking Water Act and a reformed Superfund program.

And the Vice President is right. We must also work with the private sector to connect every classroom, every clinic, every library, every hospital in America into a national information superhighway by the year 2000.

Think of it, instant access. The information will increase productivity, will help to educate our children. It will provide better medical care. It will create jobs. And I call on the Congress to pass legislation to establish that information superhighway this year.

As we expand opportunity and create jobs, no one can be left out. We must continue to enforce fair lending and fair housing and all civil rights law because America will never be complete in its renewal until everyone shares in its bounty.

But we all know, too, we can do all these things, put our economic house in order, expand world trade, target the jobs of the future, guarantee equal opportunity. But if we're honest, we'll all admit that this strategy still cannot work unless we also give our people the education, training and skills they need to seize the opportunities of tomorrow.

We must set tough world-class academic and occupational standards for all our children. And give our teachers and students the tools they need to meet them. Our Goals 2000 proposal will empower individual school districts to experiment with ideas like chartering their schools to be run by private corporations or having more public school choice, to do whatever they wish to do as long as we measure every school by one high standard: Are our children learning what they need to know to compete and win in the global economy?

Goals 2000 links world-class standards to grass-roots reforms, and I hope Congress will pass it without delay.

Our school-to-work initiative will for the first time link school to the world of work, providing at least one year of apprenticeship beyond high school. After all, most of the people we're counting on to build our economic future won't graduate from college. It's time to stop ignoring them and start empowering them.

We must literally transform our outdated unemployment system into a new re-employment system. The old unemployment system just sort of kept you going while you waited for your old job to come back. We've got to have a new system to move people into new and better jobs because most of those old jobs just don't come back, and we know that the only way to have real job security in the future, to get a good job with a growing income, is to have real skills and the ability to learn new ones.

So we've got to streamline today's patchwork of training programs and make them a source of new skill for our people who lose their jobs. Re-employment, not unemployment, must become the centerpiece of our economic renewal. I urge you to pass it in this session of Congress.

And just as we must transform our unemployment system so must we also revolutionize our welfare system. It doesn't work; it defies our values as a nation.

If we value work, we can't justify a system that makes welfare more attractive than work if people are worried about losing their health care. If we value responsibility, we can't ignore the $34 billion in child support absent parents ought to be paying to millions of parents who are taking care of their children. If we value strong families, we can't perpetuate a system that actually penalizes those who stay together.

Can you believe that a child who has a child gets more money from the Government for leaving home than for staying home with a parent or a grandparent? That's not just bad policy, it's wrong, and we ought to change it.

I worked on this problem for years before I became President —with other governors and with members of Congress of both parties, and with the previous Administration of another party. I worked on it with people who were on welfare, lots of them.

And I want to say something to everybody here who cares about this issue: The people who most want to change this system are the people who are dependent on it. They want to get off welfare, they want to go back to work, they want to do right by their kids.

I once had a hearing when I was a Governor and I brought in

people on welfare from all over America who had found their way to work. And the woman from my state who testified was asked this question: "What's the best thing about being off welfare and in a job?"

And without blinking an eye, she looked at the 40 governors, and she said, "When my boy goes to school and they say what does your mother do for a living, he can give an answer."

These people want a better system, and we ought to give it to them.

Last year, we began this. We gave the states more power to innovate because we know that a lot of great ideas come from outside Washington, and many states are already using it.

Then this Congress took a dramatic step: Instead of taxing people with modest incomes into poverty, we helped them to work their way out of poverty by dramatically increasing the earned-income tax credit. It will lift 15 million working families out of poverty, rewarding work over welfare, making it possible for people to be successful workers and successful parents. Now that's real welfare reform.

But there is more to be done.

This spring, I will send you a comprehensive welfare reform bill that builds on the Family Support Act of 1988 and restores the basic values of work and responsibility.

We'll say to teen-agers: If you have a child out of wedlock, we'll no longer give you a check to set up a separate household. We want families to stay together.

Say to absent parents who aren't paying their child support: If you're not providing for your children, we'll garnish your wages, suspend your license, track you across state lines and, if necessary, make some of you work off what you owe.

People who bring children into this world cannot and must not walk away from them.

But to all those who depend on welfare, we should offer ultimately a simple compact: We'll provide the support, the job training, the child care you need for up to two years; but after that, anyone who can work must—in the private sector wherever possible, in community service if necessary. That's the only way we'll ever make welfare what it ought to be: a second chance, not a way of life.

I know it will be difficult to tackle welfare reform in 1994 at the same time we tackle health care. But let me point out I think it is inevitable and imperative.

It is estimated that one million people are on welfare today, because it's the only way they can get health care coverage for their children. Those who choose to leave welfare for jobs without health benefits—and many entry-level jobs don't have health benefits—find themselves in the incredible position of paying taxes that help to pay for health care coverage for those who made the other choice to stay on welfare. No wonder people leave work and go back to welfare—to get health care coverage.

We've got to solve the health care problem to have real welfare reform.

So this year, we will make history by reforming the health care system. And I would say to you—all of you, my fellow public servants—this is another issue where the people are way ahead of the politicians. That may not be popular with either party, but it happens to be the truth.

You know the First Lady has received now almost a million letters from people all across America and from all walks of life. I'd like to share just one of them with you.

Richard Anderson of Reno, Nevada, lost his job and with it his health insurance. Two weeks later, his wife, Judy, suffered a cerebral aneurysm. He rushed her to the hospital where she stayed in intensive care for 21 days.

The Andersons' bills were over $120,000. Although Judy recovered and Richard went back to work at $8 an hour, the bills were too much for them and they were literally forced into bankruptcy.

"Mrs. Clinton," he wrote to Hillary, "no one in the United States of America should have to lose everything they've worked for all their lives because they were unfortunate enough to become ill."

It was to help the Richard and Judy Andersons of America that the First Lady and so many others have worked so hard and so long on this health care reform issue. We owe them our thanks and our action.

I know there are people here who say there's no health care crisis. Tell it to Richard and Judy Anderson. Tell it to the 58 million Americans who have no coverage at all for some time each year. Tell it to the 81 million Americans with those pre-existing conditions. Those folks are paying more or they can't get insurance at all, or they can't ever change their jobs because they or someone in their family has one of those pre-existing conditions.

Tell it to the small businesses burdened by skyrocketing costs of insurance. Most small businesses cover their employees and they pay on average 35 percent more in premiums than big businesses or government.

Or tell it to the 76 percent of insured Americans, three out of four whose policies have lifetime limits, that means they can find themselves without any coverage at all just when they need it the most.

So if any of you believe there's no crisis, you tell it to those people because I can't.

There are some people who literally do not understand the impact of this problem on people's lives. And all you have to do is go out and listen to them. Just go talk to them anywhere in any Congressional district in this country. They're Republicans and Democrats and independents; it doesn't have a lick to do with party. They think we don't get it, and it's time we show them that we do get it.

From the day we began, our health care initiative has been designed to strengthen what is good about our health care system: the world's best health care professionals, cutting-edge research and wonderful research institutions, Medicare for older Americans. None of this, none of it should be put at risk.

But we're paying more and more money for less and less care. Every year fewer and fewer Americans even get to choose their doctors. Every year doctors and nurses spend more time on paperwork and less time with patients because of the absolute bureaucratic nightmare the present system has become. This system is riddled with inefficiency, with abuse, with fraud and everybody knows it.

In today's health care system, insurance companies call the shots. They pick whom they cover and how they cover them. They can cut off your benefits when you need your coverage the most. They are in charge.

What does it mean? It means every night millions of well-insured Americans go to bed just an illness, an accident or a pink slip away from having no coverage or financial ruin. It means every morning millions of Americans go to work without any health insurance at all, something the workers in no other advanced country in the world do. It means that every year more and more hard-working people are told to pick a new doctor because their boss has had to pick a new plan and countless others turn down better jobs because they know if they take the better job they'll lose their health insurance.

If we just let the health care system continue to drift, our country will have people with less care, fewer choices and higher bills. Now, our approach protects the quality of care and people's choices.

It builds on what works today in the private sector to expand employer-based coverage, to guarantee private insurance for every American. And I might say, employer-based private insurance for every American was proposed 20 years ago by President Richard Nixon to the United States Congress. It was a good idea then, and it's a better idea today.

Why do we want guaranteed private insurance? Because right now, 9 out of 10 people who have insurance get it through their employers. And that should continue. And if your employer is providing good benefits at reasonable prices, that should continue, too. That ought to make the Congress and the President feel better.

Our goal is health insurance everybody can depend on, comprehensive benefits that cover preventive care and prescription drugs, health premiums that don't just explode when you get sick or you get older; the power no matter how small your business is to choose dependable insurance at the same competitive rates governments and big business get today; one simple form for people who are sick, and most of all, the freedom to choose a plan and the right to choose your own doctor.

Our approach protects older Americans. Every plan before the Congress proposes to slow the growth of Medicare. The difference is this: We believe those savings should be used to improve health care for senior citizens. Medicare must be protected, and it should cover prescription drugs, and we should take the first steps in covering long-term care.

To those who would cut Medicare without protecting seniors, I say the solution to today's squeeze on middle-class working people's health care is not to put the squeeze on middle-class retired people's health care. We can do better than that.

When it's all said and done, it's pretty simple to me. Insurance ought to mean what it used to mean: You pay a fair price for security, and when you get sick, health care is always there, no matter what.

Along with the guarantee of health security, we all have to admit, too, there must be more responsibility on the part of all of us in how we use this system. People have to take their kids to get immunized. We should all take advantage of preventive care. We must all work together to stop the violence that explodes our emergency rooms. We have to practice better health habits, and we can't abuse the system.

And those who don't have insurance under our approach will get coverage, but they'll have to pay something for it, too. The minority of businesses that provide no insurance at all and in so doing shift the cost of the care of their employees to others should contribute something. People who smoke should pay more for a pack of cigarettes.

Everybody can contribute something if we want to solve the health care crisis. There can't be any more something for nothing. It will not be easy, but it can be done.

Now in the coming months, I hope very much to work with both Democrats and Republicans to reform a health care system by using the market to bring down costs and to achieve lasting health security. But if you look at history, we see that for 60 years this country's tried to reform health care. President Roosevelt tried. President Truman tried. President Nixon tried. President Carter tried.

Every time the special interests were powerful enough to defeat them. But not this time.

I know that facing up to these interests will require courage; it will raise critical questions about the way we finance our campaigns and how lobbyists yield their influence.

The work of change, frankly, will never get any easier until we limit the influence of well-financed interests who profit from this current system. So I also must now call on you to finish the job both houses began last year by passing tough and meaningful campaign finance reform and lobbying reform legislation this year.

You know, my fellow Americans, this is really a test for all of us. The American people provide those of us in government service with terrific health care benefits at reasonable cost. We have health care; it's always there. I think we need to give every hardworking, tax-paying American the same health care security they have already given to us.

I want to make this very clear. I am open—as I have said repeatedly—to the best ideas of concerned members of both parties. I have no special brief for any specific approach even in our own bill except this: If you send me legislation that does not guarantee every American private health insurance that can never be taken away, you will force me to take this pen, veto the legislation and we'll come right back here and start all over again.

But I don't think that's going to happen. I think we're ready to act now. I believe that you're ready to act now. And if you're ready to guarantee every American the same health care that you have, health care that can never be taken away, now—not next year or the year after—now is the time to stand with the people who sent us here. Now.

As we take these steps together to renew our strength at home, we cannot turn away from our obligation to renew our leadership abroad. This is a promising moment. Because of the agreements we have reached this year—last year—Russia's strategic nuclear missiles soon will no longer be pointed at the United States nor will we point ours at them.

Instead of building weapons in space, Russian scientists will help us to build the international space station.

Of course, there are still dangers in the world: rampant arms proliferation, bitter regional conflicts, ethnic and nationalist tensions in many new democracies, severe environmental degradation the world over and fanatics to seek to cripple the world's cities with terror.

As the world's greatest power, we must, therefore, maintain our defenses and our responsibilities. This year we secured indictments against terrorists and sanctions against those who harbor them. We worked to promote environmentally sustainable economic growth. We achieved agreements with Ukraine, with Belarus, with Kazakhstan to eliminate completely their nuclear arsenals. We're working to achieve a Korean peninsula free of nuclear weapons. We will seek early ratification of a treaty to ban chemical weapons worldwide. And earlier today we joined with over 30 nations to begin negotiations on a comprehensive ban to stop all nuclear testing.

But nothing, nothing, is more important to our security than our nation's armed forces. We honor their contributions, including those who are carrying out the longest humanitarian airlift in history in Bosnia, those who will complete their mission in Somalia this year and their brave comrades who gave their lives there.

Our forces are the finest military our nation has ever had. And I have pledged that as long as I am President they will remain the best-equipped, the best-trained and the best-prepared fighting force on the face of the earth.

Last year, I proposed a defense plan that maintains our post-cold-war security at a lower cost. This year, many people urged us to cut our defense spending further to pay for other government programs. I said no.

The budget I sent to Congress draws the line against further defense cuts. It protects the readiness and quality of our forces. Ultimately, the best strategy is to do that. We must not cut defense further. I hope the Congress without regard to party will support that position.

Ultimately—ultimately the best strategy to insure our security and to build a durable peace is to support the advance of democracy elsewhere. Democracies don't attack each other; they make better trading partners and partners in diplomacy. That is why we have supported, you and I, the democratic reformers in Russia and in the other states of the former Soviet bloc. I applaud the bipartisan support this Congress provided last year for our initiatives to help Russia, Ukraine and the other states through their epic transformations.

Our support of reform must combine patience for the enormity of the task and vigilance for our fundamental interests and values. We will continue to urge Russia and the other states to press ahead with economic reforms, and we will seek to cooperate with Russia to solve regional problems while insisting that if Russian troops operate in neighboring states, they do so only when those states agree to their presence and in strict accord with international standards.

But we must also remember as these nations chart their own futures—and they must chart their own futures—how much more secure and more prosperous our own people will be if democratic and market reforms succeed all across the former Communist bloc.

Our policy has been to support that move, and that has been the policy of the Congress. We should continue it.

That is why I went to Europe earlier this month—to work with our European partners, to help to integrate all the former Communist countries into a Europe that has the possibility of becoming unified for the first time in its entire history—its entire history—based on the simple commitments of all nations in Europe to democracy, to free markets and to respect for existing borders.

With our allies, we have created a partnership for peace that invites states from the former Soviet bloc and other non-NATO members to work with NATO in military cooperation. When I met with Central Europe's leaders, including Lech Walesa and

Vaclav Havel, men who put their lives on the line for freedom, I told them that the security of their region is important to our country's security.

This year we must also do more to support democratic renewal and human rights and sustainable development all around the world. We will ask Congress to ratify the new GATT accord. We will continue standing by South Africa as it works its way through its bold and hopeful and difficult transition to democracy.

We will convene a summit of the Western Hemisphere's democratic leaders from Canada to the tip of South America, and we will continue to press for the restoration of true democracy in Haiti.

And as we build a more constructive relationship with China, we must continue to insist on clear signs of improvement in that nation's human rights record.

We will also work for new progress toward the Middle East peace. Last year, the world watched Yitzhak Rabin and Yasir Arafat at the White House when they had their historic handshake of reconciliation. But there is a long, hard road ahead, and on that road I am determined that I and our Administration will do all we can to achieve a comprehensive and lasting peace for all the people of the region.

Now there are some in our country who argue that with the cold war America should turn its back on the rest of the world. Many around the world were afraid we would do just that.

But I took this office on a pledge that had no partisan tinge to keep our nation secure by remaining engaged in the rest of the world, and this year because of our work together—enacting Nafta, keeping our military strong and prepared, supporting democracy abroad—we have reaffirmed America's leadership, America's engagement, and as a result, the American people are more secure than they were before.

But while Americans are more secure from threats abroad, I think we all know that in many ways we are less secure from threats here at home. Every day the national peace is shattered by crime. In Petaluma, Calif., an innocent slumber party gives way to agonizing tragedy for the family of Polly Klaas. An ordinary train ride on Long Island ends in a hail of 9-millimeter rounds. A tourist in Florida is nearly burned alive by bigots simply because he is black. Right here in our nation's capital a brave young man named Jason White, a policeman, the son and grandson of policemen, is ruthlessly gunned down.

Violent crime and the fear it provokes are crippling our society, limiting personal freedom and fraying the ties that bind us. The crime bill before Congress gives you a chance to do something about it, a chance to be tough and smart.

What does that mean? Let me begin by saying I care a lot about this issue. Many years ago when I started out in public life I was the Attorney General of my state. I served as the Governor for a dozen years. I know what it's like to sign laws increasing penalties, to build more prison cells, to carry out the death penalty. I understand this issue. And it is not a simple thing.

First, we must recognize that most violent crimes are committed by a small percentage of criminals, who too often break the laws even when they're on parole. Now those who commit crimes should be punished. And those who commit repeated violent crimes should be told when you commit a third violent crime you will be put away and put away for good. Three strikes, and you are out.

Second, we must take serious steps to reduce violence and prevent crime beginning with more police officers and more community policing. We know—we know right now that police who work the streets, know the folks, have the respect of the neighborhood kids, focus on high crime areas—we know that they are more likely to prevent crime as well as catch criminals. Look at the experience of Houston, where the crime rate dropped 17 percent in one year when that approach was taken.

Here tonight is one of those community policemen, a brave young detective, Kevin Jett, whose beat is eight square blocks in one of the toughest neighborhoods in New York. Every day he restores some sanity and safety, and a sense of values and connection to the people whose lives he protects. I'd like to ask him to stand up and be recognized tonight. Thank you, sir.

You will be given a chance to give the children of this country, the law-abiding working people of this country—and don't forget, in the toughest neighborhoods in this country, in the highest-crime neighborhoods in this country, the vast majority of people get up every day and obey the law, pay their taxes, do their best to raise their kids—they deserve people like Kevin Jett. And you're going to be given a chance to give the American people another 100,000 of them, well-trained, and I urge you to do it.

You have before you crime legislation which also establishes a police corps to encourage young people to get an education, pay it off by serving as police officers, which encourages retiring military personnel to move into police forces, an inordinate resource for our country. One which has a safe-schools provision which will give our young people the chance to walk to school in safety and to be in school in safety instead of dodging bullets. These are important things.

The third thing we have to do is to build on the Brady Bill, the Brady Law. To take further steps—to take further steps to keep guns out of the hands of criminals.

I want to say something about this issue. Hunters must always be free to hunt. Law-abiding adults should always be free to own guns and protect their homes. I respect that part of our culture; I grew up in it.

But I want to ask the sportsmen and others who lawfully own guns to join us in this campaign to reduce gun violence. I say to you: I know you didn't create this problem, but we need your help to solve it. There is no sporting purpose on earth that should stop the United States Congress from banishing assault weapons that out-gun police and cut down children.

Fourth, we must remember that drugs are a factor in an enormous percentage of crimes. Recent studies indicate, sadly, that drug use is on the rise again among our young people. The crime bill contains—all the crime bills contain more money for drug treatment for criminal addicts and boot camps for youthful offenders, that include incentives to get off drugs and to stay off drugs.

Our Administration's budget, with all its cuts, contains a large increase in funding for drug treatment and drug education. You must pass them both; we need them desperately.

My fellow Americans, the problem of violence is an American problem. It has no partisan or philosophical element. Therefore, I urge you to find ways as quickly as possible to set aside partisan differences and pass a strong, smart, tough crime bill.

But further, I urge you to consider this: As you demand tougher penalties for those who choose violence, let us also remember how we came to this sad point. In our toughest neighborhoods, on our meanest streets, in our poorest rural areas, we have seen a stunning and simultaneous breakdown of community, family and work—the heart and soul of civilized society.

This has created a vast vacuum which has been filled by violence and drugs and gangs. So I ask you to remember that even as we say no to crime, we must give people, especially our young people, something to say yes to.

Many of our initiatives from job training, to welfare reform, to health care, to national service will help to rebuild distressed communities, to strengthen families, to provide work. But more needs to be done. That's what our community empowerment agenda is all about, challenging businesses to provide more investment through empowerment zones; insuring banks will make loans in the same communities their deposits come from; passing legislation to unleash the power of capital through community development banks to create jobs; opportunity and hope where they're needed most.

But I think you know that to really solve this problem we'll all have to put our heads together, leave our ideological armor aside and find some new ideas to do even more. And let's be honest, we all know something else, too. Our problems go way beyond the reach of government. They're rooted in the loss of values, in the disappearance of work and the breakdown of our families and our communities.

My fellow Americans, we can cut the deficit, create jobs, promote democracy around the world, pass welfare reform and health care, pass the toughest crime bill in history and still leave too many of our people behind. The American people have got to want to change from within if we're going to bring back work and family and community.

We cannot renew our country when within a decade more than half of the children will be born into families where there has been no marriage. We cannot renew this country when 13-year-old boys get semiautomatic weapons to shoot 9-year-olds for kicks. We can't renew our country when children are having children and the fathers walk away as if the kids don't amount to anything. We can't renew the country when our businesses eagerly look for new investments and new customers abroad but ignore those people right here at home who would give anything to have their jobs and would gladly buy their products if they had the money to do it.

We can't renew our country unless more of us, I mean all of us, are willing to join churches and the other good citizens, people like all the—like ministers I've worked with over the years or the priests and the nuns I met at Our Lady of Help in East Los Angeles or my good friend Tony Campolo in Philadelphia. Unless we're willing to work with people like that, people who are saving kids, adopting schools, making streets safer. All of us can do that. We can't renew our country until we realize that governments don't raise children, parents do.

Parents who know their children's teachers and turn off the

television and help with the homework and teach their kids right from wrong. Those kind of parents can make all the difference. I know, I had one.

And I'm telling you we have got to stop pointing our fingers at these kids who have no future and reach our hands out to them. Our country needs it, we need it, and they deserve it.

And so I say to you tonight, let's give our children a future. Let us take away their guns and give them books. Let us overcome their despair and replace it with hope. Let us by our example teach them to obey the law, respect our neighbors and cherish our values.

Let us weave these sturdy threads into a new American community that can once more stand strong against the forces of despair and evil, because everybody has a chance to walk into a better tomorrow.

Oh, there will be naysayers who fear that we won't be equal to the challenges of this time. But this misreads our history, our heritage, even today's headlines. All of those things tell us we can and we will overcome any challenge.

When the earth shook and fires raged in California, when I saw the Mississippi deluge the farmlands of the Midwest in a 500-year flood, when the century's bitterest cold swept from North Dakota to Newport News, it seemed as though the world itself was coming apart at the seams. But the American people? They just came together. They rose to the occasion, neighbor helping neighbor, strangers risking life and limb to save total strangers, showing the better angels of our nature.

Let us not reserve the better angels only for natural disasters, leaving our deepest and most profound problems to petty political fighting.

Let us instead be true to our spirit, facing facts, coming together, bringing hope and moving forward.

Tonight, my fellow Americans, we are summoned to answer a question as old as the Republic itself: What is the state of our union? It is growing stronger, but it must be stronger still. With your help and God's help it will be.

Thank you, and God bless America.

AN ECONOMIC SECURITY PLATFORM[1]
Bill Bradley[2]

A major concern of many American workers in 1993–1994 was the condition economic insecurity brought about by the end of the Cold War, an explosion in world markets, the knowledge revolution, the mushrooming national debt, and the proposed North American Free Trade Agreement.

Recognizing these uncertainties and fears, Senator Bill Bradley set out to start a debate within the government about how to address them. Reportedly, Senator Bradley spent several weeks preparing the address. Coming from a senior member of the Senate Finance Committee and one of President Clinton's most reliable supporters in the Senate, the speech could be expected to attract national attention, which it did.

Bradley delivered the address to the Center for National Policy at a monthly "Newsmakers" luncheon in the Hyatt Regency Hotel on Capital Hill in Washington, D.C. at 12:00 noon on October 7, 1993. The Center for National Policy is a Washington "think tank" that conducts research on major issues. Its policies are generally regarded as liberal. Approximately 150 members of the Center, together with supporters, ambassadors, and Clinton staff, attended the luncheon.

Senator Bill Bradley's speech: George Fatemi went to work for a major U.S. steel company when he was 19. He lost that job when big steel couldn't compete with new technology from Japan during the 1970s. He got another job with a glass company, but they laid him off during the 1982 recession. In both cases, he couldn't take his pension benefits with him because he hadn't worked long enough to vest. George then hooked up with a defense contractor making missiles until 1992, when the defense cutbacks axed him. Three jobs and three layoffs. George was left with a minuscule pension and payments of $460 a month if he wants to continue health coverage for his family.

[1]Delivered to the Center for National Policy at 12:00 noon, October 7, 1993, in the Hyatt Regency Hotel, Washington, D.C.
[2]For biographical note, see Appendix.

Five years ago, Mary and Charles Jones lived the American dream in New Jersey. Mary did marketing for AT&T; Charles was a lawyer with IBM. They had a house in the suburbs, two children, and a three-week family vacation every August. Then both of them lost their jobs.

Today Charles works for a small business selling computer software, and Mary consults, but not often. No more vacations, no health benefits from the jobs. Mary's father lost his pension benefits due to an LBO and a loophole in the pension law. The two kids are now in high school, and the oldest wants to go to MIT, but the family can't afford it.

Louise Pearl is a single mother who works as a secretary to the president of a construction firm. The office construction boom of the early 1980s has turned into a construction depression in the '90s, and in the last 18 months, the firm has shrunk from 46 workers to 15. If the company goes under, Louise will need training to get a new job, but she won't have the money to pay for it.

These composite portraits of Louise Pearl, George Fatemi, and the Joneses are not unusual. There are millions of Americans who find economic security an unattainable dream. It is as if Americans are adrift on a gigantic river of economic transformation that carries away everything that resists the swirling currents of its mighty flow. Americans are being buffeted by new economic forces as surely as the communities along the Mississippi last summer were being hit by a 100-year flood. Not since the age of democratic revolution coincided with the industrial revolution, nearly 200 years ago, has the river of economic change flowed so powerfully. What makes the experience so hard is that we have to cope with four fundamental transformations taking place in the world simultaneously.

The first is the end of the age of ideology. With the fall of Marxist-Leninist communism and the triumph of democratic liberalism, the content of the U.S.-Russian conflict disappears.

Yet peace doesn't reign. Ask any ethnic or religious warrior in Bosnia, or Georgia, or Tibet, or Northern Ireland. But conflict has a less cataclysmic implication. The garrison state of the Soviet Union, with its missiles aimed at the United States, has evolved into a nationalist Russia whose hopes of meeting human needs take precedence over its bombast in preparing for Armageddon.

With peace breaking out, people feel more secure, and the arsenals of the United States and Russia can be dramatically reduced. But for millions of people who work in the defense sector, peace has an even more personal consequence than freedom from first strike. It has cost them their jobs. In 1987, there were 7.2 million people working in what President Eisenhower called the military-industrial complex. In 1992, it was 6.3 million, and in 1997, it will be 4.4 million. The economic impact of the West's triumph is the downsizing of an entire sector of our economy.

The second transformation is the explosion of world markets. There are three billion more people in the world market today than just ten years ago, and most of them will become our customers by the turn of the century. That means thousands of jobs.

During the last decade, not only have communist societies crumbled and their replacements opened up to the world, but authoritarian and protectionist regimes in Latin America and Asia have also fallen. Instead of billions of people living in closed economies, unwilling to trade and bent on producing everything they need domestically, with a politics that argues over which subsidies go to which monopolists, country after country— Poland, Mexico, Argentina, India, Vietnam—has liberalized economically. They are encouraging exports, accepting imports, and seeking capital worldwide.

A market of three billion more people represents billions of potential sales of computers, cars, Coca-colas, and CDs, as well as capital goods to electrify a continent, to build more ports and highways, to equip new hospitals, and to build new homes. But it also means a billion more workers ready to challenge our own workers in the production of tradeable goods. Clearly, some American workers will lose their jobs. But far more will be created by a competition that not only provides higher quality and lower prices to consumers, but also demands greater efficiency from our own companies and more complex skills from our work force.

Not since the end of the 19th century has the world economy been as open or the potential for worldwide human betterment through open markets been as great. Since political openness usually follows economic openness, democracy's roots are extending deeper and deeper into more societies than ever before. And yet there are dangers too.

In the early 20th century, ethnic tension and nationalist fervor snuffed out the flame of hope represented by open trade. Both irrational impulses remain alive today. Ethnic tension threatens to engulf more and more nations in costly conflict: witness Bosnia. Nationalistic fervor in its Ross Perot-Pat Buchanan form calls for protection from international competition and advocates trade only with developed countries "like us." Witness the debate over NAFTA.

It's possible that we will be closed off to this wider market and not accept the challenge, but to do so has consequences: a lower standard of living, a fraying social fabric, and a refusal to lead in a new world.

The third transformation is driven by man's advancing ability to shape his world. It is the knowledge revolution. Through knowledge applied to telecommunications, we communicate without travel. Through knowledge we combine elements in new ways to make materials that don't exist in nature to do jobs with less energy and less assembly. Through knowledge we transform genetic material and worry less about pest control.

For centuries, the determinants of national wealth have been capital, natural resources, and an abundance of labor. Today none of them is as important as knowledge, which has changed the production process and multiplied the types of services available. Applied knowledge can make society cleaner, wealthier, and more humane.

Manual labor serving a machine, whether it's in Detroit or Kuala Lumpur can never produce as efficiently as a computer serving man. It's just that simple. That's why in the future the biggest economic problems will be found in countries where the most unskilled workers live.

America is further through that revolution than most people imagine. Manufacturing remains essential to our economy. We continue to make things, but we do it with fewer people. When George Fatemi lost his job at the steel company, there were 721,000 steel workers in America, and today there are only 374,000. But those 374,000 are highly efficient. Partly as a result, imports today supply only 15 percent of the U.S. market. This story is being told over and over again in our economy as companies in order to compete become leaner, producing more with less.

To resist the trend toward knowledge-based production is to give the future to those in other countries who capitalize on the inexorable transformation. Yet the challenge to our economy is clear. If we produce the same product with less labor, then there have to be more, not fewer, jobs, producing more new products or serving more new needs.

An exploding knowledge sector built on a sound economic foundation can create these jobs, but the skill requirements will be higher. A worker tomorrow will require a substantial amount of formal knowledge and the capacity and opportunity for continuous learning. Successful work careers will exist only for those who can match what they know to what needs to be done. The days of the 40-year career on the assembly line of one company making one product are over. Sequential jobs with different companies, even sequential careers, will be the norm.

The fourth transformation has to do with the connection between economic growth and debt. America is mired in a five-year period of low growth. After the collapse of 1980s' false optimism, people are reluctant to spend or to invest. Usually a government would jump start an economy out of recession either by lowering interest rates, or by giving a tax cut or spending more money on government projects. But interest rates are at a 30-year low, and increasing the deficit to stimulate the economy risks a no-confidence vote from millions of world-wide investors. In short, the gigantic national debt has robbed us of savings just when we need them most for new investment and new training.

America got hooked on the narcotic of debt in the 1980s. It became our worst addiction. Between 1980 and 1987 consumer credit increased 95 percent. Government debt went from $800 billion in 1980 to $4 trillion in 1992. Personal debt began to decrease in the early 1990s as companies and individuals slammed on the brakes. Government kept spending. As 1993 began, the debt over the next five years was expected to go from $4 trillion to $5.4 trillion, and even after the 1993 Clinton budget, it will go to $4.9 trillion. The thing that most appalls me is the public and social policy consequences that these numbers imply. The General Accounting Office told me that if nothing were done about the debt, by 2020 every American's income would be 40 percent less than it otherwise would be. We will get poorer as we send more and more of our tax dollars to creditors and invest less and less in job-creating, wealth-producing assets. The existence of the debt literally transforms our prospects. It mortgages our children's future and robs them of the expectation that hard work usually yields reward.

So there they are: the end of the ideological cold war, the explosion of world markets, the knowledge revolution, and the gigantic debt. We feel so unprepared, even disoriented, by these four transformations, because no one predicted their cascading impacts on our prospects. No one told us, not even the best of our intelligence analysts, that the Soviet Union would disappear without a whisper and leave us little need for a vast military machine. No one told us that Adam Smith would replace Marx on the third world's best-seller list. No one told us that companies resisting change would stumble even if their names were AT&T or IBM. No one told us that gigantic American budget deficits would be financed gladly by the rich of the world and that Americans would continue merrily and irresponsibly consuming our future. No one told us that we could spend more than anyone else in the world on health care and still have millions with no coverage. No one told us that just as we educated more Americans to college level than any other country, the mediocre quality of many American elementary and high schools would be apparent to all. No one told us that the Japanese would be accepted into ASEAN or that China would be burgeoning forward to become an economic superpower. No one told us that the Europeans of Brussels could not displace the French of Paris, the British of London, and the Germans of Berlin as the centers of tribal action, political and economic drama.

Each of these events has shaped what we produce, how we trade, and pushed us further into uncharted economic waters, with more workers anxious that it will be their job that the swirling river of economic transformation will sweep away next. To survive, we must lighten our load, fix our steering wheel, and get used to living without the certainties of another time. General Motors, General Electric, Dupont no longer assure lifetime jobs. Natural resources won't be decisive in the coming economic competition. Workers can't be seen as simply discardable cogs in a machine. The cheap labor of larger and larger numbers of unskilled workers won't produce economic growth or generate higher productivity any place in the world for long. Military might won't provide substantial benefits for an economy. A democracy in time of peace and in absence of clear threat won't ever spend $310 billion on defense again. Ethnic and racial tension can't be viewed as irrelevant to the economic potential of our workers or the collective capacity of our citizens.

What we've always assumed about each generation of Americans having a higher standard of living is not guaranteed. New realities can prevail. Our leaders must be honest with us, and we must be honest with ourselves. Above all, we have to resist the temptation to believe that the only course is to hold on to what we have and how we do things now. To hold on means to lose, as individuals, as companies, and as a nation. No matter how good a worker George Fatemi was in his third career, when the missile orders stopped, so did his job. The Joneses who worked for IBM and AT&T couldn't have secure employment when IBM failed to see the technology shift, and AT&T, with deregulation, stood unprepared for worldwide competition. To believe that a labor-intensive apparel shop can compete with a modernized factory is, however well-intentioned, a delusion. The idea that we should trade only with countries "like us" of equivalent living standards ignores that other nations "*like us*" have absolutely no intention of limiting their trade and economic interaction *to us*. Underfunded pensions; deficits that can only be financed abroad; educational concepts that presume formal learning ends at 24; personal behavior that leads to skyrocketing health care costs: all of these cannot continue. If we hold onto these misconceptions and destructive patterns, we risk awaking one morning like a town after the river's flood recedes to find our communities broken and the health of our families failing.

For those in the midst of the turmoil, our heart must go out to them. They aren't interested in theories. They have to worry about putting food on the table and a roof over the heads of their families. For too long policy makers have ignored their needs and mistaken their loyalty for indifference. But the morning after, when the tears of compassion dry up, what people want most is a direction to follow that makes sense, a path to take that leads to a job. We must get about the business of dealing with our reality, not hiding from it or denying it or cursing it.

Without minimizing the difficulty, we need to see these transformations as part of a consistent and continuing American saga. We always were a nation suspicious of ideology (as Alexis D'Toqueville said). We always did seek competition to protect liberty (as James Madison stressed). We have always sought to be recognized, not for our muscle, but for our wit and agility and values (as Thomas Jefferson argued). We hate being in debt and desperately want to pay our own way (as Andrew Jackson demanded). These transformations are then "in character" for America (as they are not for much of the world). They are at once fundamental to the American crisis and at the same time a key to America's renewal. We simply have to know where we want to go and to build a platform that can allow us successfully to navigate the currents of our present economic waters.

I believe government has a role in this time of transformation. It must assure all Americans access to an "economic security platform." Given our gigantic national debt, we must build this platform with precision and hard-headedness, conserving our resources at every juncture. As platform designers, we must not respond to the siren calls of political expediency or short-term palliatives; we must steer between too many government interventions, subsidies, and entitlements and too few to liberate Americans from feeling so vulnerable and paralyzed. We must establish a set of initiatives that does not hobble the efficiency of market forces, but liberates our workers so they can realize their potential.

Who among us doesn't believe that Mary and Charles Jones have a lot more to contribute to our economy than their current employment would allow? Can we afford to let a worker like George Fatemi not work? Does any of us believe that our economy should be deprived of Louise Pearl's talents just because she cannot afford to update her 1970's skills for a 1990s' job?

What specifically do I mean by an economic security platform? My economic security platform has three planks. It consists of, and is limited to, a guarantee of basic health coverage, an opportunity for lifetime education, and a guarantee of pension security.

First is health care. It should be available to all Americans. If any American loses a job, changes a job, grows old, experiences a serious illness or a difficult childbirth, confronts an injury to a spouse, or needs regular checkups, that American should be guaranteed access to quality health care. And we simply must control its costs. We cannot compete economically if we pay a health "tariff" of 4 to 7 percent more of our GNP for health costs than in other developed countries. This premium amounts to a giant health tax on all our goods.

Second is lifetime education. We can't survive with 40 percent of Americans with high wages, 40 percent with low wages, and 20 percent unemployable. The only sure way that America will guarantee its workers higher wages is if they have higher skills. The more American workers with superior talents, the higher productivity will be, and the higher worker productivity, the faster the economy will grow.

Given the demands of a knowledge economy, the opportunity to advance and learn anew must be available for workers at every stage of a career. Lifetime education means counseling, training, and relocation. Counseling means making it clear that sequential careers will be the norm; that changing a job usually won't be the worker's fault and might not even be the company's; that is just in the nature of things in an economy that rewards innovation during a time of rapid change. Counseling also means deciding on the skill to be obtained and determining where to get it. Training means actually learning a new skill and using government financial assistance to help pay for it. Relocation means finding a new job that employs the newly acquired skills. Access to lifetime education can be assured with income contingent self-reliance loans where any American can get a loan if he or she agrees to pay a small percentage of future income to the government until it's repaid. Other times access amounts simply to assuring adequate information and coordinating the 123 existing education programs so that people know how to apply for them.

Third is pension security. One hallmark of the new age must be labor mobility. That means that when someone works and gets pension benefits, they should be portable. The worker should have his or her benefits guaranteed, companies should fund their pensions adequately, and government should assure that promises of income security for the aged are kept. The trends toward defined contribution plans and stagnating participation levels challenge this promise, as does the state of the Pension Benefit Guarantee Corporation. Greater participation in the system would provide more security and increase our private savings rate.

Our current patchwork pension system is failing large numbers of our workers. Too many are facing uncertainty in their later years. One sharp correction in the stock market, and our current federal insurance program would be in grave danger and the budget deficit would skyrocket. With the lessons of the S&L debacle in mind, we need to strengthen the pension system today rather than wait for it to falter tomorrow. It may take public funds; it will at the very least require government ingenuity. But we must begin.

With an economic security platform, people can live with less anxiety because job loss won't be fraught with the danger of catastrophic health costs or lost pensions, and lifetime education will offer the chance to start anew if you want to work for it. The economic security platform is individual and family focused. It deals with issues that erupt in people's faces. It assumes that failure has some limits and bad luck can't run its full course. It gives the middle class, as well as working people who are poor, a place to stand—a foundation from which they can regroup and then move forward on their own behalf.

But the economic security platform is limited. It is not a slippery slope back to expanded government entitlements. It does not attempt to avoid all risks. It does not guarantee income or prevent failure or oversee how people live. The nest level of both security and opportunity must come from building strong communities where people live and work.

Government programs do not create self-worth; that's what families, neighbors, and communities do. That's why neighborhood leadership and community structures are so important and should be encouraged. This is as true for the problems of rebuilding urban America as it is for the problems of small towns whose factories have closed. Communities are to humane living what markets are to international competition; both work optimally when given the freedom and the incentives to find paths that meet specific needs best.

In this sense, the economic security platform is different from a social safety net. The safety net of government subsidies is where you end up if everything is falling out from under you and you're about to hit bottom. The economic security platform is where you rest before you advance. It gives reassurance before a continued pursuit of success within our national community.

Health care, lifetime education, and pension security. "Is that it?" one asks. "Aren't there hundreds of anecdotes about failed lives that, if only there had been this or that government program, someone could have pursued happiness or someone else could have avoided tragedy?" Perhaps. But the economic security platform is strictly and intentionally limited because of resources —we have a gigantic debt—and because of theory—the market's dynamism must not be lost. I have tried only to build a platform on which a nation can steer through troubled waters. To add a house of additional new programs, mandates, and work rules would create a structure that would not be seaworthy.

What America should not do is emulate Europe. In America, overall wages have been stagnant since 1973. During the 1980s, the knowledge superstars arrived. Vast salaries went to the brightest, and no raises went to the unskilled. In Europe, unemployment has been high. Today it's 11 percent. The joblessness is caused in part because European governments have created a rigid labor market that discourages the hiring of new workers and prevents the shedding of incompetent workers, while at the same time it burdens business with cumbersome work rules even to the point of determining the required number of vacation days. In addition, income-support payments go on forever and fearsome restrictions confront anyone who wants to start a new business. Such over-regulation stifles an economy's ability to adjust to new circumstances. America's challenge is to raise take-home pay and to reduce the disparity of income without creating the disincentives to job creation that exist in Europe. Only a healthy economy that creates jobs will dampen people's worries. Only an economy that creates new businesses will create new jobs.

Beyond finding a balance between encouraging business and job creation, and providing every American some security in times of transformation, government needs to get its own fundamentals correct.

Government needs to spend less money overall with more of the money it does spend going to public investment in infrastructure, education, and R&D, which stagnated even as our population grew over the last two decades. Less money should go to transfers from one group of taxpayers to another, particularly if those transfers are unrelated to need.

Taxes should not penalize job creation, but rather hit consumption. Payroll taxes should be replaced by consumption taxes. With less tax penalty for hiring, more workers can be hired and wages can rise too.

All government spending programs should be sunsetted— presumed to expire unless reauthorized. The President should have a line-item veto both for appropriations and for special interest tax loopholes, both of which increase the debt.

International markets should stay open and competition fierce so that the highest quality and lowest price can be assured and export jobs can grow. That means assigning absolute priority to approving the North American Free Trade Agreement and completing the GATT round, which reduces barriers to worldwide trade.

I cannot help but see NAFTA as the test case of whether we hold on and lose, or transform and win. To defeat NAFTA will solve none of the problems generated by the four transformations. To pass NAFTA will improve the chances for more jobs in America and a stronger economy to deal with the real threats to American jobs coming from Europe, Japan, and China. To defeat NAFTA will darken the chances for GATT, and the defeat of both will deny America its major source of job creation during the next few years. Ultimately, if world trade expands, everyone can win. To pass NAFTA is to take the challenge head on.

People such as Louise Pearl, George Fatemi, and the Joneses will be helped by the economic security platform. Their children will be helped by keeping the market open and businesses unburdened by excessive regulation. Their children will be helped by more public investment and less transfers. Their children will be helped by reducing payroll taxes and increasing taxes on consumption. Their children will be helped by a major reduction of the national debt.

With an economic security platform to help us navigate the surging river of economic change and a healthy, dynamic market awaiting us at our destination, we all have reason to hope. America is relatively better off than our competition. We've turned transformations to our advantage before. Remember the ages of industrialization and automation. We are more flexible than the rigidified economies of Europe and more ethnically diverse than the economies of Asia. Because of those strengths, we are better able to penetrate markets worldwide with goods that are high quality and reasonably priced. What is needed for us to catch the next wave of growth is national leadership that levels with the people, that tells the hard truths as well as the good news, that guides as well as empathizes, and that sees our path clearly and shows the energy to persevere.

One final image. Odysseus, when he was sailing where the siren songs were sure to be too seductive, plugged the ears of his sailors and had them tie him to the mast so that neither they nor he would plunge into the water and drown. I have painted a picture of turbulent waters where many people on their own, without a security platform, will in fact drown. I have suggested that we cannot fail to get into the middle of this new world of international competition or knowledge production because each promises hope as well as anxiety. I have said that if we heed the siren song of every new idea of what government should do, we will never navigate these waters. If we tie ourselves to the mast of efficient government, which does what has to be done and jettisons the rest, we will not need to plug our ears in order to survive and prosper.

I continue to believe in a strong, intelligent, and caring America—one that sets its compass and pursues a course that can provide leadership by example to the world as well as sustenance and security to ourselves. A national economy free of the burden of debt, populated by educated citizens ready to work and to care for their neighbors must be our goal. A dynamic, market-driven economy that remains open to the world must be our destination. A transformed and transforming America can get beyond the river's turbulent waters with our optimism intact and our future prospects bright.

COMBATTING CRIME[1]
JANET RENO[2]

The United States Conference of Mayors is composed of the mayors of cities with populations of over 300,000 and is designed to improve municipal government through cooperation between cities and the federal government. The Conference provides educational information and services to cities, conducts research, and compiles statistics. It holds two meetings every year.

The 62nd annual winter meeting in Washington, D.C., held on January 27, 1994, came shortly on the heels of President Clinton's State of the Union address. The issues of crime, youth violence, and gun control dominated the meeting's agenda. The conference was scheduled to hear addresses by two of President Clinton's leading advisers, Lee Patrick Brown, Director of the Office of National Drug Control Policy, and United States Attorney General Janet Reno.

Reno, the first woman to serve as Attorney General, had traveled extensively throughout the country in the opening months of her appointment, addressing issues related to her office. She delivered her speech to the Conference in the Congress and Senate Rooms of the Capital Hilton Hotel at 10:55 a.m. She was interrupted six times by applause and received a standing ovation at the end. Describing Reno's typical speech delivery, Lincoln Caplan wrote:

She is tall (6 foot 1½) and large boned, and as she looks out at her

---

[1]Delivered at the winter meeting of the United States Conference of Mayors in the Congress and Senate rooms of the Capital Hilton Hotel in Washington, D.C., at 10:55 A.M. on January 27, 1994.

[2]For biographical note, see Appendix.

audience with an intense, darting gaze, she appears to embody the power of Attorney General of the United States. But with her feet spread at parade rest, and self-conscious hunch to her shoulders and her arms dangling awkwardly, she seems unvarnished and unthreatening. . . . Reno speaks without notes in a slow Florida twang. . . . Reno's presentations bear touches of an experienced speechifier. . . . But she is no orator; her speeches brim with runon sentences, are loosely constructed, and dwell on themes she recycles again and again. ("Janet Reno's Choice," *New York Times Magazines* May 15, 1994, p. 42)

Janet Reno's speech: I thank you so much for that warm applause. I thank you, too, for letting me know how difficult it is to be mayor. It is also difficult to be a prosecutor who has 26 mayors in her jurisdiction.

I learned a lot in 15 years. I learned that mayors have one of the toughest jobs of anybody in government, particularly in these last 5 years as the federal government has shifted programs to the states without monies, the states to the counties without monies, and the counties have said, "cities, you do it." And what is so exciting to me is that everywhere I have visited throughout this nation, and I have already had the chance to say hello to mayors who have made me feel welcome, Republicans and Democrats, cities are making such an incredible difference because you have your back up against the wall. You don't have money, but you are bringing people together and showing what Americans can do. With the spirit of innovation, of working together, you cut across lines of diversity to bring people together. And what is happening in American cities today is one of the most heartwarming, encouraging signs that I have seen.

You've made me feel like I was off on the right track. There were some people that were saying I was perhaps soft on crime for talking about prevention. On May the 4th of this year some mayors came to see me from your conference. I think there were six or seven mayors, balanced Republicans and Democrats, and they started talking about prevention. And I said, "Hey, I am not too far wrong."

You have led the way in your plan that you presented to the President, to myself, and to Dr. Brown this December. Every time I turn around you are doing incredible things, and I, for one, tell you all I know how difficult the job is and I appreciate it so very, very much.

I would like to talk to you today in response really to your plan. I've spoken to many of you in broader concepts, and I'd like to be as specific as I could today to give you information and to discuss with you and to develop thoughts for the future that might be helpful, first of all, with respect to funding for police.

Ladies and gentlemen, Mayor [Jerry] Abramson has already called for it, a number of you have already joined me in calling for immediate, swift passage of a good, sound crime bill that provides for police on the streets in ways that you can use them and use them as soon as possible.

Those of you who have community policing initiatives under-way know what they have done—what they can do in terms of reducing crime. You know how they can bring a community together as community police involve the neighborhood and create a spirit of cooperation that we have not seen for some time. We cannot let this bill get stalled in Congress. We have got to get it passed and we need everybody's help in getting it passed, to get drug courts, provisions for drug courts that can be seen throughout the land as evidence of what was done in Dade County and has now been expanded to 37 jurisdictions; more drug treatment monies, and Dr. Brown [Lee] will be expanding on that; boot camps that let our youngsters know that there is going to be punishment but also provide after-care and followup and jobs so they can return to the community with a chance of not becoming involved in a revolving door. Let's get that bill passed. Let's get the ban on assault weapons passed. The American people have spoken, and they have spoken so eloquently through you.

But let's go to the issue of police funding. First of all, with respect to the issue of rounds 2 and 3 on the $150 million supplement, I am going to revisit with our staff what we can do to speed that up. But we are trying to do it in as thorough a way as possible. We are learning a lot because apparatus was not there for its distribution.

I would welcome, mayors, the opportunity to have a continuing dialogue with you as to anything we can do to improve any process we have in which we deal with cities, whether it is in distribution of these monies or in other efforts, so that we can cut through red tape. What we tried to do in the police funding procedure was to develop hotlines so that communities throughout this country could call us directly, get immediate answers. We then tried to provide followup to see how these calls have worked to make sure that we are doing it the right way. And I invite you to work with us in every way possible to ensure a smooth dialogue between the cities and the Department of Justice.

In these next weeks, I am going to need your help in framing issues with respect to the flexibility you need to use the dollars as soon as possible, as wisely as possible, whether it be for new technology or overtime or for actual bodies on the streets. There are disputes and disagreements about that, but I understand that each city is different. There are problems in each city that don't match the others. We've got to be—I just don't think that we've got to say we're defeated because we're too big to be direct and personal in our contact with mayors, and I want to try to do everything I can.

On issues such as waivers and other methods that we might use to tailor grants to your community so that it can make a difference, on whether we also count as part of the 100,000 police officers prosecutors and the backup people to go with it, that's another consideration that's important. I don't know what the answer will be, but I understand just how important flexibility is.

With respect to firearms, it is because of your second point in your plan, it is because of your leadership and so many others, that the Brady bill is now the Brady law. Isn't that a nice sound?

We've tried to gear up working with the FBI to ensure smooth implementation and the prompt implementation of that bill without bureaucratic snags along the way. But we have got to move ahead and not rest on our laurels with Brady. We've got to get that ban on assault weapons passed. We have got to make sure that we develop attitudes and procedures that make sure that it is at least as difficult to get a gun as it is to get a driver's license in America and that you ought to be able to demonstrate that you know how to safely and lawfully use a weapon before you buy a weapon, just like you know how to safely and lawfully use a car before you get a driver's license.

It is leadership from amongst you that is leading the nation in saying let's get rid of the guns that police confiscate. When you look at the number of guns in your property rooms across this nation, and if you think what would happen if we'd start melting them down or start dumping them on the reefs what we could do in terms of beginning to get the millions out of circulation. Let us all join together and start now in getting rid of the guns that way.

Dr. Brown will be talking, too, about expanded drug control efforts. But I would like to describe for you what we have tried to do within the Department of Justice. When I was in Miami as a prosecutor, as some of you know, the DEA and the FBI would fight and everybody would fuss at each other and they would have turf battles. And I swore that if I didn't do anything else in Washington I wanted to try to end the turf battles, at least within the Justice agencies. I think we're well on our way to doing that.

But we're reaching out beyond the Justice agencies to say to other agencies, "Look, we don't want to take you over. We want to work hand in hand with you because there is too much to do in terms of crime and drugs in America. We've all got enough to do. If we use our resources wisely, if we share information amongst ourselves and with local law enforcement we can make a difference."

We have developed the Office of Investigative Agency Policy and we had the most remarkable ceremony, and it wasn't just ceremony because when I walked into the room they were all standing around talking together. With the announcement of Tom Constantine as the new Administrator of DEA we had all the federal agencies there. We had representatives of the police organizations, state and local prosecutors, the state attorneys general, it was one of the most exciting ceremonies that I have seen in a long time.

Lest I get carried away with ceremony, I'm also told by experienced career people in the Department of Justice that they had never seen such coordination in many, many years, and we want to continue to improve it. But as a local prosecutor in heart and soul, I think it is terribly important that the federal government form a true partnership with local and state law enforcement around this nation in sharing information and backing each other up, in doing what each does best but doing it in a coordinated way. And I commit myself to working with your law enforcement officials in every way possible in that regard.

One of the plans that you suggest there is in terms of more DEA agents working closer with local law enforcement. This afternoon there will be an announcement of how we are trying to begin to get federal agents to the field. We are going to do everything we can to get support to the field in places that it can count. We will work with local prosecutors to make sure that we handle the cases we're supposed to be handling, they handle the cases best suited for State court, and we do it the right way.

Your third point is restructuring the criminal justice system. You have a man probably more experienced than anybody in this room, and that's Judge Si Gelber who is now Mayor Gelber of Miami Beach, and he and I have worked long and hard in the area of juvenile justice. Both of us have seen the concept of juvenile justice change, and your remarks and this plan go to the heart of what he and I feel; that for too long now too many police officers have come to us and said, "Look, these kids come in at 13 and 14 having committed violent crime and they just laugh at us saying, 'hey, man, nothing's going to happen to me, nothing ever happens to anybody in the juvenile justice system.'"

We have got to join together, and I pledge to you to work with your law enforcement agencies through our Office of Juvenile Justice and Delinquency Prevention to establish appropriate responses to youth violence, to let young people know that if they commit a crime by putting a gun up beside somebody's head and hurting them they are going to be punished. But it will be a fair, humane, certain, firm punishment that lets them know there is a consequence for their act.

You all know, far better than anybody else, how important it is if you punish them and then you put them back out on the streets without jobs, without job training, without addressing their substance abuse problem, without addressing their family situation, it is going to recur and you're going to waste money. Community police are joining with others in developing after-care programs. We've got to make sure that boot camp provision in the crime bill has after-care provisions and followup. And we have all got to make clear to everybody who might disagree with us that we will never begin to solve the problem of youth violence unless we provide real job opportunity and the job training and the child development to go with it to give people the skills to fill the jobs.

You, more than any other single group of public servants I know, understand how we've got to balance punishment and prevention. And it's not an either/or choice. It's both and doing it the right way, and I thank you for your leadership in this effort.

You've asked that we do much through the Office of Juvenile Justice and Delinquency Prevention in your plan, and I have already given it a high profile. I have met with them. They say it's the first time they've seen an Attorney General in years, it's the first time they've been asked to submit a budget, and it is a unit and a bureau that I care deeply about. But the challenges are new, for a new problem that we've never seen in the juvenile justice area before, and we're going to join with you in trying to address that problem.

Your last two points go to the issue of long-term strategies and partnerships to prevent violent crime, and I blend those two together. I think you all wrote my speeches over the last 8 years. I have never seen anything like it in terms of an understanding of public officials, public officials Republican and Democrat who have to run for office, who know what it's like to go to the people, to tell people the real facts, to explain to them that it can't be done with 30-second sound bytes, that you need long-term strategies that can make a difference.

I have been to your cities—to Ft. Worth, to Salt Lake City, to Wichita—and I've watched what you're doing in your communities as you build neighborhood coalitions, as you reach out to the federal government through weed and seed initiatives, as you do your own weed and seed initiatives. As the mayor of Ft. Worth has said, "Weed and seed is not just a program, it is a concept and a philosophy." And so many of you around this nation are evidencing that philosophy of bringing disciplines together, of going to the people, of involving the people and what you do, and you are setting an example for the nation. And, Mr. Mayor, I'd like to do everything I can to continue to work with the conference to support you in every way possible.

It is a difficult process, because I had enough problems dealing with my 26 cities in Dade County plus Miami. Now, I've got all of you plus many others around the nation, and how we design a federal structure where the federal government can truly be responsive to the people and to mayors and to local communities is one of the most difficult tasks we face. I've often likened it, however—my dream would be that we could have a Ft. Worth desk in Washington, and that instead of going from HUD to Labor to Justice with hat in hand, the city of Ft. Worth could come up with its plan of its needs and resources, what it needs to do the job.

There could be one Ft. Worth expert in Washington who represented the different agencies that could touch on the situation in Ft. Worth. We would try to figure out how federal resources, limited, too, could go together to fill the cracks and how we could support each other. We could challenge Ft. Worth to leverage dollars by providing matches. We could do so much if we learn from high technology how we can communicate and say that this Nation hasn't become too big that this government can't work with cities throughout the nation on an individual basis, recognizing the strength and wonder and beauty of the small and large cities throughout the nation.

This past week we had a meeting of United States Attorneys. They all came to Washington and the snow helped keep everybody in and we had a wonderful 3-day discussion. What we talked about primarily was a violence initiative, and I would like to share with you a concept that many of you are undertaking now. The Center for Disease Control and Prevention is undertaking some remarkable work in violence. Dr. Mark Rosenberg is leading this effort, and I commend to you all contact with the Center for developing further information that might be useful to you.

Sometimes, we think the problem of violence is overwhelming us. But if we take it and look at the hard facts and if we approach it from the point of view of good public servants that are also interested in the scientific background of it, I think we can make a significant difference in utilizing our shrinking resources far more wisely than we have.

Each community can oftentimes identify the core of career criminals that are causing the problem, and through proactive initiatives with the Alcohol, Tobacco, and Firearms Bureau, with the FBI, we want to join with you in focusing on those people. And whether it be state or federal court, whatever is best for the case, we want to make sure those people are put away for the longest possible time we can get them away. Those 10 percent of the criminals are committing as much as 40 percent of your crime. Too many of your police officers engage in a revolving door effort. As they pick them up and put them in they come right back. Let's get them put away.

There are many cities that are focusing on violent traffickers where the federal agencies have come together working with local law enforcement to look at violent drug gangs. Getting those people put away has seen a reduction in the violent crime in that community. But it becomes a more effective reduction when you move in after you've gotten a drug organization off that street corner, move in with something positive so that the organization down the street doesn't start filling the vacuum. The balanced punishment and prevention approach that you call for in this plan can make a significant difference.

Let us look and realize that organized crime hasn't gone away. It's coming on in new and different forms, and we've got to be prepared and we will be prepared to work with you and share information.

The same with gangs. It was amazing to me because my jurisdiction was 365 miles south of the nearest state border, to visit Salt Lake City and see the impact of youth gangs sweeping up from California and then across to Wichita and across to Omaha.

We can share information with you that can forecast, and we can work with you in using limited resources to focus on this type of violence.

What impressed me so much about this plan is you all don't forget anything. You understand that domestic violence is critical to all these issues because I'll bet every one of your police chiefs have told you how many of their calls involve response to family violence and that these are oftentimes the most dangerous and difficult calls they make. We can't ignore that any more. We have got to develop domestic intervention programs, domestic courts, prosecutors trained in these efforts. Most of these cases can be handled better by local government. But in any way I can support you in that effort, I want to do so.

Some of your jurisdictions—I was in one recently—has [sic] an incredible incidence of child abuse. We can focus on that, provide followup, work with you, and do everything possible.

But here are the statistics that stagger my imagination, that I think we all have to understand. Because there are many of your cities that have experienced a reduction in violence. But what you haven't seen is a reduction in youth violence. Instead, you have seen an escalation. And people wonder why the American people are so concerned about violence if it is on the decline. The reason they are concerned is because they are seeing youngsters do things that we could never, ever dream that youngsters did. Youngsters who have never developed the conscience and the concept of reward and punishment. And we're all grappling with what to do.

But I would urge you again to work with the Center for Disease Control to understand what the situation is in your community. This is the report that has been furnished to me: Taking young American males age 15 to 24 in 1986, there were 22 deaths—homicides—of young American males between the ages of 15 to 24. By 1991, that number had grown to 37 per 100,000 for all young American males. It was only 17 per 100,000 for young white American males between the ages of 15 and 24. It was 159 per 100,000 for young black males between the ages of 15 and 24, and you have the strategy to deal with this terrible tragedy more than anybody else that I have seen. You understand the problem.

What the Center for Disease Control found was that the victim and the assailant were acquainted, for the most part, it was the same race, predominantly male, that it started from arguments, that it was usually not felony related; that alcohol was usually involved, and that firearms were usually present. Of the 159 total, 139 per 100,000 involved firearms.

Those are figures that we can understand, and we can begin to devise strategies that do something about it. But for the first time firearm deaths for young teenagers, both white and black, now exceeds the deaths in those age groups for all natural causes. And it won't be long before firearms deaths exceed motor vehicle deaths for that category. If we focus on this in terms of doing it right, of getting rid of the partisanship in crime, in getting rid of the 30 second sound bytes, and in saying for youngsters when they first get in trouble, if we design a fair, firm, understandable punishment, if we follow through with after-care and followup and alternate housing in certain situations and jobs and case managers and make an investment in our future, we can make a difference.

Now, there are going to be your constituents that suggest, "But, wait a minute, we don't want to do that." We're not going to have a work force, much less reduce violence, unless we make an investment in our children. But you understand better than anybody else that we have also got to make an investment in prevention.

In all that you do in your national policy for children, from strong parents to prenatal care to Head Start to programs, afternoon and the evening, you understand it.

I look forward to working with you. You have given me such encouragement, in these 10 months that I have been in office, that I was on the right track. I am deeply grateful to you all, and I look forward to working with you in every way possible.

IMPROVING HEALTH CARE[1]
Hillary Rodham Clinton[2]

One of the major themes in Bill Clinton's 1992 campaign for the presidency was a promise to reform health care. After election, Clinton immediately embarked on a program to develop

[1]Delivered at the opening of the American Medical Association's annual convention in Chicago on June 13, 1993.
[2]For biographical note, see Appendix.

and ensure enactment of such legislation. A surprise to some was his choice of his wife, Hillary Rodham Clinton, to spearhead the campaign. Although she held no cabinet appointment or official position, the president assigned her the overall responsibility for this important task.

His choice should not have been entirely surprising. During the presidential campaign, the American people had come to know Hillary Rodham Clinton as an activist. An honors graduate of Wellesley College, holder of a law degree from Yale, and a successful attorney, Mrs. Clinton had been extremely influential in her husband's five terms as governor of Arkansas and in his run for the presidency.

After accepting the responsibility for leading the health care reform campaign, Mrs. Clinton embarked on a series of town meetings, speaking at dozens of colleges and medical centers to both supporters and detractors. By September 1993, she also had met more than one hundred and thirty times with members of Congress to talk about health care, and with more than eleven hundred assorted groups.

One of the key speeches in her campaign to win support for health care reform was delivered at the opening of the American Medical Association's convention in Chicago on June 13, 1993. Approval of the President's proposal by the leaders of the powerful 290,000 member AMA was important.

A capacity crowd of 2,000, including the 436 members of the AMA's powerful House of Delegates, were present for the speech. Also in attendance was a group of school children from the Nathan Davis Elementary School. The Associated Press stated that Mrs. Clinton was interrupted by twenty-four ovations. "The doctors" according to Christopher Connell, " . . . cheered when she promised relief from antitrust laws and a new federal law regulating clinical laboratories. . . Doctors afterwards praised the first lady's bravura 45 minute performance" (*The Advocate*, Baton Rouge, Louisiana, June 14, 1994, p. 5E).

Hillary Rodham Clinton's speech: Thank you very much Mr. Speaker, all of the members of the House of Delegates, the officers and trustees of the AMA, and all whom you represent. It is an honor for me to be with you at this meeting and to have the opportunity to participate with you in an ongoing conversation about our health care system and the kinds of constructive changes that we all wish to see brought to it.

I know that you have, through Health Access America, and

through other activities and programs of the AMA been deeply involved in this conversation already, and all of us are grateful for your contribution. I'm also pleased that you invited students from the Nathan Davis Elementary School to join us here this afternoon.

I know that the AMA has a special relationship with this school, named as it is for the founder of the AMA, and that the AMA participates in its corporate capacity in the Adopt a School program here in Chicago. You have made a real contribution to these young men and women. And not only have you provided free immunizations and physicals and lectures and help about health and related matters, but you have served as role models and mentors. It is very important that all of us as adults do what we can to give young people the skills they will need to become responsible and successful adults. And I congratulate you for your efforts and welcome the students here today.

All of us respond to children. We want to nurture them so they can dream the dreams that free and healthy children should have. This is our primary responsibility as adults. And it is our primary responsibility as a government. We should stand behind families, teachers, and others who work with the young, so that we can enable them to meet their own needs by becoming self-sufficient and responsible so that they, in turn, will be able to meet their families and their own children's needs.

When I was growing up, not far from where we are today, this seemed an easier task. There seemed to be more strong families. There seemed to be safer neighborhoods. There seemed to be an outlook of caring and cooperation among adults that stood for and behind children. I remember so well my father saying to me that if you get in trouble at school, you get in trouble at home, no questions asked, because there was this sense among the adult community that all of them, from my child's perspective, were involved in helping their own and others' children.

Much has changed since those days. We have lost some of the hope and optimism of that earlier time. Today, we too often meet our greatest challenges, whether it is the raising of children or reforming the health care system, with a sense that our problems have grown too large and unmanageable. And I don't need to tell you that that kind of attitude begins to undermine one's sense of hope, optimism, and even competence.

We know now, and you know better than I, that over the last decade our health care system has been under extraordinary stress. It is one of the many institutions in our society that has experienced such stress. That stress has begun to break down many of the relationships that should stand at the core of the health care system. That breakdown has, in turn, undermined your profession in many ways, changing the nature of and the rewards of practicing medicine.

Most doctors and other health care professionals choose careers in health and medicine because they want to help people. But too often because our system isn't working and we haven't taken full responsibility for fixing it, that motive is clouded by perceptions that doctors aren't the same as they used to be. They're not really doing what they used to do. They don't really care like they once did.

You know and I know that we have to work harder to renew a trust in who doctors are and what doctors do. That is also not unique to the medical community. Just as our institutions across society are under attack and stress, all elements of those institutions are finding that they no longer can command the trust and respect, whether we talk of parents or government officials or other professionals—police officers, teachers—that should come with giving of themselves and doing a job well that needs to be done.

But focusing this afternoon on those concerns that are yours, what has happened with medicine, what is likely to happen, we need to start with a fundamental commitment to making the practice of medicine again a visible, honored link in our efforts to promote the common good. And the way to do that is to improve the entire system of which you are a part. We cannot create the atmosphere of trust and respect and professionalism that you deserve to have, and that many of you who are in this room remember from earlier years, without changing the incentives and the way the entire system operates. That has to be our primary commitment. If we do not put medicine and those who operate within medicine in the forefront of the respect they deserve to have, no matter what we do to the system on the margins will not make the differences that it should.

As you know, the president is in the process of finalizing his proposal for health care reform, and I am grateful to speak with you about that process and where it is today and where it is going. I had originally hoped to join you at your meeting in March in Washington, D.C. And I, again, want to apologize for my absence. I very much appreciated Vice President Gore attending for me, and I also appreciated the kind words from your executive officials on behalf of the entire association because of my absence.

My father was ill and I spent several weeks with him in the hospital before he died. During his hospitalization at St. Vincent's Hospital in Little Rock, Arkansas, I witnessed firsthand the courage and commitment of health care professionals, both directly and indirectly. I will always appreciate the sensitivity and the skills they showed, not just in caring for my father, not just in caring for his family, which, as you know, often needs as much care as the patient, but in caring for the many others whose names I will never know. I know that some of you worry about what the impact of health care reform will be on your profession and on your practice. Let me say from the start, if I read only what the newspapers have said about what we are doing in our plan, I'd probably be a little afraid myself, too, because it is very difficult to get out what is going on in such a complex process.

But the simple fact is this: The president has asked all of us, representatives of the AMA, of every other element of the health care system, as well as the administration, to work on making changes where they are needed, to keeping and improving those things that work, and to preserving and conserving the best parts of our system as we try to improve and change those that are not.

This system is not working as well as it did, or as well as it could: for you, for the private sector, for the public, or for the nation. The one area that is so important to be understood on a macronational level is how our failure to deal with the health care system and its financial demands is at the center of our problems financially in Washington. Because we cannot control health care costs and become further and further behind in our efforts to do so, we find our economy, and particularly the federal budget, under increasing pressure.

Just as it would be irresponsible, therefore, to change what is working in the health care system, it is equally irresponsible for us not to fix what we know is no longer working. So let us start with some basic principles that are remarkably like the ones that you have adopted in your statements, and in particularly in Health Access America. We must guarantee all Americans access to a comprehensive package of benefits, no matter where they work, where they live, or whether they have ever been sick before. If we do not reach universal access, we cannot deal with our other problems.

And that is a point that you understand that you have to help the rest of the country understand; that until we do provide security for every American when it comes to health care, we cannot fix what is wrong with the health care system. Secondly, we do have to control costs. How we do that is one of the great challenges in this system, but one thing we can all agree on is that we have to cut down on the paperwork and reduce the bureaucracy in both the public and private sectors.

We also have to be sure that when we look at costs, we look at it not just from a financial perspective, but also from a human perspective. I remember sitting in the family waiting area of St. Vincent's, talking to a number of my physician friends [who stopped] by to see how we were doing. And one day, one of my friends told me that, every day, he discharges patients who need medication to stabilize a condition. And at least once a day, he knows there is a patient who will not be able to afford the prescription drugs he has prescribed, with the result that that patient may decide not to fill the prescription when the hospital supply runs out. Or that patient may decide that even though the doctor told him to take three pills a day, he'll just take one a day so it can be stretched further.

And even though St. Vincent's has created a fund to try to help support the needs of patients who cannot afford prescriptions, there's not enough to go around, and so every day there is someone who my friend knows and you know will be back in the hospital because of their inability either to afford the care that is required after they leave, or because they try to cut the corners on it, with the net result that then you and I will pay more for that person who is back in the hospital than we would have if we had taken a sensible approach toward what the real costs in the medical system are. That is why we will try, for example, to include prescription drugs in the comprehensive benefit package for all Americans, including those over 65, through Medicare.

We believe that if we help control costs up front, we will save costs on the back end. That is a principle that runs through our proposal and which each of you knows from firsthand experience is more likely to be efficient in both human and financial terms. We will also preserve what is best in the American health care system today.

We have looked at every other system in the world. We have tried to talk to every expert whom we can find to describe how any other country tries to provide health care. And we have concluded that what is needed is an American solution for an Ameri-

can problem by creating an American health care system that
works for America. And two of the principles that underlie that
American solution are quality and choice.

We want to ensure and enhance quality. And in order to do
that, we're going to have to make some changes, and you know
that. We cannot, for example, promise to really achieve universal
access if we do not expand our supply of primary care physicians,
and we must do that. And you will have to help us determine the
best way to go about achieving that goal.

I've spoken with representatives of our medical schools, and
we have talked about how the funding of graduate medical education will have to be changed to provide incentives for the training
of more primary care physicians. I have talked with representatives of many of the associations, such as this one, about how
continuing educational opportunities could help even mid-career
physicians, once we have a real supply of primary care physicians
who are adequately reimbursed and adequately supported, how
they might even go back into primary care.

We have also very much put choice in the center of our system
so that we will have not just choice for patients as to which plan
they choose to join, but choice for physicians as to which plan they
choose to practice with, including the option of being part of
more than one plan at the same time.

Now, as we work out all of the details in the many proposals
and its parts that must come together, I am not suggesting that
you will agree with every recommendation the President makes. I
don't expect any group to do that. In fact, I suppose that if
everybody's not a little put out that means we probably haven't
done it right. But I do hope and expect that this group, as with
other groups representing physicians and nurses and other
health care professionals will find in this plan much to be ap-
plauded and supported. And I also believe that given the complexities of the problem we face, it would be difficult to arrive at a
solution that was universally accepted.

But the reason I have confidence that this house, the AMA,
and others will be supportive of the President's proposal is because we have benefited so much from what you have already
done and from the involvement of many of you and others
around the country.

Again, contrary to what you may have heard, scores of practicing physicians served on the working groups that were study-

ing health care reform. I am deeply grateful on a personal level that members of the AMA's leadership spent invaluable time coming to meeting after meeting, day after day sharing their ideas, reacting to ideas at the White House. And, of course, in the course of that we learned we had many common goals and objectives.

We will not only stand for universal coverage, but in addition the following: community rating so that we can assure all Americans they will be taken care of; eliminating restrictions based on preexisting conditions so that every American will be eligible; a nationally guaranteed comprehensive benefits package that will emphasize primary and preventive health care as well as hospitalization and other care; the kind of choice and quality assurances that we will need to have to make sure this new system not only operates well during the transition but gets a firm footing as it moves into the future and we will therefore be emphasizing more on practice parameters and outcomes research so that you, too, can know better what works.

One of the great interesting experiences I have had during the past months is as I've traveled around from state to state is having doctors coming up to me and telling me that they need more information; that all too often the information they receive doesn't come to them in forms that they believe are practical in their particular context. And what we want to do is by working with organizations like yours is be sure that the quality outcomes and the kind of research that will be done will be readily available to every practicing physician in the country.

We also believe that it will be essential to continue medical research and to use the breakthroughs in medical research, again, not just to alleviate human suffering but to save money, because you know better than I that often times a breakthrough in research, a new drug, a new procedure, is the quickest way to take care of the most people in a cost-effective manner. So we will continue to support medical research.

All of these principles arise from the same common assumption: that the status quo is unacceptable. And it is not really even any longer a status quo because we do not stand still, we drift backwards. Every month people lose their insurance; every month you have more micromanagement and regulation to put up with; every month our health care system becomes more expensive to fix.

I know that many of you feel that as doctors you are under siege in the current system. And I think there is cause for you to believe that, because we are witnessing a disturbing assault on the doctor/patient relationship. More and more employers are buying into managed care plans that force employees to choose from a specific pool of doctors. And too often, even when a doctor is willing to join a new plan to maintain his relationship with patients, he, or she I should say, is frozen out.

What we want to see is a system in which the employer does not make the choice as to what plan is available for the employee, the employee makes that choice for him or herself. But if we do not change and if the present pattern continues, as it will if we do not act quickly, the art of practicing medicine will be forever transformed. Gone will be the patients treasured privilege to choose his or her doctor. Gone will be the close trusting bonds built up between physicians and patients over the years. Gone will be the security of knowing you can switch jobs and still visit your longtime internist or pediatrician or OB/GYN.

We cannot afford to let that happen. But the erosion of the doctor/patient relationship is only one piece of the problem. Another piece is the role that insurance companies have come to play and the role that the government has come to play along with them in second-guessing medical decisions.

I can understand how many of you must feel. When instead of being trusted for your expertise, you're expected to call an 800 number and get approval for even basic medical procedures from a total stranger.

Frankly, despite my best efforts of the last month to understand every aspect of the health care system, it is and remains a mystery to me how a person sitting at a computer in some air-conditioned office thousands of miles away can make a judgment about what should or shouldn't happen at a patient's bedside in Illinois or Georgia or California. The result of this excessive oversight, this peering over all of your shoulder's is a system of backward incentives. It rewards providers for overprescribing, overtesting, and generally overdoing. And worse, it punishes doctors who show proper restraint and exercise their professional judgment in ways that those sitting at the computers disagree with.

Dr. Bob Barrinson, one of the practicing physicians who spent hours and hours working with us while also maintaining his practice, told us recently of an experience that he had as one of many. He admitted an emergency room patient named Jeff. Jeff suffered from cirrhosis of the liver, and Dr. Barrinson put him in the hospital and within 24 hours received a call from Jeff's insurance company. The insurance company wanted to know exactly how many days Jeff would be in the hospital and why. Dr. Barrinson replied that he couldn't predict the precise length of stay. A few days later the insurance company called back and questioned whether Jeff would need surgery. Again, Dr. Barrinson said he wasn't yet sure.

And what was Dr. Barrinson's reward for his honesty and his professionalism? He was placed on the insurance company's "special exceptions" list. You know, that's a list of troublesome doctors who make the insurance company wait a few days or a few weeks to determine the bottom line on a particular patient.

From that point on, the insurance company called Dr. Barrinson six times in two weeks. Each time he had to be summoned away from the patient to take the call. Each time he spoke to a different insurance company representative. Each time he repeated the same story. Each time his role as the physician was subverted. And each time the treatment of the patient was impeded.

Dr. Barrinson and you know that medicine, the art of healing, doesn't work like that. There is no master checklist that can be administered by some faceless bureaucrat that can tell you what you need to do on an hourly basis to take care of your patients; and, frankly, I wouldn't want to be one of your patients if there were.

Now, adding to these difficulties doctors and hospitals and nurses, particularly, are being buried under an avalanche of paperwork. There are mountains of forms, mountains of rules, mountains of hours spent on administrative minutiae instead of caring for the sick. Where, you might ask yourself, did all this bureaucracy come from? And the short answer is, basically, everywhere.

There are forms to ensure appropriate care for the sick and the dying; forms to guard against unnecessary tests and procedures. And from each insurance company and government agency there are forms to record the decisions of doctors and nurses. I remember going to Boston and having a physician bring into a hearing I held there the stack of forms his office is required to fill out. And he held up a Medicare form and next to it he held up an insurance company form. And he said that they are the same forms that ask the same questions, but the insurance company form will not be accepted by the government, and the government form will not be accepted by the insurance company. And the insurance company basically took the government form, changed the title to call it by its own name and requires them to have it filled out. That was the tip of the iceberg.

One nurse told me that she entered the profession because she wanted to care for people. She said that if she had wanted to be an accountant, she would have gone to work for an accounting company instead. But she, like many other nurses, and as you know so well, many of the people in your offices now, are required to be bookkeepers and accountants, not clinicians, not caregivers.

The latest statistic I have seen is that for every doctor a hospital hires, four new administrative staff are hired. And that in the average doctor's office 80 hours a month is now spent on administration. That is not time spent with a patient recovering from bypass surgery or with a child or teenager who needs a checkup and maybe a little extra TLC time of listening and counseling, and certainly not spent with a patient who has to run in quickly for some kind of an emergency.

Blanketing an entire profession with rules aimed at catching those who are not living up to their professional standards does not improve quality. What we need is a new bargain. We need to remove from the vast majority of physicians these unnecessary, repetitive, often uneven read forms and instead substitute for what they were attempting to do: more discipline, more peer review, more careful scrutiny of your colleagues. You are the ones who can tell better than I or better than some bureaucrat whether the quality of medicine that is being practiced in your clinic, in your hospital, is what you would want for yourself and your family.

Let us remove the kind of micromanagement and regulation that has not improved quality and has wasted billions of dollars, but then you have to help us substitute for it, a system that the patients of this country, the public of this country, the decision-makers of this country can have confidence in. Now, I know there are legal obstacles for your being able to do that, and we are looking very closely at how we can remove those so that you can be part of creating a new solution in which everyone, including yourself, can believe in.

In every private conversation I've had with a physician, whether it's someone I knew from St. Vincent's or someone I had just met, I have asked: "Tell me, have you ever practiced with or around someone you did not think was living up to your standards?" And, invariably, the answer is, "Well, yes, I remember in my training; well, yes, I remember this emergency room work I used to do; yes, I remember in the hospital when so-and-so had that problem." And I've said, "Do you believe enough was done by the profession to deal with that problem and to eliminate it?" And, invariably, no matter who the doctor is, I've been told, "No, I don't."

We want you to have the chance so that in the future you can say, yes, I do believe we've been dealing with our problems. It is not something we should leave for the government, and, certainly, we cannot leave it to the patient. That is the new kind of relationship I think that we need to have.

Finally, if we do not, as I said earlier, provide universal coverage, we cannot do any of what I have just been speaking about because we cannot fulfill our basic commitment you as physicians, us as a society, that we will care for one another. It should no longer be left to the individual doctor to decide to probe his conscience before determining whether to treat a needy patient. I cannot tell you what it is like for me to travel around to hear stories from doctors and patients that are right on point.

But the most poignant that I tell because it struck me so personally was of the woman with no insurance; working for a company in New Orleans; had worked there for a number of years; tried to take good care of herself; went for the annual physical every year; and I sat with her on a folding chair in the loading dock of her company along with others, all of whom were uninsured; all of whom had worked numbers of years, while she told me at her last physical her doctor had found a lump in her breast and referred her to a surgeon. And the surgeon told her that if she had insurance, he would have biopsied it but because she did not he would watch it.

I don't think you have to be a woman to feel what I felt when that woman told me that story. And I don't think you have to be a physician to feel what you felt when you heard that story. We need to create a system in which no one ever has to say that for good cause or bad, and no one has to hear it ever again.

If we move toward universal coverage, so therefore everyone has a payment stream behind them to be able to come into your office, to be able to come into the hospital, you will again be able to make decisions that should be made with clinical autonomy, with professional judgment. And we intend to try to give you the time and free you up from other conditions to be able to do that.

One specific issue I want to mention, because I feel strongly about it. If my husband had not asked me to do this, I would have felt strongly about it because of the impact in my state of Arkansas. We have to simplify and eliminate the burdensome regulations created under CLEA a well-intentioned law with many unintended consequences that have affected not only those of you in private practice but public health departments like ours in Arkansas around the country.

But again we need that new bargain. You have to help us know what should be eliminated so that we then can just focus in on a very small part of this whole situation and eliminate the rest of the regulations that were thrown on top.

So those are the kinds of issues in which we think we can make it more possible for you to practice in a more efficient, human, better manner. We also believe strongly that we have to emphasize preventive care. And we have to provide a basic policy of preventive care. And we have to be sure that all of you and those who come after you into medicine are trained well in medical school to appreciate the importance of preventive care.

Much of what is now considered outside the scope of mainstream medicine is crowding in. Many of us in this room I know exercise, try to watch our diets, do things to try to remain healthier. And yet often medical education and medicine as it's practiced does not include those new kind of common-sense approaches to health. We need to be a system that does not take care of the sick but instead promotes health wherever we can in whatever way we possibly can do it.

And finally, let me say that we will offer a serious proposal to curb malpractice problems for all of you. But let me add that it, too, must be part of this new contract. In order to do that and to do it in a way that engenders the confidence of the average American, we must have organized medicine standing ready to say we will do a better job of taking care of the problems within us.

I have read or tried to read everything I can find about all of this. And you know as well as I do there are studies all over the field. It depends upon who writes it and who it's written for and the like. But we know there's a problem. We know we're going to deal with it. But one of the stark statistics from these studies is that all too often the largest number of malpractice suits is brought against the same physicians on a repetitive basis.

Now, it may be that for some that is an unfair accusation, and we need to deal with that through reform. But for others, you need to weed them out of your profession if they cannot practice to the quality that you expect your fellow colleagues to practice to. So we will propose serious malpractice reform, and we will have to look to you to help us make sure that the problems that will still flow from people who should not be making decisions will be eliminated. That way we can give confidence back to you as a profession, that you will not be second-guessed or unfairly called into court. And we will give confidence to the public that they will be protected insofar as humanly possible. So that is what we will have to look for when we come forward with that.

Now, reaching consensus on all that should be done and putting it into a piece of legislation and moving it through the Congress is not going to be easy. There will be many groups that will nibble at the edges of it, not like the whole idea of it, want to continue to the status quo. But if we do not have the courage to change now, if we do not move toward a system that once again gives you back your professionalism to practice prudent, practical, intelligent medicine again; if we do not move toward restoring the dignity again to the doctor-patient relationship, and that encourages young people to become physicians because they want to participate in that wonderful process of healing and caring, then the entire society, but most particularly medicine, will suffer.

The reason we are doing any of this is because of children like those who are here from Nathan Davis. Most of us in this room are at least halfway through. And most of us in this room have sat in dozens and dozens of meetings just like this. We've sat and listened to people tell us what was wrong with health care or what medicine or with whatever, and we've talked about the problems at least seriously since the 1970s. And we've produced proposals like yours for Health Access America.

But while we have talked, our problems have gotten worse, and the frustration on the part of all of you and others has increased. Time and again, groups, individuals, and particularly the government, has walked up to trying to reform health care and then walked away.

There's enough blame to go around, every kind of political stripes can be included, but the point now is that we could have done something about health care reform 20 years ago and solved our problems for millions of dollars, and we walked away. Later we could have done something and solved our problems for hundreds of millions, and we walked away.

After 20 years with [the] rate of medical inflation going up and with all of the problems you know so well, it is a harder and more difficult solution that confronts us. But I believe that if one looks at what is at stake, we are not talking just about reforming the way we finance health care, we are not talking just about the particulars of how we deliver health care, we are talking about creating a new sense of community and caring in this country in which we once again value your contribution, value the dignity of all people.

How many more meetings do we need? How many alerts? How many more plans? How many more brochures? The time has come for all of us, not just with respect to health care, but with respect to all of the difficulties our country faces to stop walking away and to start stepping up and taking responsibility. We are supposed to be the ones to lead for our children and our grand-children. And the way we have behaved in the last years, we have run away and abdicated that responsibility. And at the core of the human experience is responsibility for children to leave them a better world than the one we found.

We can do that with health care. We can make a difference now that will be a legacy for all of you. We can once again give you the confidence to say to your grandsons and granddaughters, yes, do go into medicine; yes, it is the most rewarding profession there is.

So let's celebrate your profession by improving health care. Let's celebrate our children by reforming this system. Let's come together not as liberals or conservatives or Republicans or Democrats, but as Americans who want the best for their country and know we can no longer wait to get about the business of providing it.

Thank you all very much.

THE ENDURING REVOLUTION[1]
Charles W. Colson[2]

Among the many prominent government officials caught up in the Watergate scandals that led to the resignation of President Richard Nixon in 1974 was Charles W. Colson. A graduate of Brown with a law degree from George Washington University, Colson had established a successful law practice before joining the Nixon administration as Special Counsel to the President in 1973.

In the aftermath of Watergate, Colson was convicted of obstructing justice for his role in the affair. He served a seven-month prison term, during which he became, by his own account, a Christian. In 1976 he published *Born Again* in which he chronicled the events leading to his conversion. With the money earned from royalties, Colson established the Prison Fellowship Ministries, an international evangelical program designed to help prison inmates study the Bible and Christianity.

By 1993 the Prison Fellowship Ministries was established in 800 federal and state prisons with the help of 49,000 volunteers. The ministry in the United States is part of Prison Fellowship International, which operates programs in 53 other countries.

The 1993 John M. Templeton Prize for Progress in Religion was awarded to Colson for his work with the Prison Fellowship Ministries. Earlier winners of the prize included Dr. Billy Graham, Mother Teresa, and Alexander Solzhenitsyn. At one million dollars, the prize, established by American-born British financier Sir John M. Templeton, is one the world's most lucrative awards.

While the prize was actually presented to Colson at Buckingham Palace in London on May 12, 1993, it was not until nearly four months later, on September 2, 1993, that Colson delivered an acceptance speech. The occasion was a ceremony in Chicago at the Chicago Center for Religion and Science and the Lutheran School of Theology, held as part of the meeting of the Parliament

[1]Delivered to the Parliament of World's Religions meeting at the University of Chicago, Chicago, Illinois, September 2, 1993.

[2]For biographical note, see Appendix.

63

of the World's Religions. Colson began his speech to a full house of 1200 people at the University of Chicago with these words:

> I speak as one transformed by Jesus Christ, the living God. He is the way, the truth, and the life. He has lived in me for 20 years. His presence is the sole explanation for whatever is praiseworthy in my work, the only reason for my receiving this award.

The speech was inserted in the *Congressional Record* by Congressman Frank R. Wolf of Virginia, who had nominated Colson for the award.

Charles W. Colson's speech: I speak as one transformed by Jesus Christ, the living God. He is the way, the truth, and the life. He has lived in me for 20 years. His presence is the sole explanation for whatever is praiseworthy in my work, the only reason for my receiving this award [the Templeton Prize].

That is more than a statement about myself. It is a claim to truth. It is a claim that may contradict your own.

Yet on this, at least, we must agree: the right to do what I've just done—to state my faith without fear—is the first human right. Religious liberty is the essence of human dignity. We cannot build our temples on the ruins of individual conscience. For faith does not come through the weight of power, but through the hope of glory.

It is a sad fact that religious oppression is often practiced by religious groups. Sad and inexcusable. A believer may risk prison for his own religious beliefs, but he may never build prisons for those of other beliefs.

It is our obligation—all of us here—to bring back a renewed passion for religious liberty to every nation from which we came. It is our duty to create a cultural environment where conscience can flourish. I say this for the sake of every believer imprisoned for boldness or silenced for fear. I say this for the sake of every society that has yet to learn the benefits of vital and voluntary religious faith.

The beliefs that divide us should not be minimized. But neither should the aspirations we share: for spiritual understanding; for justice and compassion; for proper stewardship of God's creation; for religious influence—not oppression—in the right ordering of society. And for truth against the arrogant lies of our modern age.

For at the close of this century, every religious tradition finds common ground, ground in a common task: a struggle over the meaning and future of our world and our own particular culture.

Each of us has an obligation to expose the deceptions that are incompatible with true faith. It is to this end I will direct my remarks today.

Four great myths define our times: the four horsemen of the present apocalypse.

The first myth is the goodness of man. The first horseman rails against heaven with the presumptuous question: why do bad things happen to good people? He multiplies evil by denying its existence.

This myth deludes people into thinking that they are always victims, never villains; always deprived, never depraved. It dismisses responsibility as the teaching of a darker age. It can excuse any crime, because it can always blame something else—a sickness of society or a sickness of the mind.

One writer has called the modern age "the golden age of exoneration." When guilt is dismissed as the illusion of narrow minds, then no one is finally accountable, even to his conscience.

The irony is that one should come alive in this century, of all centuries, with its gulags and death camps, and killing fields. As G. K. Chesterton once said, "The doctrine of original sin is the only philosophy empirically validated by the centuries of recorded human history."

It was a Holocaust survivor who exposed the myth most eloquently. Yehiel Dinur was a witness during the trial of Adolf Eichmann. Dinur entered the courtroom and stared at the man behind the bulletproof glass—the man who had presided over the slaughter of millions. The court was hushed as a victim confronted a butcher.

Then suddenly Dinur began to sob, and collapsed to the floor. Not out of anger or bitterness. As he explained later in an interview, what struck him at that instant was a terrifying realization. "I was afraid about myself," Dinur said. "I saw that I am capable to do this. . . . Exactly like he."

The reporter interviewing Dinur understood precisely. "How was it possible for a man to act as Eichmann acted?" he asked. "Was he a monster? A madman? Or was he perhaps something even more terrifying: Was he normal?"

Yehiel Dinur, in a moment of chilling clarity, saw the skull beneath the skin. "Eichmann," he concluded, "is in all of us."

Jesus said it plainly: "That which proceeds out of man, that is what defiles the man" (Mark 7:20).

The second myth of modernity is the promise of coming utopia. The second horseman arrives with sword and slaughter.

This is the myth that human nature can be perfected by government; that a new Jerusalem can be built using the tools of politics.

From the birth of this century, ruthless ideologies claimed history as their own. They moved swiftly from nation to nation on the strength of a promised utopia. They pledged to move the world, but could only stain it with blood.

In communism and fascism we have seen the rulers who bear the mark of Cain as a badge of honor; who pursue a savage virtue, devoid of humility and humanity. We have seen more people killed in this century by their own governments than in all its wars combined. We have seen every utopian experience fall, exhausted from the pace of its own brutality.

Yet utopian temptations persist, even in the world's democracies, stripped of their terrors perhaps, but not of their risks. The political illusion still deceives, whether it is called the great society, the new covenant, or the new world order. In each case it promises government solutions to our deepest needs for security, peace, and meaning.

The third myth is the relativity of moral values. The third horseman sows chaos and confusion.

This myth hides the dividing line between good and evil, noble and base. It has thus created a crisis in the realm of truth. When a society abandons its transcendent values, each individual's moral vision become purely personal and finally equal. Society becomes merely the sum total of individual preferences, and since no preference is morally preferable, anything that can be dared will be permitted.

This leaves the moral consensus for our laws and manners in tatters. Moral neutrality slips into moral relativism. Tolerance substitutes for truth, indifference for religious conviction. And in the end, confusion undercuts all our creeds.

The fourth modern myth is radical individualism. The fourth horseman brings excess and isolation.

This myth dismisses the importance of the family, church, and community, denies the value of sacrifice, and elevates individual rights and pleasures as the ultimate social value.

But with no higher principles to live by, men and women suffocate under their own expanding pleasures. Consumerism becomes empty and leveling, leaving society full of possessions but drained of ideals. That is what Vaclav Havel calls "totalitarian consumerism."

As author George Macdonald once wrote, "The one principle of hell is 'I am on my own.'"

I have seen firsthand the kind of society these deadly myths create. In 17 years I have been in more prisons than I can count, in more nations than I can name. I have seen the face of the crisis of modernity in real human faces.

The myth of human goodness tells men and women they are not responsible for their actions, that everyone is a victim. "Poverty is the cause of crime," said a U.S. attorney general three decades ago. "Looters are not to blame for looting," said a U.S. president. Thus excused, millions refused accountability for their behavior. Crime soared and is today the great plague on civilized societies.

Utopianism, however, assures us that crime can be solved by government policy. On the left that means rehabilitation, on the right, more and tougher laws to scare people straight. But our efforts prove futile. In the past 30 years the prison population in America has increased five-fold. But the violent crime has increased just as fast.

For criminals are not made by sociological or environmental or economic forces. They are created by their own moral choices. Institutions of cold steel and bars are unable to reach the human heart, and so they can neither deter nor rehabilitate.

A decade ago, social scientist James Q. Wilson searched for some correlation between crime and social forces. He discovered that in the late nineteenth century, when the nation was rapidly industrializing, conditions that should have caused crime to increase, crime actually declined. The explanation? At the time a powerful spiritual awakening was sweeping across America, inspiring moral revival and renewal. By contrast, in the affluent 1920s, when there should have been less economic incentive for lawlessness, crime increased. Why? In the wake of Freud and Darwin, religion fell from favor. In Wilson's words, "The educated classes have began to repudiate moral uplift."

A similar study in England by Professor Christie Davies found that crime was lowest a century ago when three out of four young Britons were enrolled in Sunday school. Since then, Sunday school attendance has declined, and crime has correspondingly increased.

Crime is a mirror of a community's moral state. A society cannot long survive if the demands of human dignity are not written on our hearts. No number of people can enforce order. No threat of punishment can create it. Crime and violence frustrate every political answer, because there can be no solution apart from character and creed.

But relativism and individualism have undermined the traditional beliefs that once informed our character and defined our creed. There are no standards to guide us. Dostoyevsky's diagnosis was correct: without God, everything is permissible; crime is inevitable.

These myths constitute a threat for all of us regardless of our culture or the faith communities we represent. The four horsemen of the present day apocalypse lead away from the cloud and fire of God's presence into a barren wilderness. Modernity was once judged by the heights of its aspirations. Today it must be judged by the depths of its decadence. That decadence has marked the West most deeply. This makes it imperative that we understand the struggle for the soul of the western civilization.

We stand at a pivotal moment in history, when nations around the world are looking westward. In the past five years the balance of the world power shifted dramatically. Suddenly, remarkably, almost inexplicably, one of history's most sustained assaults on freedom collapsed before our eyes.

The world was changed, not through the militant dialect of communism, but through the power of unarmed truth. It found revolution in the highest hopes of common men. Love of liberty steeled under the weight of tyranny; the path of the future was charted in prison cells.

This revolution's symbolic moment was May Day 1990. Protesters followed the tanks, missiles, and troops rumbling across Red Square. One, a bearded Orthodox Monk, darted under the reviewing stand where Gorbachev and other Soviet leaders stood. He thrust a huge crucifix into the air, shouting above the crowd, "Mikhail Sergeyevich!" Christ is risen!

Gorbachev turned and walked off the platform.

Across the continent the signal went. In defiant hope a spell was broken. The lies of the decades were exposed. Fear and terror fled. And millions awoke from a long nightmare.

Their waking dream is a world revolution. Almost overnight the western model of economic, political, and social liberty has captured the imagination of reformers and given hope to the oppressed. We saw it at Tiananmen Square, where a replica of the Statue of Liberty, an icon of western freedom, became a symbol of Chinese hope. We saw it in Czechoslovakia when a worker stood before a desolate factory and read to a crowd, with tears in his eyes, the American Declaration of Independence.

This is one of history's defining moments. The faults of the West are evident. But equally evident are the extraordinary gifts it has to offer the world: the gift of markets that increase living standards and choices, the gift of political institutions where power forms from the consent of the governed, not the barrel of the gun, the gift of social beliefs that encourage tolerance and individual autonomy.

Free markets. Free governments. Free minds.

But just at this moment—after the struggle of the century, just at this moment, with a new era of liberty our realistic hope, just at this moment—the culture that rationed this freedom is being overrun by the four horsemen. It has embraced the destructive myths of modernity, which are poisoning its wellspring of justice and virtue and stripping away its most essential humanizing, civilizing influence.

Make no mistake. This humanizing, civilizing is the Judeo-Christian heritage. It is a heritage brought to life anew in each generation by men and women whose lives are transformed by the living God and filled with holy conviction.

Despite the failures of some of its followers—the crusades and the inquisitions—this heritage has laid the foundations of freedom in the West. It has established a standard of justice over both men and nations. It has proclaimed a higher law that exposes the pretensions of tyrants. It has taught that every human soul is on a path of immortality, that every man and woman is to be treated as the child of a king.

The muscular faith has motivated excellence in art and discovery in science. It has undergirded an ethic of work and an ethic of service. It has tempered freedom with internal restraint, so our laws could be permissive while our society was not.

Christian conviction inspires public virtue: the moral impulse to do good. It has sent legions into battle against disease, oppression, and bigotry. It ended the slave trade, built hospitals and orphanages, tamed the brutality of mental wards and prisons.

In every age is given divine mercy a human face in the lives of those who follow Christ: from Francis of Assisi to the great social reformers Wilberforce and Shaftesbury to Mother Teresa to the tens of thousands of Prison Fellowship volunteers who take hope to the captives and who are the true recipients of this award.

Christian conviction also shapes personal virtue: the moral imperative to be good. It subdues an obstinate will. It ties a tether to self-interest and violence.

Finally, Christian conviction provides a principled belief in human freedom. As Lord Acton explained, "Liberty is the highest political end of man. . . . (But) no country can be free without religion. It creates and strengthens the notion of duty. If men are not kept straight by duty, they must be by fear. The more they are kept, by fear, the less they are free. The greater the strength of duty, the greater the liberty."

The kind of duty to which Acton refers is driven by the most compelling motivation. I and every other Christian have experienced it. It is the duty that flows from gratitude to God that He would send His only Son to die so that we might live.

This is the lesson of centuries: that ordered liberty is one of faith's triumphs. And yet, western cultural and political elites seem blinded by modernity's myths to the historic civilizing role of Christian faith. And so, in the guise of pluralism and tolerance, they have set about to exile religion from our common life. They use the power of the media and the law like steel wool to scrub public debates and public places bare of religious ideas and symbols. But what is left is sterile and featureless and cold.

The elites seek freedom without self-restraint, liberty without standards. But they find instead the revenge of offended absolutes.

Courts strike down even perfunctory prayers, and we are surprised that schools, bristling with barbed wire, look more like prisons than prisons do.

Universities reject the very idea of truth, and we are shocked when the best and the brightest of their graduates loot and betray.

Celebrities mock the traditional family, even revile it as a form of slavery, and we are appalled at the human tragedy of broken homes and millions of unwed mothers.

The media celebrate sex without responsibility, and we are horrified by sexual plagues.

Our lawmakers justify the taking of innocent life in sterile clinics, and we are terrorized by the disregard for life in blood-soaked streets.

C. S. Lewis described this irony a generation ago. "We laugh at honor," he said, "and are shocked to find traitors in our midst. . . . We castrate and bid the geldings fruitful."

A generation of cultural leaders wants to live off the spiritual capital of its inheritance, while denigrating the ideals of its ancestors. It squanders a treasure it no longer values. It celebrates its liberation when it should be trembling for its future.

Where does the stampede of the four horsemen lead us? Only one place: tyranny. A new kind of cultural tyranny finds minds, unformed by traditions and standards, easy to shape.

Philosopher Hannah Arendt described totalitarianism as a process where lonely, rootless individuals, deprived of meaning and community, welcome the captivity of ideology. To escape their inner emptiness, they seek out new forms of servitude. Trading independence for security, they blend into faceless conformity.

The lonely crowd always finds a leader. It submits to the party line and calls it freedom. America is filled with willing recruits to follow a new Grand Inquisitor.

This coming cultural tyranny already casts its shadow across university campuses where repressive speech codes stifle free debate; across court houses and legislatures where officials hunt down and purge every religious symbol; across network newsrooms and board rooms where nothing is censored except traditional belief. Our modern elites speak of enlightened tolerance while preparing shackles for those who disagree. This is what Chesterton defined as true bigotry: "The anger of men who have no conviction."

Disdaining the past and its values, we flee the judgment of the dead. We tear down memory's monuments, removing every guidepost and landmark, and wander in unfamiliar country. But it is a sterile wasteland in which men and women are left with carefully furnished lives and utterly barren souls.

And so, paradoxically, at the very moment much of the rest of the world seems to be reaching out for western liberal ideals, the West itself, beguiled by myths of modernity, is undermining the very foundation of those ideals.

This is irony without humor, farce without joy. Western elites are carefully separating the wheat from the chaff and keeping the chaff. They are performing a modern miracle of turning wine into water.

This crisis is not only alarming, it is also urgent. In earlier times, social patterns were formed over centuries by tradition and intellectual debate, then gradually filtered to the masses. Now, through technology, a social revolution can be wired directly to the brain. It comes through satellites and videos, through pleasing images and catchy tunes. Refugees on a boat from southern China were recently intercepted by the U.S. Coast Guard: their entire knowledge of the English language consisted of one acronym: MTV.

The world's newly developing nations are in a revolution of rising expectations that may become a trap of misplaced hope.

Nations that import a western ideal stripped of its soul will find out only what we have found: pleasures as shallow as the moment, emptiness as deep as eternity.

I say to you assembled here today from every part of the globe that this is a challenge facing all of us. At this extraordinary moment in world history, many nations once enslaved to ruthless ideologies have now been set free, only to face a momentous decision. Each must decide whether to embrace the myths of modernity or turn to a deeper, older tradition: the half-forgotten teachings of saints and sages.

I say to my compatriots in the West that we bear a particular responsibility, for modernity's myths have found fertile soil in our lands, and we have offered haven to the four horsemen who trample the dreams and hopes of men and women everywhere. As the world looks to us, let us summon the courage to challenge our comfortable assumptions, to scrutinize the effect we have on our global neighbors, and then to recover that which has been the very soul and conscience of our own civilization.

For the West today is like Janus, with a two-sided face. One offering futility, empty secularism and death. The other offering freedom, rich, biblically rooted spiritually, and life. Commentators have described the internal conflict between these two as a culture war. Some have declared the war over. The four horsemen, they tell us, are the victors at this chapter in our history.

Admittedly the signs are not auspicious, as I have been at pains to show, and it is easy to become discouraged. But a Christian neither has the reason nor the right, for history's cadence is called with a confident voice. The God of Abraham, Isaac, and Jacob reigns. His plan and purpose robs the future of its fears.

By the cross He offers hope, by the Resurrection He assures His triumph. This cannot be resisted or delayed. Mankind's only choice is to recognize Him now or in the moment of ultimate judgment. Our only decision is to welcome His rule or to fear it.

But this gives every one of us hope. For this is a vision beyond a vain utopia or a timid new world order. It is a vision of an enduring revolution. One that breaks the chains of sin and death. And it proclaims liberation that the cruelest person cannot contain.

The Templeton Prize is awarded for progress in religion. In a technological age, we often equate progress with breaking through barriers in science and knowledge. But progress does not always mean discovering something new. Sometimes it means discovering wisdom that is ancient and eternal. Sometimes, in our search for advancement, we find it only where we began. The greatest progress in religion today is to meet every nation's most urgent need: A revolution that begins in the human heart. It is the enduring revolution.

In the aftermath of the tragedy in Waco, Texas, and terrorist bombings in New York, we heard dire warnings, even from the president of the United States, of religious extremism. But that, with due respect, is not the world's gravest threat. Far more dangerous is the decline of true religion and of its humanizing values in our daily lives. No ideology, not even liberal democracy, is sufficient. Every noble hope is empty apart from the enduring revolution.

This revolution reaches across centuries and beyond politics. It confounds the ambitions of kings, and rewards the faith of a child. It clothes itself in the rags of common lives, then emerges with sudden splendor. It violates every jaded expectation with the paradox of its power.

The evidence of its power is humility. The evidence of its conquest is peace. The evidence of its triumph is service. But that still, small voice of humility, of peace, of service becomes a thundering judgment that shakes every human institution to its foundation.

The enduring revolution teaches that freedom is found in submission to a moral law. It says that duty is our sharpest weapon against fear and tyranny. This revolution raises an unchanging and eternal moral standard *and* offers hope to everyone who fails to reach it. This revolution sets the content of justice *and* transforms the will to achieve it. It builds communities of character and of compassion.

On occasion, God provides glimpses of this glory. I witnessed one in an unlikely place—a prison in Brazil like none I've ever seen.

Twenty years ago in the city of San Jose dos Campos, a prison was turned over to two Christian laymen. They called it Humaita, and their plan was to run it on Christian principles.

The prison has only two full-time staff. The rest of the work is done by inmates. Every prisoner is assigned to another inmate to whom he is accountable. In addition, every prisoner is assigned a volunteer family from the outside that works with him during his term and after his release. Every prisoner joins a chapel program, or else takes a course in character development.

When I visited Humaita, I found the inmates smiling—particularly the murderer who held the keys, opened the gates, and let me in. Wherever I walked, I saw men at peace. I saw clean living areas. I saw people working industriously. The walls were decorated with biblical sayings from Psalms and Proverbs.

Humaita has an astonishing record. Its recidivism rate is 4 percent compared to the 75 percent in the rest of Brazil and the United States. How is that possible?

I saw the answer when my inmate guide escorted me to the notorious punishment cell once used for torture. Today, he told me, that block houses only a single inmate. As we reached the end of the long concrete corridor and he put the key into the lock, he paused and asked, "Are you sure you want to go in?"

"Of course," I replied impatiently. "I've been in isolation cells all over the world." Slowly he swung open the massive door, and I saw the prisoner in that punishment cell: a crucifix, beautifully carved by the Humaita inmates, the prisoner Jesus, hanging on the cross.

"He's doing time for all the rest of us," my guide said softly.

In that cross carved by loving hands is a holy subversion. It heralds change more radical than mankind's most fevered dreams. Its followers expand the boundaries of a kingdom that can never fall. A shining kingdom that reaches into the darkest corners of every community, into the darkest corners of every mind. A kingdom of deathless hope, of restless virtue, of endless peace.

This work proceeds, this hope remains, this fire will not be quenched. The enduring revolution of the cross of Christ.

THE DANGERS OF RELIGION[1]
ROBERT H. MENEILLY[2]

Although the United States Constitution provides for the separation of church and state, religion has always been a force in American politics. Historically, religious groups have sought to affect political questions including slavery, temperance, and immigration.

[1]Delivered to the congregation of The Village Church, Prairie Village, Kansas, on the morning of Sunday, August 15, 1993.
[2]For biographical note, see Appendix.

Religious leaders have often mobilized their followers on be-half of one or another political cause. One of the most successful at this in recent years was the group called Moral Majority orga-nized by the Reverend Jerry Falwell. The group dissolved in the 1980s when Falwell proclaimed it had accomplished its goals.

In 1988 a new group, the Christian Coalition, was spawned from mailing lists used in the Reverend Pat Robertson's failed campaign for the Republican presidential nomination. By April 1993, the coalition had grown to 350,000 members with 750 local chapters, full-time staffs in 15 states, and an annual budget said to be over 8 million dollars.

Although the Christian Coalition claims tax-exempt status as a religious-education organization, some critics argue that its ac-tivities are largely political and cite among other evidence a 1991 fund-raising letter to members, in which Pat Robertson wrote: "We are training people to be effective—to be elected to school boards, to city councils, to state legislatures, and to key positions in political parties." Later in the letter, he predicted that by the end of the decade "the Christian Coalition will be the most power-ful political organization in America" (Robert Sullivan, "An Army of the Faithful," *New York Times Magazine* April 25, 1993, p. 34).

Some accuse the group of trying to gain control of the Repub-lican Party by running highly conservative candidates for local and state offices who conceal their right-wing affiliations and beliefs. These "stealth" candidates have been unusually success-ful, winning according to some reports more than 40 percent of the races they have entered (Elena Neuman, "A Holy Terror from the Right," *Insight on the News*, January 11, 1993, p. 4).

The political activities of the so-called Religious Right on be-half of candidates in the Kansas City, Kansas, area led the Rever-end Robert H. Meneilly to deliver a sermon to his congregation on August 15, 1993. The sermon attracted considerable atten-tion. It was printed in full two days later locally and subsequently in the *New York Times* and other newspapers around the country.

The Reverend Meneilly gave his sermon at a regular Sunday morning worship service to some 2,300 members of The Village Church (Presbyterian Church, U.S.A.), Prairie Village, Kansas. Meneilly, who has been with the church since 1947, is its first and only minister.

Robert H. Meneilly's speech: Let it be made clear from the outset that this is a sermon on religion, not politics. What is good about religion is good for the republic, and what is good about a republic is good for religion. However, we believe fervently in the American way, which stands for the separation of religion and state. Naturally, we are to live out our beliefs within the political state as private citizens, but we do not attempt to use the state's political system to enforce our belief system upon our pluralistic neighbors.

Religion can be the greatest thing on earth, or the worst. It can be the greatest healing therapy in society, or the greatest hazard to a society's health. It can be a democratic republic's greatest good, or its worst threat.

Look at the hot spots of the earth today and you see religious extremists lighting the fuses, whether in Northern Ireland, Israel, Bosnia, or California, USA. Religious extremists are breeding all kinds of "culture wars." Religion can breed all kinds of harassment, bigotry, prejudice, intolerance, and deception.

We have only to look back to Jesus' day. His greatest problems were not with the atheists or agnostics, but with religious extremists. When you have religionists who think they have all the answers and that everyone should be compelled to live by their beliefs because they have an "exclusive" on righteousness, you have the worst dangers knocking at your door.

Religion is peculiar. When it is not in earnest, it doesn't hurt anyone; but it doesn't do any good either. When it is in earnest, it is a most powerful force for good or evil. If religion can persuade someone that an idea is the will of God, that person, not wanting to displease Almighty God, may feel compelled to act on it.

We Christians must face up to the fact that our Christianity has propagated, in the name of Jesus, devilish acts, bloody wars, awful persecutions, hate crimes, and political chaos. We have seen this evidenced on television with leaders of Operation Rescue harassing neighbors and demonstrating at women's clinics in most detestable and criminal ways, in the name of Jesus! The hate which certain extreme elements of the Christian community have cultivated toward neighbors of a homosexual orientation resembles the environment of hell. It causes the community to wonder if they have ever heard of the first and second greatest commandments of God.

One of the not-so-obvious Christian religious movements in our country is what has become known as the Religious Right, or the New Right. So many wonderfully good and well-meaning people are being drawn in and are supporting their agenda without realizing what they are doing or considering the ultimate consequences. The movement is led by some very charismatic leaders like Pat Robertson, James Dobson, Tim LaHaye, Jimmy Swaggart, and Jerry Falwell. Their message sounds good, righteous, and very Christian on the surface. What unthinking person can listen to clean-shaven, well-dressed and patriotic-sounding Pat Robertson talk about his Christian Coalition and not think, "That it is exactly what this country needs. This is good old American patriotism?" The thousands of good Christians who will gather in Kansas City or other cities to hear James Dobson talk of his "Focus on the Family" crusade may think, "Wow, that's the greatest, and every American should hear and heed." "Discipline our kids, don't spare the rod and spoil the child; indoctrinate them with our exclusive doctrines; make divorce impossible; don't teach about sex until kids are more mature and can understand it; don't permit the teaching of sexuality to youth in public school, because it will end up making them prematurely curious, and that leads to promiscuity. Preach 'Mom at home in the kitchen and Dad bringing home all the bacon' orthodoxy."

"Focus on the Family," on the surface, appears to be a commendable mission. But it is a mission which is out to get the state to legislate what Dobson's religion can't seem to do. Any religion that needs the government to support and subsidize it doesn't deserve to survive. It is not the state's business to carry out the churches' ministries!

The Religious Right's mission is twofold. First, it seeks to gain control of the Republican Party apparatus at the state and local levels, with the eventual goal of claiming control of the Republican National Committee itself. Its second objective is to win for its candidates election to hundreds, even thousands, of lower level public offices. Once elected, they can begin to implement Robertson's Christian Coalition extremist views. And from there, they can seek higher offices. They have put out a detailed manual, spelling out how to get in and manipulate the democratic political process. They seem to think that any means justify their ends. They campaign quietly, very much within the safety of their own church communities. They are referred to as "stealth" candidates. They have been concentrating upon school boards throughout the country. No one hears of them, except their own church sponsors, and with the low turnout of voters for school board elections, they are suddenly seen for the first time after being elected.

To be sure, any person should be free to run for an office, whatever his or her political party or religious affiliation. But stealth candidates, who conceal their ultimate purpose until elected, are mighty dangerous for local communities and the nation.

Once in office, these New Right folks "come out of their closets." They begin pushing their agenda on our schools, ranging from censorship of selected novels and textbooks to the teaching of creationism, gutting sex education programs, and putting an end to school breakfast programs for the needy and day care for children of working parent families on the grounds that such programs undercut the family. Children should eat at home with their parents, when there may be no parents there, or no food. The Religious Right's general agenda includes, among other things, antipornography. What sane person does not detest child pornography? Yet people buy into the general agenda on the basis that an antipornography program is worthy of support. They are against any woman having a say about what goes on in her own body and insist that abortions, performed for any reason, should be judged as "murder in the first degree." In turn, single-issue antiabortion folks may jump on their bandwagon. However, it should be noted that many pro-life antiabortionists will not have anything to do with Robertson's Christian Coalition. It should also be noted that a majority of conservative citizens do not want to be equated with the Religious Right. The Religious Right are also opposed to the Equal Rights Amendment and would deprive those who are not "their kind of people" of certain inalienable rights guaranteed by our Constitution.

The Religious Right are determined to get their prayers and their Bible reading back into the public schools, by hook or by crook. They are big on censorship of books, including any fantasy yarns involving witches, even those in the long tradition of children's literature, such as *Snow White* and *Hansel and Gretel*. They claim that these lead to devil worship and witchcraft.

The newest code words of the New Right, used to hook those who might not hear them otherwise, are the environment, the deficit, and the economy. Since there is hardly one among us who is not interested in these issues, some of the finest of persons are hooked into the New Right agenda based on a single concern.

The Religious Right extremists always refer to the United States as a "Christian nation." This always appeals to the white Anglo-Saxon Protestant! But look at history honestly. The very idea that the United States should be officially Christian was explicitly rejected by James Madison, one of the primary designers of our Constitution, and the other framers, who insisted on a system of separation of church and state that guarantees religious freedom for all individuals and groups, Christian and non-Christian alike. The "Christian nation" concept has never been endorsed by the Supreme Court as officially binding judicial policy. "Christian nation," like "family values," have been code words for an evangelical socioreligious perspective and have been used to marginalize, if not blackball, all of their nonconformists.

Ours has always been a pluralistic country of all nationalities and religions. We used to pride ourselves in being "the melting pot of the world," and considered our diversity our strength and uniqueness. The genius of our American system is that in religious matters the government remains neutral. This allows all citizens to practice their religious faiths freely and not impose them on government.

The Religious Right always employ the expression "Christian nation," referring to their desire to see the national laws reflect the narrow sectarian principles which they themselves hold, not just saying that a majority of Americans identify with Christian denominations. These misguided religionists and patriots are trying to say that only persons with the correct religious views are real Americans and should hold public offices. The historic position of this nation is that the government as a legal organization is independent of all religions. Our constitution specifically provides that "Congress shall make no law respecting an establishment of religion or prohibiting the free exercise thereof." In the words of Thomas Jefferson, the First Amendment was intended to "erect a wall of separation between church and state." The person's right to freedom of belief is to be beyond the reach of government and majoritarian rule.

The Religious Right extremists have been conniving in every political way to get state-mandated prayer and Bible reading back into the public school ever since the 1963 Supreme Court decision declared it to be unconstitutional. Let's face it, Christian Protestants, that old tradition, clearly promoted a generic form of Protestantism without any concern for our Roman Catholic, Mormon, Jewish, Unitarian, or Muslim neighbors. The Pennsylvania law that was challenged by the Supreme Court was explicit: "At least ten verses from the Holy Bible shall be read, without comment, at the opening of each school day."

Actually, voluntary prayer in public schools has always been legal. Children are perfectly free to say grace after lunch and read the Bible in their free time. We need to resist government-prescribed prayer programs in our public schools. That 1963 Supreme Court [decision] put the responsibility back upon parents, where it belongs, giving fathers and mothers the right to determine what religious exercises are taught. A religion that must depend upon the state to do what it cannot do is not worthy of existence. Even Christianity.

The Religious Right are running down the public schools toward the end of getting government money for the private and parochial schools. It is called the "voucher" system. The head of the National Education Association has said, "Since the New Right can't get the public schools to go along with their religious views, they want to privatize education, to get money from the public treasury for religious schools." Private and parochial schools may be excellent, but they ought not expect public funding, for soon the funding state is sure to impose its regulations. Any subsidizer soon regulates, and religion loses! Every election within the Shawnee Mission and Blue Valley school districts and Johnson County Community College has stealth candidates. The Republican Party in Johnson County has been captured by the New right and stealth candidates. This osmosis will continue if the religious and nonreligious set by and do not insist on knowing exactly where a candidate is coming from and heading toward. Surely, any patriotic American believes that no individual or organization should promote or impose their religious or personal beliefs on others through deceptive practices, personal attacks, political connivery or stealthy activities.

Now, folks, the issue of this sermon is not politics, but religion. If we continue to let the historic wall between church and state erode away, religion will suffer more than the State. The new Religious Right extremists want nothing less than to force our American society to enact into law their exclusive religious views, and thereby impose them on everyone. But ours is a constitutional republic made up of many different religions, where every individual's rights are guaranteed and all voices are heard. The Religious Right seeks a theocracy that legislates and enforces their particular vision of God's law.

This New Right confronts us with a threat far greater than the old threat of Communism. When the state and the church would become entwined, it is religion that will be the loser.

I tremble for my country when I hear zealous religionists

plaguing good neighbors and women's health clinics in the name of Jesus, who said, "A new commandment I give to you: love one another as I have loved you." I tremble for our nation when I hear extremists discredit our public school system—the only truly ecumenical program left in our community. The public schools take the poor and the handicapped, the abused and foster children, the Christian and the Muslim, the Roman Catholic and the Jew. They do more of the Lord's work every day than most other institutions. I fear for our public school system if we afford government support to private schools, either secular or religious. It is our freedom of religion that will ultimately lose.

Americans need to be reminded that no group, religious or secular, can insist upon majority rule. One does not keep the Ten Commandments by any majority rule! The Bill of Rights aims precisely to protect the religious freedom, rights, and sensibilities of the minority against the whims of the majority. The protection afforded individuals under the First Amendment is not subject to majority rule. Government agencies, including public school authorities, do not have liberty to promote the religious perspective of any group, majority or minority.

It may sound judgmental for one religionist in a pulpit to stand up and warn people about the threat of differing religionists. I pray that what I do today is discernment in love, not judgment in any hate. We must not let the Pat Robertsons, James Dobsons, Tim La Hayes, or Jimmy Swaggarts be ignored. It is our Christian commission to put in a good word for Jesus Christ, our Savior and Lord. We are to share our faith in Jerusalem, Judea, and to the ends of the earth, but not at the expense of another faith. To love our neighbors as ourselves requires tolerance, but it also requires looking out for the best ultimate welfare of both state and church. It means being humble, not self-righteous.

Recently, the "born-again" Watergate burglar, Southern Baptist, evangelical writer and Republican, Charles Colson, predicted that "if evangelicals don't begin to attend to their own houses of worship, they will be eclipsed." Colson said that the role of the church is not to win political battles or even make people happy; it is to make people holy.

I have saved my biblical text for this sermon until last: Love your neighbor as yourself. When we abide by those words, we will do best by our religion and by our country.

Lord, we have certainly sought your guidance in preparing this sermon. If, in our own sinful nature, we have missed your

wisdom, save us all. If we have perceived your true word, let it be
heard and bring it to its fullest fruition. Grant that, in the midst of
our differences within the Christian community, we may discipline ourselves, with the aid of your grace, to love all of our
neighbors, not just in theory but in practice. Grant that in every
family, even our church family, we may agree to disagree and still
love one another. We beg of you, teach us the truth that sets us
free. Amen

REMEMBERING THE HOLOCAUST[1]
ALBERT GORE, JR.[2]

Each year, the United States Holocaust Memorial Council or-
ganizes a ceremony in connection with the annual Days of Re-
membrance to remember the six million victims of the Holocaust.

March 19th marked the fiftieth anniversary of the beginning
of the Holocaust in Hungary. By the time Budapest was liberated
ten months later, the number of Jews in Hungary had dropped
from 750,000 to just 139,000. The 1994 ceremony was dedicated
to the Hungarian Jewish Community.

Ceremonies remembering the Holocaust in Hungary were
held in various cities around the country. Probably the most important was the observance at the rotunda in the Capitol building
on April 6, 1994. The principal speaker was Vice President Albert
Gore, Jr. His audience included members of the House and Senate, cabinet members, ambassadors, and prominent Hungarian
and American Jewish leaders.

Albert Gore, Jr's speech: Eva Heyman kept a diary during those last
weeks before the Nazis rounded up the Jews of Nagyvarad, then
inside Hungary, near its Romanian border. It was during the days
when Jews could still live in their homes, but things were awful. In
May 1944, Eva wrote: "Every time I think this is the end, things
couldn't possibly get worse. And then I find out that it's always
possible for everything to get worse."

Sometimes she couldn't sleep. Lying awake in her bed, she

[1]Delivered in the rotunda of the Capitol, Washington, D.C., April 6, 1994.
[2]For biographical note, see Appendix.

would hear the adults talking. "They said that the people aren't only beaten, but also get electric shocks," she wrote:

People are brought to the hospital bleeding at the mouth and ears . . . some of them also with teeth missing and the soles of their feet swollen so they can't stand . . . in the ghetto pharmacy there is enough poison and Grandpa gives poison to the older people who ask for it. Grandpa also said it would be better if he took cyanide and also gave some to Grandma.

On this Spring day here in Washington, we think of Eva Heyman, listening in her bed, and wish we could somehow go back in time and rescue her.

But she wrote during the last spring she would ever know. The gendarmes came for her family three weeks later, and marched her into the gas chamber at Auschwitz on October 17. She was thirteen years old.

To read what happened to the Jews of Hungary is to read of the most unspeakably barbaric acts: of Arrow Cross members, in black boots and green shirts, herding Jewish women, children and old men through the streets of Budapest, prodding them with rifle butts, shooting those who could not keep up the pace.

Or the ritual executions. Arrow Cross guards would line up three Jewish victims, and wire their wrists together. The rifleman would fire into the back of one. The dead person would slump forward and pull others in the Danube where the freezing river and weight of the corpse finished the others. That saved two bullets.

What is the lesson of these acts for us, fifty years later?

Certainly on this week after Passover, a commemoration of freedom from slavery three thousand years old, there is this lesson: tell the story. The purpose of this memorial of this day is to tell the story to each generation.

We tell the story, in part, to remember those who died. We also tell it to remember the need for vigilance. And for the Jewish people there is a need for vigilance. Is there any people who have been persecuted for so long and in so many places, driven from nation to nation, whether from Babylon or Rome, England or Spain, or by the pogroms throughout Eastern Europe?

There are those who argue that Jews were victims, going passively to their death. This is a lie. Jews fought back. They fought back in Warsaw. They fought back throughout Eastern Europe.

They even recorded accounts of their fighting back. A merchant and aspiring writer, Zalman Gradowski, who fell in a revolt at Auschwitz he spearheaded, buried four manuscript accounts of life in death, on which he had inscribed these words: "Take heed of this document, for it contains valuable material for the historian." Because of what he and others did, we can refute the liars with a wealth of detail that is unassailable.

To a Christian reading about the resistance, it is natural to ask: what did others do? The past twelve months have brought America stories of heroism by Gentiles in some powerful new ways. One was the portrayal by Steven Spielberg of a hero of the Nazi occupation, Oskar Schindler.

And of course, those walking through the Holocaust Museum are reminded of another hero, Raoul Wallenberg, who saved hundreds of thousands of Hungarian Jews.

Their heroism is beyond dispute.

The images in Spielberg's film of Schindler and Yitzchak Stern together pecking out on the typewriter the names of those who could be saved; the images of Wallenberg in Hungary, mounting trains bound for Auschwitz and ordering guards to release people with "Swedish" passports give the lie to the myth that everyone was indifferent.

But we must be careful not to exaggerate either their numbers or their impact. The fact is, that in most cases, nothing was done. And we must confront that, as well.

Why was so little done? For a Christian, this is an agonizing question as I confront it. For if we believe, as I do, that religion is a powerful force for good, why did so many believers and churchgoers remain silent in the face of such unalloyed evil?

One lesson learned from such massive failure is expressed by the famous words attributed to Pastor Niemoller:

When Hitler attacked the Jews . . . I was not a Jew, therefore I was not concerned. And when Hitler attacked the Catholics, I was not a Catholic and therefore I was not concerned. . . . Then Hitler attacked me and the Protestant church and there was nobody left to be concerned.

Powerful words.

But for some there is an implication in that paragraph that makes it seem insufficient. For one way to read it is as a morality play with self interest at its core: we must defend others, so others will defend us.

But we all know self-interest isn't enough. It is essential that those who feel in no danger at all rise in defense of the persecuted. The passion for justice and tolerance must be so ingrained in society that even those feeling most secure will take action to preserve it.

And we must put in place safeguards—of law, of values—that make it impossible for the human race to give vent to its most barbaric impulses during those times when the individual conscience or even the sum of those consciences is too weak, or cowed, or terrorized to resist.

Elie Weisel, talking about how Christians should react to the Holocaust, quotes the Hasidic story about a great person who said:

Look, I know how to bring about a change that would benefit the whole world. But the whole world is a huge place, so I'll begin with my country. I don't know my whole country, though; so I'll begin with my town. My town has so many streets; I'll begin in my own street. There are so many houses on my street; I'll begin in mine. There are so many people in my house; I'll begin with myself.

"You begin with yourself," Weisel says.

He is certainly right.

But of course, while we begin with ourselves, we cannot end there. Not in a world where there are those who argue the Holocaust never happened; that cyanide was used for fumigation and that the pictures of gas chambers are fabrications.

There are people who organize themselves as the enemy of truth. We must confront their lies.

We must also confront the temptation to acknowledge intellectually—but only intellectually—that the Holocaust happened, and accept it humbly, without the outrage that can prevent another one.

It is too easy for Americans, shielded for over 130 years from warfare inside our own borders, to say it can't happen here; that the Holocaust happened fifty years ago and in countries without the safeguards that make it impossible to happen in America.

But remember: the Holocaust originated in the country of Goethe and Beethoven, a country that prided itself on its refinement. We can never give in to complacency. No country is exempt from hatred or from demagogues.

And yet, when we look at America, we are certain in our hearts that if a Holocaust happened here it would not be in the America we know. It would not be in the America that has carefully separated and balanced the powers of the state and protected the freedom of its citizens. It would not be in the America whose Declaration of Independence calling for the "inalienable rights of life, liberty, and the pursuit of happiness" is venerated not simply within our National Archives, but lives and breathes in our national character.

It would not be the America whose courts have time and again affirmed the separation of church and state that has been one of our most sacred traditions. It would not be the America whose liberating forces entered the death camps in 1945 to free the survivors and provide witness that the worst stories we had heard were true.

And it would not be the America that has placed a Holocaust museum in its national capitol.

It was a controversial step. There were those who argued this was not an American experience. "Who will want to see it?" they asked. "Who, surrounded by places like the Air & Space Museum, would subject themselves to images of death?"

Those questions have been answered. They have been answered by those who crowd in to the Holocaust Museum every weekend, who stand patiently in line, people of every national origin, every color and every religion to expose their children to exhibits of the most savage things done to children in history.

The Holocaust is not an event to be remembered just by those who survived, or just by Jews or by Gypsies. Its memorial should continue to be part of the American experience for everyone.

And there is no better place for it than Washington, to remind those who make the agonizing decisions of foreign policy of the consequences of their decisions.

One remembers, of course, not just to ward off dire consequences. We remember also so we can be inspired. And that is the meaning of Raoul Wallenberg.

As opposed to Schindler, who seems to have gradually become aware of his responsibility, Wallenberg knew right from the beginning.

In Kati Marton's book about Wallenberg, she tells of the night he got a terrified call from Tibor Vandor, one of his office workers. Agnes Vandor was having a baby. They were afraid to go to the hospital.

Wallenberg brought the pregnant woman into his own bedroom, found a Jewish doctor, then paced the corridor outside all night, standing guard, while she gave birth.

The grateful parents insisted Wallenberg help name the baby, and he did: Yvonne.

Years later, this story appeared in the newspapers, and

Yvonne recognized the details, came forward, and identified herself.

But, she said, there was one detail that was wrong. She wasn't Jewish.

She had nothing against Jews, in fact, she had married one herself. But she was sure her parents were Catholic.

It was only then that she learned how terrified her parents had been in postwar Hungary to admit that they were Jewish. They didn't even dare tell her.

The effects of the Holocaust did not end when the killing ended. It scarred those who survived. It caused a generation of Jews to feel they could never again trust the countries in which they lived. Some didn't even dare admit their own heritage to their children.

The value of a Raoul Wallenberg is to inspire us so we never again fail those who need our trust. Looking back with the perspective of half a century, we remember him and others in order to strengthen us when we need strength.

Because the need for heroes is not dead. You see it in Sarajevo. You see it in Somalia. You see it in the Middle East where the courageous leaders of Israel and its Arab neighbors are taking bold risks for peace.

For much of the world the ideals of America, though not always its practices, have stood as its polar opposite. In the long, upward journey of the human experiment, our ideals—freedom, equality, tolerance, justice for all—represent a destiny.

To reach that destiny we must never forget where human beings have failed. So, on this day we allow, even force, ourselves to again remember the Holocaust in all its barbaric detail. We should not shrink from it. We remember Eva Heyman and mourn the barbarism inflicted on her because only then will we know the terrible capabilities that can lie coiled in the human soul.

But we also remember the acts of heroism like those of Raoul Wallenberg. Because that teaches us what we are capable of doing. And that means when the need occurs we won't flinch from our moral responsibility. We will meet our obligations, in our daily lives or in the business that takes place under the marble dome of this building, and make ourselves, in the words of Isaiah, "as hiding places from the winds and shelters from the tempests; as rivers of water in dry places; as shadows of a great rock in a weary land."

GETTING BEYOND RACISM[1]
CAROL MOSELEY-BRAUN[2]

Most speeches delivered on the floor of the United States Senate do not attract national attention. Because differences on major legislative proposals usually have been worked out beforehand in committee, debate in the Senate is more likely to be concerned with the details of a proposed bill rather than substantial issues. Even when a member succeeds in getting the full Senate to challenge a bill reported out of committee, seldom does a speech by an individual senator have a significant influence on the outcome of the vote.

An exception was a speech by Senator Carole Mosely-Braun given on July 22, 1993. Her speech, as presented here, was not a single set address, but the sum of two major arguments, interrupted by comments and contentions from the Senate floor. Unlike most of the addresses included in this collection, several other speakers participated in the heated exchange.

The issue was the largely symbolic one of whether to renew a patent on the logo of the United Daughters of the Confederate flag. As required by patent law the patent had been routinely renewed every 14 years since 1898. In May of 1993 Mosely-Braun persuaded the Senate Judiciary Committee to reject the request.

The first and only African-American woman in the United States Senate, Mosely-Braun, a freshman Democratic senator from Illinois, and deeply conscious of her race, had made her maiden speech in the Senate in January in tribute to the late Thurgood Marshall, the first African-American Supreme Court Justice. (See *Representative American Speeches, 1992–1993*, pp. 123–127.)

Mosely-Braun probably thought the matter of the logo patent was settled after its rejection by the Judiciary Committee. However, on July 22, 1993, while she was attending a confirmation hearing, Mosely-Braun learned that Senator Jesse Helms of North Carolina, supported by Senator Strom Thurman of South Carolina, had attached an amendment to President Clinton's national service bill that would renew the logo's patent.

[1]Delivered to the United States Senate, Washington, D.C., July 22, 1993.
[2]For biographical note, see Appendix.

Surprised by the news, Mosely-Braun rushed to the Senate chamber to challenge the amendment. Speaking without a prepared text or even notes, Mosely-Braun argued that the Senate should not renew the patent and that the amendment should be tabled. However, the motion to table was rejected by a vote of 52 to 48.

After the vote, Mosely-Braun resumed her speaking but in a different tone. "She was mad through and through," reported an aide (Stephen Braden, March 18, 1994). In her early remarks, she sounded conciliatory; when she resumed, she:

Took the floor in outrage at the defense of a symbol of slavery. Shouting and crying, she told the Senate: "On this issue there can be no consensus. It is an outrage. It is an insult. It is absolutely unacceptable to me and to millions of Americans, black and white, that we should put the imprint of the United States on a symbol of this kind of idea. (*New York Times,* July 23, 1993, p. A10)

While only about half of the Senate had been in attendance to hear Mosely-Braun's first speech, as word of the debate spread, more and more senators came to the floor. When the debate was over and the second vote came, the Senate killed the Helms amendment 75 to 25, with 27 senators changing their votes over a two-hour period. Senator Joseph Biden, a 21-year Senate veteran, said he had never seen the Senate reverse itself because of a speech by one senator (Elaine Harrington and Elaine S. Povich, *Chicago Tribune,* July 23, 1993, p. 1).

Moseley-Braun's speech was broadcast nationwide on cable television and received widespread press coverage and highly favorable response, from the public in the form of a flow of flowers, faxes, telephone calls, and accolades to the Senator's office.

Readers should realize that only the remarks of Senator Mosely-Braun during the entire two-hour debate have been reprinted here. Her speech has been edited to eliminate interruptions above procedural matters not relevant to the issue. All such omissions are indicated by ellipses. (For a complete text of the debate, see the *Congressional Record,* July 22, 1993, pp. 59252-S9270.)

Carol Moseley-Braun's speech: Mr. President, I would like to respond to this amendment and to suggest that it is absolutely ill-founded and to oppose the amendment.

Mr. President, I understand that we do not have a germaneness rule here in the Senate. But I would submit that, in the first instance, this amendment is not germane, either to this bill or, frankly, to anything else.

The real bottom line with regard to this amendment and to the request for a design patent extension by the United Daughters of the Confederacy is that it is not needed. This was recognized by the Judiciary Committee when, on the 12th of May of this year, it considered the extension of design patents and, by a vote of 13 to 2, I believe, rejected the appeal of the United Daughters of the Confederacy for renewal and extension of this particular design patent.

I think it is important to note what a design patent is. It is not just a matter of simple recognition. It is a rare honor given to an organization. There are very few of them given. In fact, design patents have only been conferred on fewer than 10 organizations in this century. They are given for a period of some 14 years. And it just is rarely done, in any event, for any organization.

There are a number of fine organizations throughout this country that are well known that do not enjoy or do not have design patents. But this organization, by a matter of oversight or whatever, has—this last year, as was brought to the attention of the Judiciary Committee, and the design patent was refused or withheld. Now the Senator from South Carolina has come to the floor attempting to undo the work of the Judiciary Committee, attempting to undo the decision of that committee that a design patent was not necessary in this case.

I submit further that the design patent is not needed in terms of the work of the organization. The Senator from South Carolina has gone on at great length to talk about the charitable work of the United Daughters of the Confederacy. The fact of the matter is the refusal to extend this extraordinary honor by this body does not stop them from doing whatever it is they do, from continuing their work in the community and the like.

The Senator has not explained, however, why the Daughters need this extraordinary congressional action to continue the work of their organization or protect against the unauthorized use of their insignia. He has not addressed at all the conclusions that have been set forth from the Treasury, which were addressed in the committee, that say it is not only extraordinary but probably inappropriate to have a design patent issued in this regard.

When members of the United Daughters of the Confederacy came to my office to discuss this issue when we were involved with consideration of the issue before the Judiciary Committee, they could not even then answer the question why it was necessary to have a design patent. They can continue to fundraise. They can continue to exist. They can continue to use the insignia. Nothing changes in terms of what it is they do. The only issue is whether or not this body is prepared to put its imprimatur on the Confederate insignia used by the United Daughters of the Confederacy.

I submit to you, Mr. President, and the members who are listening to this debate, as I did in the Judiciary Committee, that the United Daughters of the Confederacy have every right to honor their ancestors and to choose the Confederate flag as their symbol if they like. However, those of us whose ancestors fought on a different side in the Civil War, or who were held, frankly, as human chattel under the Confederate flag, are duty bound to honor our ancestors as well by asking whether such recognition by the U.S. Senate is appropriate.

The United Daughters of the Confederacy did not require this action to either conduct the affairs of their organization or to protect their insignia against unauthorized use. As the Patent Commissioner, Mr. Kirk, wrote in a letter issued April 30:

In the absence of design patent protection and regardless of statutory protection . . . nonprofit organizations have still other options for obtaining protection for their badges, insignias, logos, and names.

So this is not an issue about protecting the insignia of the United Daughters of the Confederacy, nor is it an issue about whether or not they do good works in the community, nor is it an issue of whether or not the organization has a right to use this insignia. I think the answer in all those cases is they have a right to use whatever insignia they want, they have a right to organize in any way they want, they have a right to conduct whatever business they want. But at the same time it is inappropriate for this Senate, this U.S. Congress, to grant a special, extraordinary imprimatur, if you will, to a symbol which is as inappropriate to all of us as Americans as this one is.

I have heard the argument on the floor today with regard to the imprimatur that is being sought for this organization and for this symbol, and I submit this really is revisionist history. The fact of the matter is the emblems of the Confederacy have meaning to Americans even 100 years after the end of the Civil War. Everybody knows what the Confederacy stands for. Everybody knows what the insignia means. That matter of common knowledge is not a surprise to any of us. When a former Governor stood and raised the Confederate battle flag over the Alabama State Capitol to protest the Federal Government support for civil rights and a visit by the Attorney General at the time in 1963, everybody knew what that meant. Now, in this time, in 1993, when we see the Confederate symbols hauled out, everybody knows what that means.

So I submit, as Americans we have an obligation. No. 1, to recognize the meaning, not to fall prey to revisionist history on the one hand, and also really to make a statement that we believe the Civil War is over. We believe that as Americans we are all Americans and have a need to be respectful of one another with regard to our respective histories, just as I would.

Whether we are black or white, northerners or southerners, all Americans share a common history and we share a common flag. The flag which is behind you right now, Mr. President, is our flag. The flag, the Stars and Stripes forever is our flag, whether we are from the north or south, whether we are African-American or not—that is our flag. And to give a design patent, that even our own flag does not enjoy, to a symbol of the Confederacy seems to me just to create the kind of divisions in our society that are counterproductive, that are not needed.

So I come back to the point I raised to begin with. What is the point of doing this? Why would we give an extraordinary honor to a symbol which is counter to the symbol that we as Americans, I believe, all know and love, which would be a recognition of the losing side of the war, a war that I hope—while it is a painful part of our history—I hope as Americans we have all gotten past and we can say as Americans we come together under a single flag. And this organization, if it chooses to honor the losing side of the Civil War, that is their prerogative. But it is inappropriate for that organization to call on the rest of us, on everybody else, to give our imprimatur to the symbolism of the Confederate flag.

Symbols are important. They speak volumes. They speak volumes to the people in our country. They speak volumes to the people outside of our country who follow and who care about what happens in this, the greatest nation in the world. It seems to me the time has long passed when we could put behind us the debates and arguments that have raged since the Civil War, that we get beyond the separateness and we get beyond the divisions and we get beyond fanning the flames of racial antagonism. I submit that to use the insignia of the United Daughters is their prerogative. However, it is not their prerogative to force me and the other members of this body to assent to an extraordinary honor of their own revisionist history. That is the purpose of the design patent.

Mr. President, I will have printed in the *Record* a letter to me dated April 30, 1993, from Mr. Kirk, of the U.S. Department of Commerce, Patents and Trademark Office. And, while Senator Metzenbaum is on the floor—and I do not know whether he wants to speak or not—I would like not only to have this letter printed in the *Record,* but I would like also to share with the membership what it is the Patent Office says about design patents.

Mr. President, I ask unanimous consent the letter be printed in the *Record* at the conclusion of my remarks. . . .

Mr. President, he answered this question: Is it common practice for nonprofit groups to obtain design patents for their insignia and logos?

The answer is this:

First, logos are generally words or word combinations and are not articles of manufacture. As a consequence, they cannot be protected by design patents, but may be appropriate subject matter for trademark protection.

I point out that this is a design patent involved in this situation.

Obtaining design patent protection for a nonprofit group's insignia and emblems used to be more frequent in past years than today. However, obtaining renewal and extension of design patents for the insignia of such groups is the exception rather than the rule. This may well be due to the fact that numerous organizations have acquired exclusive rights to their seals, emblems and badges under title 36, U.S. Code, which pertains to patriotic societies and observances. It should be noted, however, that under this statute some organizations are granted exclusive rights to their names, emblems, seals and badges, while others have exclusive rights to their names only.

In other words, what he is saying is that most organizations have other kinds of protections and do not have this design patent, which is sought today by the United Daughters of the Confederacy.

He goes on:

For example, 36 U.S.C., section 48 confers to the American Legion only the exclusive right to its name.

The Boy Scouts have exclusive right to their name. But neither of these organizations enjoy a design patent.

He goes on:

"In that regard, the Boy Scouts"—with regard to their fleurde-lis emblem—". . . did not obtain an extension" of the design patent that they had at the turn of the century when it expired.

So this organization has now had a design patent, from what I understand, for two renewals and they are extraordinary in their request to have it renewed.

The next question asked in the letter is: Are design patents typically renewed? The answer to this question I think is significant to this body:

> You are correct in understanding that design patents normally terminate after 14 years and, as a rule, are not renewed.

So while I will not finish reading the rest of the letter, because I have no intent right now to stand here and filibuster this issue, I think it is important to note that these patents are rarely renewed.

This is more than a second renewal for this organization. It is not necessary to begin with. They can continue to use their insignia. It does not interfere with their fundraising. It does not interfere with their charitable activities. It interferes in no way with their real activities. But rather is a symbolism of what is sought here with this amendment, which is so troublesome.

I submit to the body that the Judiciary Committee, in voting 13 to 2, recognized how singularly inappropriate it would be to renew the patent for the United Daughters of the Confederacy and it is singularly inappropriate for this amendment to be accepted.

At this time Senators Helms and Thurman were granted four minutes each. Both spoke in support of the amendment. Immediately after their speeches, the Senate voted 52 to 48 against recall of the amendment. The presiding officer then recognized Senator Mosely-Braun.

Madam President, I really had not wanted to have to do this because in my remarks I believe that I was restrained and tempered. I talked about the committee procedure. I talked about the lack of germaneness of this amendment. I talked about how it was not necessary for this organization to receive the design patent extension, which was an extraordinary extension of an extraordinary act to begin with.

What I did not talk about and what I am constrained now to talk about with no small degree of emotion is the symbolism of what this vote . . . That is what this vote really means.

I started off—maybe—I do not know—it is just my day to get to talk about race. Maybe I am just lucky about that today.

I have to tell you this vote is about race. It is about racial symbolism. It is about racial symbols, the racial past, and the single most painful episode in American history.

I have just gone through—in fact in committee yesterday I leaned over to my colleague Dianne Feinstein and I said, "You know, Dianne, I am stunned about how often and how much race comes up in conversation and debate in this general assembly." Did not I say that?. . .

So I turned to my colleague, Dianne Feinstein. You know, I am really stunned by how often and how much the issue of race, the subject of racism, comes up in this U.S. Senate, comes up in this body and how I have to, on many occasions, as the only African-American here, constrain myself to be calm, to be laid back, to talk about these issues in very intellectual, nonemotional terms, and that is what I do on a regular basis, Madam President. That is part and parcel of my daily existence.

But at the same time, when the issue of the design patent extension for the United Daughters of the Confederacy first came up, I looked at it. I did not make a big deal of it. It came as part of the work of the Judiciary Committee. I looked at it, and I said, well, I am not going to vote for that.

When I announced I was not going to vote for it, the chairman, as is his due, began to poll the members. We talked about it, and I found myself getting drawn into a debate that I frankly never expected.

Who would have expected a design patent for the Confederate flag? And there are those in this body who say this really is not the Confederate flag. The other thing we did know was a Confederate flag.

I did my research, and I looked it up as I am wont to do, and guess what? That is the real Confederate flag. The thing we see all the time and are accustomed to is the battle flag. In fact, there is some history on this issue. I would like to read the following quote from the *Flag Book of the United States*.

The real flower in the southern flag began in November 1860, when the election of Lincoln to the Presidency caused widespread fear the federal government will try to make changes in the institution of slavery. The winter of 1860 to 1861, rallies and speeches were held throughout the South and, frankly, the United States flag was replaced by a local banner.

This flag is the real flag of the Confederacy. If there is anybody in this chamber anybody, indeed anybody in this world, that has a doubt that the Confederate effort was around preserving the institution of slavery, I am prepared and I believe history is prepared to dispute them to the nth. There is no question but that battle was fought to try to preserve our nation, to keep the states from separating themselves over the issue of whether or not my ancestors could be held as property, as chattel, as objects of commerce and trade in this country.

And people died. More Americans died in the Civil War than any war they have ever gone through since. People died over the proposition that indeed these United States stood for the proposition that every person was created equal without regard to race, that we are all American citizens.

I am sorry, Madam President. I will lower my voice. I am getting excited, because, quite frankly, that is the very issue. The issue is whether or not Americans, such as myself, who believe in the promise of this country, who feel strongly and who are patriots in this country, will have to suffer the indignity of being reminded time and time again, that at one point in this country's history we were human chattel. We were property. We could be traded, bought, and sold.

Now, to suggest as a matter of revisionist history that this flag is not about slavery flies in the face of history, Madam President.

I was not going to get inflammatory. In fact, my staff brought me this little thing earlier, and it has been sitting here. I do not know if you noticed it sitting here during the earlier debate in which I was dispassionate and tried my level best not to be emotional and lawyering about and not get into calling names and talking about race and racism. I did not use it to begin with. I do want to share it now. It is a speech by the Vice President of the Confederate States of America, March 21, 1861, in Savannah, GA.

"Slavery, the Cornerstone of the Confederacy." And this man goes on to say:

> The new Confederate constitution has put to rest forever all agitating questions relating to our peculiar "institution," which is what they called it, African slavery as it exists among us, the proper status of a negro in our form of civilization. This was the immediate cause of the late rupture and present revolution.
>
> The prevailing ideas entertained by Thomas Jefferson and most of the leading statesmen at the time of the formation of the old Constitution were that the enslavement of the African was in violation of the laws of nature, that it was wrong in principle, socially, morally, and politically.

And then he goes on to say:

> Our new government is founded upon exactly the opposite idea. Its foundations are laid, its cornerstone rests upon the great truth that the

negro is not equal to the white man, that slavery, subordination to the superior race is his natural and moral condition.

This was a statement by the Vice President of the Confederate States of America.

Madam President, across the room on the other side is the flag. I say to you it is outrageous. It is an absolute outrage that this body would adopt as an amendment to this legislation a symbol of this point of view and, Madam President, I say to you that it is an important issue. It is a symbolic issue up there. There is no way you can get around it.

The reason for my emotion—I have been here almost 7 months now, and my colleagues will tell you there is not a more congenial, laid back, even person in this entire body who makes it a point to try to get along with everybody. I make it a point to try to talk to my colleagues and get beyond controversy and conflict, to try to find consensus on issues.

But I say to you, Madam President, on this issue there can be no consensus. It is an outrage. It is an insult. It is absolutely unacceptable to me and to millions of Americans, black or white, that we would put the imprimatur of the United States Senate on a symbol of this kind of idea. And that is what is at stake with this amendment, Madam President.

I am going to continue—I am going to continue because I am going to call it like I see it, as I always do. I was appalled, appalled at a segment of my own Democratic Party that would go take a walk and vote for something like this.

I am going to talk for a minute first about my brethren, my close-in brethen and then talk about the other side of the aisle and the responsibility of the Republican Party.

The reason the Republican Party got run out on a rail the last time is the American people sensed intolerance in that party. The American people, African-Americans sensed there was not room for them in that party. Folks took a look at the convention and said, "My God, what are these people standing for? This is not America." And they turned around and voted for change. They elected Bill Clinton president and the rest of us to this chamber. The changes they were speaking out for was a change that said we have to get past racism, we have to get past sexism, the many issues that divide us as Americans, and come together as Americans so we can make this country be what it can be in the 21st century.

That is the real reason, Madam President, that I am here

today. My state has less than 12 percent African-Americans in it, but the people of Illinois had no problem voting for a candidate that was African-American because they thought they were doing the same thing.

Similarly, the state of California sent two women, two women to the U.S. Senate, breaking a gender barrier, as did the state of Washington. Why? Because they felt that it was time to get past the barriers that said that women had no place in the conduct of our business.

And so, just as our country is moving forward, Madam President, to have this kind of symbol shoved in your face, shoved in my face, shoved in the faces of all the Americans who want to see a change for us to get beyond racism, is singularly inappropriate.

I say to you, Madam President, that this is no small matter. This is not a matter of little old ladies walking around doing good deeds. There is no reason why these little old ladies cannot do good deeds anyway. If they choose to wave the Confederate flag, that certainly is their right. Because I care about the fact that this is a free country. Free speech is the cornerstone of democracy. People are supposed to be able to say what they want to say. They are supposed to be able to join associations and organizations that express their views.

But I daresay, Madam President, that following the Civil War, and following the victory of the United States and the coming together of our country, that that peculiar institution was put to rest for once and for all; that the division in our nation, the North versus the South, was put to rest once and for all. And the people of this country do not want to see a day in which flags like that are underwritten, underscored, adopted, approved by this U.S. Senate.

That is what this vote is about. That is what this vote is about.

I say to you, Madam President, I do not know—I do not want to yield the floor right now because I do not know what will happen next.

I will yield momentarily to my colleague from California, Madam President, because I think that this is an issue that I am not going—if I have to stand here until this room freezes over, I am not going to see this amendment put on this legislation which has to do with national service. . . . If I have to stand here until this room freezes over, Madam President, I am going to do so. Because I will tell you, this is something that has no place in our modern times. It has no place in this body. It has no place in the Senate. It has no place in our society.

And the fact is, Madam President, that I would encourage my colleagues on both sides of the aisle—Republican and Democrat; those who thought, "Well, we are just going to do this, you know, because it is no big deal"—to understand what a very big deal indeed it is—that the imprimatur that is being sought here today sends a sign out to the rest of this country that that peculiar institution has not been put to bed for once and for all; that, indeed, like Dracula, it has come back to haunt us time and time and time again; and that, in spite of the fact that we have made strides forward, the fact of the matter is that there are those who would keep us slipping back into the darkness of division, into the snake pit of racial hatred, of racial antagonism and of support for symbols—symbols of the struggle to keep African-Americans, Americans of African descent, in bondage.

PEACE IN THE MIDDLE EAST

BUILDING PEACE IN THE MIDDLE EAST[1]
William J. Clinton, Shimon Peres, Mahmoud Abbas, Yitzhak Rabin, and Yasir Arafat[2]

On September 13, 1994, in a triumph of diplomacy and hope over controversy and history, President Bill Clinton presided over a ceremony in which Prime Minister Yitzhak Rabin of Israel, and Chairman Yasir Arafat of the Palestine Liberation Organization, shook hands on the White House lawn, sealing the first agreement between Jews and Palestinians to end their conflict and share the Holy Land along the River Jordan.

The ceremony reminded some observers of the historic Camp David Peace Accord between Egypt and Israel in 1979. (See *Representative American Speeches, 1978–1979,* p. 142.) In fact, the new agreement was signed on the same wooden table on which the Camp David agreement had been signed. In actuality, the two occasions differed: the Camp David accord had been worked out on American soil under the leadership of President Carter and U.S. diplomats, while the 1993 Palestine agreement was largely the result of secret negotiations by Norway. Only the signing ceremony was held in the United States.

The ceremony itself took place at 11:43 A.M. on the South Lawn of the White House. Some of the participants—including Shimon Peres, Foreign minister of Israel, and Mahmoud Abbas, the chief P.L.O. negotiator—met briefly for coffee and juice in the Blue Room of the White House, though the two delegations—Israeli and PLO—continued to shun each other. It wasn't until all of the other dignitaries had filed out to be introduced, leaving President Clinton with Arafat and Rabin that the two antagonists exchanged their first words.

More than 3,000 guests, including former Presidents Jimmy Carter and George Bush, watched as the two leaders signed a "Declaration of Principles" on Palestinian self-rule in Israeli-

---

[1]All of the speeches were delivered at a ceremony on the south lawn of the White House, Washington, D.C., beginning at 11:43 A.M. on September 13, 1993.

[2]For biographical notes, see Appendix.

occupied Gaza and the West Bank. Millions of others in the United States and around the world watched the ceremony on television. Perhaps, the highlight was the handshake that Arafat and Rabin exchanged, with some coaxing from President Clinton, after the signing.

The ceremony was generally hailed as a great triumph. Maureen Dowd wrote of the ceremony: "It was not a day the earth stood still, but it was close. It was the day that Washington was not cynical. . . . The jaded were awed. Even for a New Age presidency, there were a lot of men in the audience crying." William Safire, political columnist and former presidential speech writer, declared Clinton's address "the best of his life" (*New York Times,* September 16, 1993, p. A15).

President Clinton's speech: Prime Minister Rabin, Chairman Arafat, Foreign Minister Peres, Mr. Abbas, President Carter, President Bush, distinguished guests: On behalf of the United States and Russia, co-sponsors of the Middle East peace process, welcome to this great occasion of history and hope. Today we bear witness to an extraordinary act in one of history's defining dramas. A drama that began in a time of our ancestors when the word went forth from a sliver of land between the River Jordan and the Mediterranean Sea. That hallowed piece of earth, that land of light and revelation, is the home to the memories and dreams of Jews, Muslims, and Christians throughout the world.

As we all know, devotion to that land has also been the source of conflict and bloodshed for too long. Throughout this century bitterness between the Palestinian and Jewish people has robbed the entire region of its resources, its potential, and too many of its sons and daughters. The land has been so drenched in warfare and hatred, the conflicting claims of history etched so deeply in the souls of the combatants there that many believe the past would always have the upper hand. Then, fourteen years ago, the past began to give way when, at this place and upon this desk, three men of great vision signed their names to the Camp David accords. Today we honor the memories of Menachem Begin and Anwar Sadat. And we salute the wise leadership of President Jimmy Carter.

Then, as now, we heard from those who said that conflict would come again soon. But the peace between Egypt and Israel has endured. Just so, this bold new venture today, this brave gamble that the future can be better than the past, must endure.

Two years ago in Madrid another president took a major step on the road to peace by bringing Israel and all her neighbors together to launch direct negotiations. And today we also express our deep thanks for the skillful leadership of President George Bush.

Ever since Harry Truman first recognized Israel, every American president, Democrat and Republican, has worked for peace between Israel and her neighbors. Now the efforts of all who have labored before us bring us to this moment—a moment when we dare to pledge what for so long seemed difficult even to imagine: that the security of the Israeli people will be reconciled with the hopes of the Palestinian people, and there will be more security and more hope for all.

Today the leadership of Israel and the Palestine Liberation Organization will sign a declaration of principles on interim Palestinian self-government. It charts a course toward reconciliation between two peoples who have both known the bitterness of exile. Now both pledge to put old sorrows and antagonisms behind them and to work for a shared future shaped by the values of the Torah, the Koran, and the Bible. Let us salute also today the government of Norway, for its remarkable role in nurturing this agreement.

But above all, let us today pay tribute to the leaders who had the courage to lead their people toward peace, away from the scars of battle, the wounds and the losses of the past, toward a brighter tomorrow. The world today thanks Prime Minister Rabin, Foreign Minister Peres, and Chairman Arafat.

That tenacity and vision has given us the promise of a new beginning. What these leaders have done now must be done by others. Their achievement must be a catalyst for progress in all aspects of the peace process. And those of us who support them must be there to help in all aspects, for the peace must render the people who make it more secure. A peace of the brave is within our reach. Throughout the Middle East there is a great yearning for the quiet miracle of a normal life. We know a difficult road lies ahead. Every peace has its enemies, those who still prefer the easy habits of hatred to the hard labors of reconciliation. But Prime Minister Rabin has reminded us that you do not have to make peace with your friends. And the Koran teaches that if the enemy inclines toward peace, do thou also incline toward peace.

Therefore, let us resolve that this new mutual recognition will be a continuing process in which the parties transform the very way they see and understand each other. Let the skeptics of this peace recall what once existed among these people. There was a time when the traffic of ideas and commerce and pilgrims flowed uninterrupted among the cities of the fertile crescent. In Spain, in the Middle East, Muslims and Jews once worked together to write brilliant chapters in the history of literature and science. All this can come to pass again.

Mr. Prime Minister, Mr. Chairman, I pledge the active support of the United States of America to the difficult work that lies ahead.

The United States is committed to insuring that the people who are affected by this agreement will be made more secure by it, and to leading the world in marshaling the resources necessary to implement the difficult details that will make real the principles to which you commit yourselves today. Together let us imagine what can be accomplished if all the energy and ability the Israelis and the Palestinians have invested into your struggle can now be channeled into cultivating the land and freshening the waters; into ending the boycotts and creating new industry; into building a land as bountiful and peaceful as it is holy. Above all, let us dedicate ourselves today to your region's next generation. In this entire assembly, no one is more important than the group of Israeli and Arab children who are seated here with us today.

Mr. Prime Minister, Mr. Chairman, this day belongs to you. And because of what you have done, tomorrow belongs to them. We must not leave them prey to the politics of extremism and despair, to those who would derail this process because they cannot overcome the fears and hatreds of the past. We must not betray their future.

For too long the young of the Middle East have been caught in a web of hatred not of their own making. For too long they have been taught from the chronicles of war. Now we can give them the chance to know the season of peace. For them we must realize the prophecy of Isaiah, that the cry of violence shall no more be heard in your land, nor wrack nor ruin within your borders. The children of Abraham, the descendants of Isaac and Ishmael, have embarked together on a bold journey. Together today with all our hearts and all our souls, we bid them shalom, salaam, peace.

Shimon Peres's speech: Mr. President, your excellencies, ladies and gentlemen: Mr. President, I would like to thank you and the great

American people for peace and support. Indeed I would like to thank all those who have made this day possible. What we are doing today is more than signing an agreement; it is a revolution. Yesterday a dream, today a commitment.

The Israeli and the Palestinian peoples who fought each other for almost a century have agreed to move decisively on the path of dialogue, understanding, and cooperation. We live in an ancient land and as our land is small, so must our reconciliation be great. As our wars have been long, so must our healing be swift. Deep gaps call for lofty breezes. I want to tell the Palestinian delegation that we are sincere, that we mean business. We do not seek to shape your lives or determine your destiny. Let all of us turn from bullets to ballots, from guns to shovels. We shall pray with you. We shall offer you our help in making Gaza prosper and Jericho blossom again.

As we have promised, we shall negotiate with you a permanent settlement, and with all our neighbors a comprehensive peace, peace for all. We shall support the agreement with an economic structure. We shall convert the bitter triangle of Jordanians, Palestinians, and Israelis into a triangle of political triumph and economic prosperity.

We shall lower our barriers and widen our roads so goods and guests will be able to move freely all about the places holy and other places. This should be another Genesis. We have to build a new commonwealth on our old soil: a Middle East of the people and a Middle East for their children. For their sake we must put an end to the waste of arms races and invest our resources in education.

Ladies and gentlemen, two parallel tragedies have unfolded. Let us become a civic community. Let us bid once and for all farewell to wars, to tricks, to human misery. Let us bid farewell to enmity and may there be no more victims on either side.

Let us build a Middle East of hope where today's food is produced and tomorrow's prosperity is guaranteed, a region with a common market, a Near East with a long-range agenda. We owe it to our own soldiers, to the memories of the victims of the Holocaust. Our hearts today grieve for the loss of lives of young and innocent people yesterday in our own country. Let their memory be our foundation we are establishing today; a memory of peace on fresh and old tombs.

Suffering is first of all human. We also feel for the innocent loss of Palestinian lives. We begin a new day. The day may be long and the challenges enormous. Our calendar must meet an intensive schedule.

Mr. President, historically you are presiding over a most promising day in the very long history of our region, of our people. I thank all or ladies and gentlemen, and let's pray together. Let's add hope to determination as all of us since Abraham believe in freedom, in peace, in the blessing of our great land, and great spirit.

[*Speaking in Hebrew*]. From the eternal city of Jerusalem, from this green, promising lawn of the White House, let's say together in the language of our Bible: "Peace, peace to him that is far off and to him that is near," sayeth the Lord, "and I will hear."

Thank you.

Mahmoud Abbas's speech: Mr. President, ladies and gentlemen: In these historic moments with feelings of joy that are mixed with a maximum sense of responsibility regarding events that are affecting our entire region, I greet you and I greet this distinguished gathering. I hope that this meeting in Washington will prove to be the onset of a positive and constructive change that will serve the interests of the Palestinian and Israeli peoples.

We have come to this point because we believe that peaceful coexistence and cooperation are the only means for reaching understanding and for realizing the hopes of the Palestinians and the Israelis. The agreement we will sign reflects the decision we made in the Palestine Liberation Organization to turn a new page in our relationship with Israel.

We know quite well that this is merely the beginning of a journey that is surrounded by numerous dangers and difficulties. And yet, our mutual determination to overcome everything that stands in the way of the cause for peace, our common belief that peace is the only means to security and stability, and our mutual aspiration for a secure peace characterized by cooperation, all this will enable us to overcome all obstacles with the support of the international community. And here I would like to mention, in particular, the United States government, which will shoulder the responsibility of continuing to play an effective and distinct role in the next stage, so that this great achievement may be completed.

In this regard, it is important to me to affirm that we are looking forward with a great deal of hope and optimism to a date that is two years from today, when negotiations over the final status of our country are set to begin. We will then settle the remaining fundamental issues, especially those of Jerusalem, the refugees, and the settlements. At that time, we will be laying the last brick in the edifice of peace whose foundation has been established today.

Economic development is the principal challenge facing the Palestinian people after years of struggle during which our national infrastructure and institutions were overburdened and drained. We are looking to the world for its support and encouragement in our struggle for growth and development, which begins today.

I thank the government of the United States of America and the government of the Russian Federation for the part they played and for their efforts and their sponsorship of the peace process. I also appreciate the role played by the government of Norway in bringing about this agreement. And I look forward to seeing positive results soon on the remaining Arab-Israeli tracks so we can proceed together with our Arab brothers on this comprehensive quest for peace.

Thank you.

Yitzhak Rabin's speech: President of the United States, your excellencies, ladies and gentlemen: This signing of the Israeli-Palestinian declaration of principle here today, it's not so easy, neither for myself as a soldier in Israel's war nor for the people of Israel, nor to the Jewish people in the diaspora, who are watching us now with great hope mixed with apprehension. It is certainly not easy for the families of the victims of the war's violence, terror, whose pain will never heal, for the many thousands who defended our lives in their own and have even sacrificed their lives for our own. For them this ceremony has come too late.

Today on the eve of an opportunity, opportunity for peace and perhaps end of violence and war, we remember each and every one of them with everlasting love. We have come from Jerusalem, the ancient and eternal capital of the Jewish people. We have come from an anguished and grieving land. We have come from a people, a home, a family that has not known a single year, not a single month, in which mothers have not wept for their sons. We have come to try and put an end to the hostilities so that our children, our children's children, will no longer experience the painful cost of war: violence and terror. We have come to secure their lives and to ease the soul and the painful memories of the past: to hope and pray for peace.

Let me say to you, the Palestinians, we are destined to live together on the same soil in the same land. We, the soldiers who have returned from battles stained with blood; we who have seen our relatives and friends killed before our eyes; we who have attended their funerals and cannot look in the eyes of their parents; we who have come from a land where parents bury their children; we who have fought against you, the Palestinians, we say to you today, in a loud and clear voice: enough blood and tears. Enough.

We have no desire for revenge. We harbor no hatred towards you. We, like you, are people, people who want to build a home. To plant a tree. To live, live side by side with you. In dignity. In empathy. As human beings. As free men. We are today giving peace a chance, and saying to you and saying again to you: enough. Let us pray that a day will come when we all will say farewell to the arms. We wish to open a new chapter in the sad book of our lives together, a chapter of mutual recognition, of good neighborliness, of mutual respect, of understanding. We hope to embark on a new era in the history of the Middle East. Today here in Washington at the White House, we will begin a new reckoning in the relations between children who will not know war.

President of the United States, ladies and gentlemen, our inner strength, our high moral values, have been the right for thousands of years, from the book of the books. In one of which, we read: To everything there is a season and a time to every purpose under heaven: a time to be bourn and a time to die, a time to kill and a time to heal, a time to weep and a time to laugh, a time to love and a time to hate, a time of war and a time of peace. Ladies and gentlemen, the time for peace has come.

In two days the Jewish people will celebrate the beginning of a new year. I believe, I hope, I pray that the new year will bring a message of redemption for all peoples, a good year for you, for all of you; a good year for all the peoples of the Middle East; a good year for our American friends who so want peace, and are helping to achieve it.

For presidents and members of previous administrations, especially for you, President Clinton, and your staff, for all citizens of the world, may peace come for all citizens of the world, may

peace come to all your homes. In the Jewish tradition it is customary to conclude our prayers with the word Amen. With your
permission, men of peace, I shall conclude with the words taken
from the prayer recited by Jews daily. And whoever of you who
volunteer, I would ask the entire audience to join me in saying
Amen. [*Speaking in Hebrew*] May He who brings peace to His
universe bring peace to us and to all Israel. Amen.

Yasir Arafat's speech: [*Delivered in Arabic, translated by a State Department interpreter.*] In the name of God most merciful, the passion-
ate. Mr. President, ladies and gentlemen: I would like to express
our tremendous appreciation to President Clinton and to his administration for sponsoring this historic event, which the entire
world has been waiting for. Mr. President, I am taking this opportunity to assure you and to assure the great American people that
we share your values for freedom, justice, and human rights:
values for which my people have been striving.

My people are hoping that this agreement, which we are signing today, marks the beginning of the end of a chapter of pain
and suffering which has lasted throughout this century. My
people are hoping that this agreement which we are signing today
will usher in an age of peace, coexistence, and equal rights. We
are relying on your role, Mr. President, and on the role of all the
countries which believe that without peace in the Middle East,
peace in the world will not be complete.

Enforcing the agreements and moving toward the final settlement, after two years to implement all aspects of U.N. resolutions
242 and 338 in all of their aspects, and resolve all the issues of
Jerusalem, the settlements, the refugees and the boundaries, will
be a Palestinian and an Israeli responsibility. It is also the responsibility of the international community in its entirety to help the
parties overcome the tremendous difficulties which are still
standing in the way of reaching a final and comprehensive settlement.

Now, as we stand on the threshold of this new historic era, let
me address the people of Israel and their leaders, with whom we
are meeting today for the first time. And let me assure them that
the difficult decision we reached together was one that required
great and exceptional courage.

We will need more courage and determination to continue
the course of building coexistence and peace between us. This is

possible. And it will happen with mutual determination and with the effort that will be made with all parties on all the tracks to establish the foundations of a just and comprehensive peace. Our people do not consider that exercising the right to self-determination could violate the rights of their neighbors or infringe on their security. Rather, putting an end to their feelings of being wronged and of having suffered an historic injustice is the strongest guarantee to achieve coexistence and openness between our two peoples and future generations.

Our two peoples are awaiting today this historic hope. And they want to give peace a real chance.

Such a shift will give us an opportunity to embark upon the process of economic, social, and cultural growth and development. And we hope that international participation in that process will be as extensive as it can be. This shift will also provide an opportunity for all forms of cooperation on a broad scale and in all fields.

I thank you Mr. President. We hope that our meeting will be a new beginning for fruitful and effective relations between the American people and the Palestinian people.

I wish to thank the Russian Federation and President Boris Yeltsin. Our thanks also go to Secretary Christopher and Foreign Minister Kozyrev, to the government of Norway, and to the Foreign Minister of Norway for the positive part they played in bringing about this major achievement.

I extend greetings to all the Arab leaders, our brothers, and to all the world leaders who contributed to this achievement.

Ladies and gentlemen, the battle for peace is the most difficult battle of our lives. It deserves our utmost efforts because the land of peace, the land of peace yearns for a just and comprehensive peace.

[*Speaking in English*] Mr. President, thank you. Thank you. Thank you.

President Clinton: We have been granted the great privilege of witnessing this victory for peace. Just as the Jewish people this week celebrate the dawn of a new year, let us all go from this place to celebrate the dawn of a new era, not only for the Middle East but for the entire world. The sound we heard today, once again as in ancient Jericho, was of trumpets toppling walls, the walls of anger and suspicion between Israeli and Palestinian, between

Arab and Jew. This time, praise God, the trumpets herald not the destruction of that city, but its new beginning.

Now let each of us here today return to our portion of that effort, uplifted by the spirit of the moment, refreshed in our hopes, and guided by the wisdom of the Almighty, who has brought us to this joyous day. Go in peace. Go as peacemakers.

CHALLENGES TO THE MEDIA

VIOLENCE ON TELEVISION AND FILM:
AN APPEAL FOR RESPONSIBILITY[1]
Paul Simon[2]

Increasing concern over violence on television and its influence on American society led to a one-day conference in Beverly Hills, California, on August 2, 1993. The conference brought together representatives from all segments of the broadcasting, cable, production, and distribution industries, as well as child advocates and experts in the fields of law, education, medicine, and government. The sponsor of the conference, the National Council for Families and Television, is a non-profit, educational organization.

During the course of the meeting, more than thirty speakers and panelists appeared. The keynote speaker was Senator Paul Simon of Illinois, one of the leading advocates for reduced violence on television. Although the conference was planned to accomplish only an exchange of views, with more and more government leaders criticizing the amount of violence and threatening to create an outside group to monitor television, broadcasting executives in attendance may have felt intimidated.

Simon's speech was delivered to a luncheon meeting attended by 650 in a banquet room of the Beverly Hilton Hotel at 1 P.M. on August 2, 1993. The speech was carried on C-SPAN and was covered by all the major newspapers.

Paul Simon's speech: I am grateful to those who have convened this unprecedented session. You have an opportunity to make a significant contribution to a better nation and world, trite as that sounds.

Many across this country are aware of this meeting, and a considerable portion of them are hoping that a marked reduction

[1]Delivered to a conference on the influence of television and film, sponsored by the National Council for Families and Film at the Beverly Hilton Hotel in Los Angeles at 1 P.M. on August 2, 1993.

[2]For biographical note, see Appendix.

in the video violence transported into their homes will follow. They are entitled to some progress.

No one suggests that there should be no violence on television. A film on the Civil War is likely to have violence. But there should be less violence on the screen and, more important, it should not be glamorized. No one suggests that television violence is the sole cause of crime in our society. We have, as a people and government, ducked the problems of handgun proliferation and that of other weapons; we concentrate the poor into our central cities and then ignore their problems. To deal with drug abuse, rather than placing a heavy emphasis on education and treatment, we choose to spend billions on more and more prisons. We now have a higher number incarcerated than any nation and a higher percentage of our population in jails and prisons than any nation—and the crime rate has escalated, not declined. Other reasons for crime could be mentioned. But one of the causes is violence on the entertainment screen. Television, like political leaders, can appeal to the best in each of us or to our worst impulses and weaknesses.

Ted Turner recently told a House subcommittee: "As a parent with five children, I don't need experts to tell me that the amount of violence on television today, and its increasingly graphic portrayal, can be harmful to children." Of this gathering, he showed pessimism: "Unless you keep the gun pointed at their heads, all you'll get is mumbly, mealy-mouthed BS. They just hope the subject will go away." On this conclusion, I hope you will prove him wrong.

In the magazine *Mother Jones*, Carl Cannon writes: "Actors and producers seem to be constantly speaking out for noble causes. . . . But in the one area over which they have control—the excessive violence in the entertainment industry—Hollywood activists remain silent. . . . The liberals in Hollywood don't act like progressive thinkers; they act like the National Rifle Association: Guns don't kill people, people kill people. We don't cause violence in the world, we just reflect it."

Here are a few basic questions, and then I shall make seven recommendations to you.

Is television violence harmful?

When we watch a news program from Bosnia showing the tragedy of violence, we understand the pain, the anguish and the senselessness of violence. When we watch entertainment violence, in the majority of cases, it is sanitized and made attractive. On entertainment television our heroes and heroines, with whom we identify, do not suffer and die. In fact, our heroes and heroines are often portrayed as justified perpetrators of violence. When death occurs, it is usually quick and clean. No relatives with tears are seen at the side of the victim. And just as 30 seconds of attractive portrayal of a bar of soap sells soap, and 30 seconds of the attractive portrayal of a car sells that car, 25 minutes of the attractive portrayal of violence sells violence.

This is no longer theory. The evidence that television violence does harm is now just as overwhelming as the evidence that cigarettes do harm. Dr. Deborah Prothrow-Stith of Harvard, commenting on the harmful effects of television violence, noted: "No one is immune. Some are more susceptible than others, children most of all." As recently as July 23, a Harvard publication quoted developmental psychologist Ron Slaby: "Television violence has significantly contributed to the violence in American society."

The National Institute of Mental Health has twice warned us about the harmful effects, as have more than 85 additional substantial studies. The American Medical Association calls television violence an environmental hazard. The most recent study I have seen, from the Department of Psychiatry of Pennsylvania State University, showed, once again, child behavioral problems associated with watching violence on television.

But, you say, the people in the industry are decent people who are good parents and grandparents. They wouldn't do anything to harm society.

Unfortunately, that description also applies to the people who manufacture cigarettes and nuclear bombs and handguns. Sometimes people on the outside, with no financial stake, have to call attention to the harm that can occur.

Isn't the television/film industry simply reflecting reality?

That is partially true, but you also are shaping reality by sometimes glamorizing violence. Television also gives the impression that the person to be feared for violence is the stranger, when the reality is that a family member or an acquaintance is much more likely to commit the violent act. Television portrays the single woman at great risk, but the reality is that the married woman is at greater risk. Urban children and urban teen-agers are too often portrayed negatively, and sometimes they live up to the expectations television creates. The industry should have a higher and more noble calling than simply reflecting reality, even if that argument were completely valid. You should improve reality. The industry should be a beacon for the nation, not simply a mirror.

Isn't the industry responding to the anti-trust exemption that Congressman Dan Glickman and I sponsored and which is now law?

Yes and no.

The broadcast networks have adopted joint standards, which are good but very subjective. What is "gratuitous violence?" Compared to the British standards, for example, they are not strong. But I sense what does give them meaning is a willingness to face the problem and a commitment—at least by some—to make these standards meaningful.

The agreement for a warning to parents is helpful and takes on added significance when you understand that generally advertisers are not eager to buy on programs with warnings. That gives this commitment greater meaning than is immediately apparent.

The Association of Independent Television Stations has created a set of guidelines on violent material and is encouraging its members to agree with these standards.

Network affiliates have not been significantly involved up to this point, but their participation is important because they are responsible for programming shown from 7 P.M. to 8 P.M. when many children watch television.

Syndication is a total question mark. The "reality-based" shows can do real harm.

Jack Valenti is convening meetings of various branches of the movie industry, and I am hopeful for positive results there.

In all these cases, more needs to be done.

In some ways, cable presents greater problems with violence than broadcast, and the agreement by the majors among cable to have the message of caution is welcomed, as is their hiring of George Gerbner to monitor their activities.

Is censorship the answer?

I am, in the words of George Bush, "a card-carrying member of the ACLU." Few nations have as little regulation of their television and movies as we do. I want to maintain that freedom. I want our creative community to flourish. So far, no member of the House or Senate has introduced legislation suggesting formal, general censorship, but many ideas short of that have been floated, including Congressman Ed Markey's chip suggestion to permit parents to prevent violent programs; Congressman Joe Kennedy's idea for a 1-800 number to the FCC that people could call to make a record of complaints on violence, to be considered when a station seeks re-licensing; Senator Byron Dorgan's and Congressman Dick Durbin's suggestion that the FCC calculate incidents of violence and then regularly report to the public on which programs are the most violent, and who the sponsors are; Senator Dave Durenberger's bill would require visual and sound warnings on programs that are violent or which involve unsafe gun practices; Senator Carl Levin and Congressman Charles Schumer each has legislation drafted concerned with television violence, which they may introduce; Senator Kent Conrad has initiated a petition drive on the issue; two Senators suggested to me that sponsors not be permitted to deduct for advertising on programs that the FCC deems violent. Others favor more extreme measures.

All or none of these may pass. I can tell you that none of the sponsors of these initiatives is losing votes back home with these ideas.

Non-lawmakers have made suggestions varying from strict censorship to the proposal that a television station must demonstrate what it is doing in its programming to discourage violence to get its license renewed. Whether or not these proposals become law rests, in large measure, with the decision-makers in this room. When you have Senators from Howard Metzenbaum to Jesse Helms—and that covers a pretty broad spectrum—saying that something has to happen to change things, the message should be clear. The July 18th *Washington Post* carries a lengthy article by staff writer Megan Rosenfeld, with the heading: "And Now, A Word From A Mother," and the subhead: "Forget the First Amendment. When It Comes to TV Violence, All I Care About Is Protecting My Kids."

Aren't the columnists right who suggest that the actions up to this point are simply public relations, that the industry isn't treating this problem seriously?

The answer is no. It is true that we have been through this exercise before. In 1954 Senator Robert Hendrickson held hearings on the subject of television and juvenile delinquency. In 1961 Senator Thomas Dodd held hearings on television violence and received assurance that change would occur. Early in 1974, the Screen Actors Guild adopted a strong resolution calling for change, describing the "degree of violence in television programming [as] . . . excessive." Senator John Pastore followed with hearings on the subject. Some assurance of action followed each set of hearings. And after a short period, violence on the screen escalated.

All of this feeds the appetite of the doubters. When I was a young reporter, the great vice of journalism was whiskey. My first newspaper boss kept a fifth of whiskey in the top drawer of his desk. He opened the drawer frequently. The whiskey of today is cynicism. For every reason they give me for cynicism, I can give them 10 more. The cynics aren't going to build a better society. However, there is legitimate reason for questioning whether we are not just going through the same motions again.

Two things have changed:

First, while many had intuitive belief that violence on television caused harm, the research was slim. There were warnings, however. The late Norman Cousins, who lived near where we meet, wrote in the *Saturday Review* in 1959: "The TV operators make all sorts of claims about the power of their medium to sell all sorts of goods. They boast about the ease with which they dominate the fashions of teenagers just by having TV stars dress in a certain way. Yet they see no cause-and-effect relationship between what they show on the screen and the increasing addiction of young people to cheap violence." About this same time, the nation's most widely-read columnist, Walter Lippmann, wrote: "Can there be any real doubt that there is a close connection between the suddenness of the increase in sadistic crimes and the new vogue of sadism among the mass media of entertainment. A continual exposure of a generation to the commercial exploitation of the enjoyment of violence and cruelty is one way to corrode the foundations of a civilized society. For my part, believing as I do in freedom of speech and thought, I see no objection in principle to censorship of the mass entertainment . . . .Until some more refined way is worked out of controlling this evil thing, the risks to our liberties are, I believe, decidedly less than the risks of unmanageable violence."

At the 1961 Congressional hearings, Frank Stanton of CBS could honestly testify: "The research that has been conducted in this field is limited in its scope, is inconclusive in its findings." And Grace Johnson of ABC, in the same hearing, said that an emotionally disturbed child may "drain off . . . elements in his behavior which cause that disturbance" by watching violence on television. At that time, there was limited research showing harm, about like the early research on cigarette smoking. Many people intuitively thought smoking cigarettes did harm, but the evidence had not accumulated. Now it has accumulated, both for violence on television and for cigarette smoking. I know of no serious student of television violence who questions the validity of the massive evidence.

The second difference from the early period is the seriousness with which at least part of the industry is addressing the question. Considerable time is being devoted to the subject, not only at the lower staff levels, but by top officials. Television executives are speaking candidly about the problem. There is almost no denial or semi-denial. Constructive steps are being taken. One network chief executive told me a few weeks ago that he decided to cancel a movie for which he had paid a good price, because he felt it was too violent. There is a changed attitude on the part of at least some key decision-makers.

But what needs to be done?

Let me make seven suggestions.

1. There should be recognition by the creative community that self-restraint is essential for a democracy to function.

Here is an analogy from the political arena. When John F. Kennedy barely defeated Richard Nixon, Nixon could have gone on television proclaiming what harm would come to the nation with Kennedy as President, asking people to turn to the streets with peaceful protest. He did not. While he did not feel like congratulating John F. Kennedy, he did it, and we had a peaceful transition from one administration and political party to another in the world's most powerful nation. When Richard Nixon defeated Hubert Humphrey, the same thing happened. Both Richard Nixon and Hubert Humphrey recognized that for a democracy to function effectively, it is unwise to exercise freedom to its extreme.

In Ken Auletta's recent article in the *New Yorker* he tells of approaching those who produce and asking what violent or shocking stunt wouldn't they put on the screen to make money. He refers to the embarrassed pause he often received when he asked that question.

In response to a *Los Angeles Times* editorial titled, "Televised Violence Can Have Violent Consequences; Does Anyone Care?", one reader who monitored standards for a network wrote: "I wept on occasion with the inadequacy of my role as we were forced to accept so much violence just to maintain viewers' enthusiasm for the program so they wouldn't switch channels." In his book, *Hollywood vs. America,* Michael Medved quotes Director Alan

J. Pakula: "Movie violence is like eating salt. The more you eat, the more you need to eat to taste it. People are becoming immune to the effects: The death counts have quadrupled, the blast power is increasing by the megaton, and they're becoming deaf to it. They've developed an insatiability for raw sensation." We have spawned an arms race on American television and, like every arms race, no one wins.

I am told that the English word "obscene" comes from two Greek words, "a skene," which means off stage. In the ancient Greek theater, any violent act occurred off stage, and a third party recounted the violence and then interpreted the meaning for the audience, remarkably like the British Code of Standards for television: "People should be permitted to die in private and only in the rarest circumstances should broadcasting dwell on the moment of death itself."

The creative community gathered here needs to exercise its freedom with wisdom, with a sense of public responsibility and with good taste. As FCC Commissioner Ervin Duggan observes: "The public interest is not merely what interests the public." The best way to protect your industry from the dangerous and heavy hand of government is to exercise self-restraint. The gauge of whether we are a civilized society is not to what extremes we can indulge ourselves.

2. The entire industry needs to be involved.

That means broadcasters, cable, independents, syndicators and the movies. What is somewhat disheartening is the finger-pointing that now takes place. Broadcasters say the real culprit is cable, and the other way around. Both blame the movies they get. The producers and directors blame the writers, and the writers say they produce what the networks and cable demand. I am not interested in assigning blame, but getting action. The finger-pointing all has some legitimacy and some illegitimacy, but it should not become an excuse for inaction. Chief executives in all parts of the industry must be exactly what their title implies, chief executives. Just as a publisher or editor of a newspaper has to take the responsibility for what appears in that publication, so chief executives must assert their responsibilities in the television and film industries.

If it becomes obvious that one branch of your industry loves money more than responsibility, that will not go unnoticed in Washington.

3. In some way, we need to be assured of continuity of concern and effort.

The question I cannot answer is: Can you be certain that the present interest in this subject will continue? The current concerns by industry leaders, whatever their motivation, is genuine. Buttressing that is not only the congressional effort, but the *Times-Mirror* poll that shows 80 percent of the public today believes that television violence is harmful compared to 64 percent ten years ago, and 47 percent describe it as "very harmful" compared to 25 percent ten years ago. The poll showed that the higher the level of education, the greater the concern. The Gannett chain's Sunday supplement, *USA Weekend,* did a survey of its readers and had similar results. Ninety-six percent said that television violence does not reflect reality but glorifies violence. Seventy percent said they noticed a change in their children's behavior after watching a violent television show or cartoon.

Several chief executives of major American corporations have told me recently that they are asking their public relations people to avoid advertising on programs that glamorize violence.

Some type of ongoing monitoring of the status of television violence is needed, and I would prefer that the federal government not be involved. If those gathered here would form a committee of respected citizens—perhaps called the Advisory Office on Television Violence—who would employ a small staff, headed by someone who has an understanding of the field, and that committee would report to the American people annually, in specifics, it would indicate a desire to sustain better programming. Those specifics should let us know whether glamorized violence is increasing or decreasing, on each of the broadcast and cable networks, whether there is an attempt to avoid the time periods when children are more likely to observe. They should tell us what is happening with the independents, affiliates, syndication and with the entire industry. They would play an advisory role to the industry, when requested. The person heading the effort should be someone like Walter Cronkite, John Chancellor or Newton Minow. The Committee could also develop a set of standards by which they will judge both broadcasting and cable, standards that are less subjective than those adopted by the four broadcast networks. These new standards could be guideposts for all elements of the industry, as well as for advertisers and the public. Without some type of monitoring, the lure of profits will entice those less responsible to abuse their privilege. The industry needs encouragement to a higher sense of responsibility and good taste than the financial bottom line.

The interest in dealing effectively with this issue must be

sustained. And, let me add, it will be sustained. Either you will initiate the effort for such a monitoring office, or those outside the industry will do it. I started in this effort as a somewhat lonely voice in Congress, but I now find many of my colleagues want to go much further than is healthy for a free society. My request of the television and film industries to accept some responsibility is not an assault on the First Amendment, but if within the industry you do not exercise self-restraint, neither will many of those who are concerned. Extremes in behavior invite extremes in response. The surest solution is governmental intervention, but it is also the most dangerous.

4. Glamorized violence should be avoided, the harsh realities of violence must be portrayed, and non-violent problem-solving should be encouraged.

Howard Stringer of CBS has correctly observed: "If you argue that we have no moral responsibility to sustain values, then perhaps we have an artistic responsibility. Death stings, pain hurts, loss devastates, fear terrifies. If we still insist that television merely mirrors reality, then let us reflect our reality more skillfully and honestly. Murder, even fighting, is not poetic or balletic. It is ugly and clumsy. Violence is vile."

The television/movie industry can play a positive role and should. The harmful effect of choosing the violent alternative to problem-solving should be conveyed and too rarely is.

One intensive study covering 22 years shows first, that the greatest single indicator of violent behavior at age 30—more than other indicators, such as economic status, broken home, low IQ, or race—is the amount of television watched at age eight; second, that television viewers will exaggerate the likelihood that they will become victims and are more likely to isolate themselves, not walking the streets as much and, in the words of criminologist James Q. Wilson, "excessive fear of crime contributes to crime;" third, there is the "bystander effect" to violence, a callousness to it because viewers have been hardened through viewing.

But one more important fourth effect: There is an increased appetite for violence, both as an answer to problems and as entertainment. "Make my day" is a phrase that gets used by children and a President. Its message is clear: give me the pleasure of a violent response. When small children laugh at violent action in a cartoon, they are being taught the wrong thing by the powerful teacher called television.

The positive message needs to be delivered that violence

brings no pleasure. Stories should develop constructive alternatives to violence. In hundreds of schools around the nation there
are "peer mediators," students assigned to listen to both sides in
an encounter between two other students, to work out peaceful
resolution of a conflict. It works. Including that reality in a story,
as well as other efforts at avoiding violence through peaceful
alternatives, needs to be on public display much more. Really
creative writers can make it work. And violent alternatives need
to be deglamorized.

5. Violent promos should be eliminated or reduced, and certainly avoided when children are most likely to be watching.

Some of the worst moments on television are during the 30-
second promotion pieces. The most dramatic part of the movie or
feature hopes to captivate an audience. It requires more creativity
to get that audience without offending or harming it, and this
industry is fully capable of doing that.

Ted Harbert of ABC is quoted in the *New Yorker:* "[Three-
year-old] Emily's entrance into the world totally changed the way
I look at television. I have a massive problem . . . now with violence on television. . . . If a promo comes on that I would never
let her sit there and watch, or if something comes on that is
violent . . . and this look of bewilderment comes across her face—
'What is that man doing, Daddy?'—I don't have a very good
answer."

6. The medium must be used to help educate the nation about
the harmful effects of television violence.

Cigarette smoking did not experience its dramatic drop because of a Surgeon General's statement. That statement received
extensive coverage in television shows and in public service an-
nouncements.

When the Surgeon General warns us about the harmful effects of television violence, the industry is audibly silent. That
should change. There is no similar heavily documented threat to
public health which television has so studiously ignored.

Parents should know more clearly that it is not just their instinct that says entertainment violence is harmful, but solid research. Something more than a brief mention in the evening news
or two minutes on a morning show is needed. I would like to see
60 Minutes, Prime Time and their counterparts give viewers greater
depth of understanding on this issue.

By doing this you can help create the market for less violent
entertainment. Then bright executives can also anticipate a

growth in that type of market. I would also like to see one of the broadcast networks and one major cable company put together a creative team to explore ways of marketing less violent programming. And which will be the first network or cable company to occasionally bring this simple message: "Watching too much violence on television may be harmful to your children's health?" Who will be the first with an educational film for schools that points out the dangers of glamorized television violence?

Organizations like the PTA, the American Federation of Teachers and the National Education Association can buttress such an effort with public education campaigns that urge viewership of television that plays a positive role.

7. Recognize more clearly the international dimensions of your product.

This is a complex area. Unfortunately, violence is easy to translate into any language. In contrast, comedy is not. Sixty-four percent of New Zealand's entertainment television comes from the United States, but the New Zealand Mental Health Foundation has called for a reduction in the number of U.S. television programs. Their survey concluded that U.S. television shows are three times more violent than those of other countries. One major U.S. children's program has two versions: The violent one for consumption in the United States and the non-violent one for all other nations. The spokesperson for the program told the *Christian Science Monitor:* "At home, we don't get many objections to violence on our shows. American kids are used to it. But abroad, it's a different story. The BBC wouldn't buy [it] unless they could edit out some of the violence. It's that version that we sold to the rest of the world. Otherwise [it] wouldn't have done nearly as well."

Ideas, good and bad, are hard to retain within national borders. I know of no research to support the assumption by Meg Greenfield of *Newsweek* that violence on television also causes us to be more receptive to violent answers to international problems. But without any research, my instinct tells me she is correct. And that same message is conveyed to citizens of other nations.

Before he stepped down as Prime Minister of Canada, Brian Mulroney told me in a phone conversation that while the United States is reducing the physical harm done to Canada through acid rain, the harm done to that nation's minds through violence on television is a real concern. Canada's Communications Minister has called television violence an international problem that requires an international response. The revulsion in many nations to parts of the American culture is not a reaction to the Chicago Symphony Orchestra or to Isaac Stern or to Van Cliburn, nor is it in response to our finer movies or television shows. We should ask ourselves what message we wish to send to other nations.

All of these things are easy to say for an outsider who does not understand all of your problems. But I do understand our culture. I do know the mood of the electorate and of my colleagues in government.

I also know what you have contributed to our culture in many positive ways, including making us one nation as we never were before your medium took its place of dominance, as well as spreading the word about the desirability of democracy to those who do not have it. I know what you contribute to our economy and to our balance of trade.

I also know that you have in your hands a tool that is unprecedented in the history of humanity in its power. You have helped move the nation away from smoking cigarettes, and by being more sensitive on issues of race, you ended the "Amos and Andy" era in film and conversation. You can use television's power for good or ill, and I am here today urging you, in the words of Abraham Lincoln, to use that instrument to "appeal to the better angels of our nature" to aid all of humanity.

CALL IT COURAGE[1]
DAN RATHER[2]

The most widely publicized speech at the forty-eighth annual conference of the Radio-Television News Directors Association, held from September 29 to October 2, 1993, was a strongly worded attack by the veteran CBS reporter Dan Rather. The Association is a professional society of news department executives in broadcast, cable, and network organizations.

Rather delivered his remarks at the presentation of the Ed-

[1]Delivered at the annual international convention of the Radio-Television News Directors Association in the Grand Ballroom of the Fontainbleau Hilton Hotel, Miami Beach, Florida, 7:36 P.M., September 29, 1993.

[2]For biographical note, see Appendix.

ward R. Murrow Awards in the Grand Ballroom of the Fontainebleau Hilton Hotel in Miami Beach, Florida, from 7:30 to 9:00 P.M. on September 29, 1993. Following a welcome to the audience of 1200 by the mayor of Miami Beach and the presentation of the Murrow Awards, Rather presented his remarks.

The speech was reminiscent of one given by Murrow himself to the Association 35 years before. Reports of Rather's speech described it as "an unusual condemnation of television by one of its stars" (*International Herald Tribune*, October 9, 1993); "a gutsy speech . . . roasting his television news business for pandering, greed, and cowardice" (*Boston Globe*, October 7, 1993); "by turns angry, confessional, and inspirational" (*Broadcasting and Cable*, October 4, 1993); "a stinging attack against the industry that nurtured him" (*Reuters*, September 30, 1993); and a speech that "slammed the entire TV news business and, by inference, CBS News" (*Chicago Sun Times*, October 2, 1993).

While the speech created widespread interest and some controversy, Rather's immediate audience in Miami Beach seemed to agree with him, giving the speaker a standing ovation.

Dan Rather's speech: Thank you. And thank you, members of the Radio and Television News Directors Association. This is an honor for me, and I am grateful. It is humbling to be asked to speak on this night to this group. On this night, because it is the time when the late, great Ed Murrow has a commemorative stamp issued in his name. To this group, because it was before the RTNDA that Murrow gave the best speech he ever made, the best ever made by *any* broadcaster.

Edward R. Murrow *was* the best. Sixty years after he started, thirty years after his death—and *still* the best.

He was the best reporter of his generation. The best reporter in broadcasting *or* print. He reported, he led, he *made* the best broadcasts of his time, *both* in radio *and* television. *And* those broadcasts remain, to this day, the best of *all* time. They include the "This . . . Is London" broadcasts from the Battle of Britain, the radio reports from the death camp at Buchenwald, and the television programs on Joseph McCarthy and "Harvest of Shame."

Ed Murrow was not only the founding saint of broadcast news and the best-ever practitioner of it, he also set standards for excellence and courage that remain *the* standards, the world over. And, along the way, he made the best speech ever by anyone in our business.

He was, in short, a hero. No wonder they have issued a stamp in his name.

But we should, we must remember this: he was a *real*, flesh-and-blood, flawed, vulnerable, mistake-making hero.

With all his triumphs, many and mighty, he also fought some fights he should not have fought, and he sometimes, often times, lost. Including losing at the end. In the end, his bosses and his competitors—inside as well as outside his own network—cut him up, cut him down, and finally cut him out.

And not long after that, he died. Cancer was the cause, they say.

Murrow made his memorable RTNDA speech not at the dawn, nor at midday, but in the twilight—in Chicago, October 15, 1958.

In it, he criticized what commercial television was becoming, and challenged himself, his colleagues—and us, all of us—to do better.

Ed Murrow said of television:

This instrument can teach, it can illuminate; yes, and it can even inspire. But it can do so only to the extent that humans are determined to use it to those ends. Otherwise it is merely wires and lights in a box. There is a great and perhaps decisive battle to be fought against ignorance, intolerance, and indifference. This weapon of television could be useful.

What follows now is a tribute, a biography and a fond re-membrance, prepared by CBS News, to Edward R. Murrow—a commander in the battle against ignorance, intolerance, and indifference.

The speech Ed Murrow gave at the RTNDA convention in Chicago, 1958, was a risky speech, and he knew it. It was a bold shot, and he knew it. That was part of the Murrow style, and part of what has made the Murrow mystique: the bold, brave shot.

He began that speech with the modest speculation that, and I quote, "This just might do nobody any good." I don't think Ed Murrow believed that. It was a call to arms. The most quoted line is the one about "wires and lights in a box," but the more important line is "this weapon of television." Ed Murrow had seen all kinds of battles, and if *he* lifted *his* voice in a battle cry, surely some of his own colleagues would hear him and heed him.

As with many broadcast news people of my generation, that speech has criss-crossed over the back-roads of my memory through a lifetime in the business.

I wasn't in Chicago that night. I was in Houston, serving my apprenticeship in news, a beginner in radio and television. I hadn't met Murrow yet. I could only read about his speech in the newspapers, but I absorbed every word. In my own little Texas hicktown world of journalism dreams, Murrow became protean, titanic, huge. (I still think that.) There were other great ones: William L. Shirer, Eric Sevareid, and Charles Collingwood, and Douglas Edwards; and later Walter Cronkite. Men of courage and accomplishment, of great skill and great intelligence. But Murrow was *their* leader.

As he had been for many others, Murrow had been my hero when I was just a boy. Across the radio, across the Atlantic and across half the United States, his voice came, the deep rumble and the dramatic pause just when he said, "THIS . . . is London." I never got that voice out of my head. It was like a piece of music that has never stopped playing for me. Murrow told me tales of bravery in time of war, tales more thrilling than *Captain Midnight* or *Jack Armstrong* because these were *true*.

He talked about the bravery of soldiers and citizens. He never made a big fuss about his own bravery. But even as a little boy, I knew it took bravery just to stand on that rooftop, with the bombs raining down thunder and lightning all around him . . . or to go up in that plane—"D-for-Dog"—with odds he'd never get down alive. And I never forgot that Murrow did all this because he wanted me and my family, and all of us back home in America, to know . . . the truth. For *that*, for our knowledge of the truth, *he* risked his life.

In my mind, then and now, neither Achilles nor King Arthur, not Pecos Bill or Davy Crockett, surpassed a hero like that.

The Murrow I met years later—person to person, if you will—the real Ed Murrow, was everything I wanted that hero to be. He was a quiet man: tall, strong, steady-eyed, not afraid of silence.

What separated Ed Murrow from the rest of the pack was courage.

I know what you're thinking. I've gotten in trouble before for using the word. Probably deserved it. Maybe I used it inappropriately. Maybe I'm a poor person to talk about it because I have so little myself. But I want to hear the word. I want to hear it praised, and the men and women who have courage elevated.

Ed Murrow *had* courage. He had the physical courage to face the Blitzkrieg in London and to ride "D-for-Dog." He had the professional courage to tell the truth about McCarthyism. And he had the courage to stand before the Radio and Television News

Directors Association, and to say some things those good people didn't want to hear, but needed to hear.

In our comfort and complacency, in our (dare we say it?) cowardice, we, none of us, want to hear the battle cry. Murrow had the courage to sound it anyway. And thirty-five years later, however uncomfortable, it's worth pausing to ask: how goes the battle?

In the constant scratching and scrambling for ever better ratings and money and the boss' praise and a better job, it is worth pausing to ask: how goes the *real* war, the really important battle of our professional lives? How goes the battle for quality, for truth, and justice, for programs worthy of the *best* within ourselves and the audience? How goes the battle against "ignorance, intolerance, and indifference?" The battle *not* to be merely "wires and lights in a box," the battle to make television *not just* entertaining but also, at least some little of the time, *useful* for higher, better things? How goes the battle?

The answer we know is "Not very well." In too many important ways, we have allowed this great instrument, this resource, this weapon for good, to be squandered and cheapened. About this, the best among us hang their heads in embarrassment, even shame. We all should be ashamed of what we have and have not done, measured against what we could do . . . ashamed of many of the things we have allowed our craft, our profession, our life's work to become.

Our reputations have been reduced, our credibility cracked, justifiably. This has happened because too often for too long we have answered to the worst, not to the best, within ourselves and within our audience. We are less because of this. Our audience is less, and so is our country.

Ed Murrow had faith in our country, and in our country's decision to emphasize, from the beginning, *commercial* broadcasting. He recognized *commercial* broadcasting's potential, and its superiority over other possibilities. But even as he believed in the strength of market values and the freedom of commercial broadcasting, Ed Murrow feared the rise of a cult that worshipped at the shrine of the implacable idol Ratings. He feared that the drive to sell, sell, sell—and nothing but sell—was overwhelming the potential for good, the potential for *service* of radio and television.

He decried the hours of prime-time as being full of "decadence, escapism, and insulation from the realities of the world in which we live." As you let that sink in, let's remember that he was talking about programs like *I Love Lucy* and *The Honeymooners*, that are now esteemed on a par with the best comedies of Plautus and Molière; Murrow singled out the *Ed Sullivan Show*, which is now studied and praised as a modern-day School of Athens, peopled by all the best minds and talents of the time. These are the programs that had Ed Murrow worried.

He wasn't worried about, didn't live to see *Full House* or *America's Funniest Home Videos* or *Fish Police*. He wasn't worried about, didn't live to see, the glut of inanities now in "Access" time. He never lived to see the cynicism and greed that go into the decisions to put on much of that garbage.

In 1958, Murrow was worried because he saw a trend setting in . . . avoiding the unpleasant or controversial or challenging . . . shortening news broadcasts, or jamming them with ever-increasing numbers of commercials . . . throwing out background, context, and analysis, and relying just on headlines . . . going for entertainment values over the values of good journalism . . . all in the belief that the public must be shielded, wouldn't accept anything other than the safe, the serene, and the self-evident.

Murrow knew that belief was wrong, and contrary to the principles on which this country was founded. He'd seen how honest, mature, and responsible American listeners and viewers could be when programming itself was honest, mature, and responsible. *Reducing* the amount of real-world reality on television, Murrow argued, was unconscionable.

But Murrow did not just offer criticism. He also offered solutions. Importantly, Murrow proposed that news divisions and departments not be held to the same standards of ratings and profits as entertainment and sports. He recognized that news operations couldn't be run as philanthropies. But he added:

I can find nothing in the Bill of Rights or the Communications Act which says that [news divisions] must increase their net profits each year, lest the Republic collapse.

Murrow saw turmoil, danger, and opportunity in the world; and the best means of communicating the realities to the public—the communications innovation called television—was increasingly ignoring the realities. And those few Americans who had been given the privilege of owning and operating television stations and networks, the privilege of making great wealth from them, were beginning to reduce if not downright eliminate their responsibilities to public service.

Private profit from television is fine, but there *should be* a responsibility to news and public service that goes with it. This was the core of Murrow's case.

These were words which needed to be heard. Then, and now. . . . I thought about coming here tonight—and you might have been better enlightened if I'd done this—to read you verbatim the text of Murrow's speech from 1958. It's a hell of a speech. Much of it is more true, more dire, more needed than it was when Murrow said it.

When Murrow spoke to your predecessors at RTNDA, he knew that *they* were not his problem. The people he wanted most to hear and heed his speech were not in that Chicago ballroom. They worked in boardrooms, not newsrooms. Murrow's Chicago speech was a brave, bold bid to persuade corporate executives, both at stations and networks *and* at the advertising agencies and corporate sponsors.

He failed. Not long afterward, his position inside his own network was diminished. And not long after *that,* he was out.

Little has changed since Murrow gave that report from the battlefield and issued that call to arms. And much of what *has* changed has not been for the better. More people in television now than then are doing things that deny the public service of television, that ensure that the mighty weapon of television remains nothing more than wires and lights in a box.

Even the best among decision-makers in television freely take an hour that might have been used for a documentary, and hand it over to a quote-unquote "entertainment special" about the discovery of Noah's Ark—that turns out to be a one-hundred percent *hoax.*

And the worst among the decision-makers have got us all so afraid of our own independence and integrity that at least one news director actually planned to have all his hirings reviewed by radical ideological and highly partisan political groups. (And he bragged about it.)

They've got another news director telling his staff that he didn't want stories on the Pope's visit. He wanted stories—plural—on Madonna's sex book. It's the ratings, stupid, don't you know?

And they've got us putting more and more fuzz and wuzz on the air, cop-shop stuff, so as to compete not with other news programs but with entertainment programs (including those *posing* as news programs) for dead bodies, mayhem, and lurid tales.

They tell us international news doesn't get ratings, doesn't sell, and, besides, its too expensive. "Foreign news" is considered an expletive best deleted in most local station newsrooms, and has fallen from favor even among networks.

Thoughtfully-written analysis is out, live pops are in. "Action, Jackson" is the cry. Hire lookers, not writers. Do powder-puff, not probing, interviews. Stay away from controversial subjects. Kiss ass, move with the mass, and for heaven and the ratings' sake don't make anybody mad—certainly not anybody that you're covering, and especially not the mayor, the governor, the senator, the President or Vice-President or *anybody* in a position of power. Make nice, not news.

This has become the new mantra. These have become the new rules. The post-Murrow generation of owners and managers have made them so. These people are, in some cases, our friends. They are, in all cases, our bosses. They aren't venal; they're afraid. They've got education and taste and good sense. They care about their country, but you'd never know it from the things that fear makes them do—from the things that fear makes them make *us* do.

It is fear of ratings slippage if not failure, fear that this quarter's bottom line will not be better than last quarter's—and a whole lot better than the same quarter a year ago.

A climate of fear, at all levels, has been created, without a fight. We—you and I—have allowed them to do it, and even *helped* them to do it.

The climate is now such that, when a few people at one news organization rig the results of a test to get better pictures, and are caught and rightly criticized, there's no rejoicing that a terrible, unusual journalistic practice has been caught, punished, and eradicated. Because we all know that, with only a slight relaxation of vigilance and a slight increase of fear, those journalistic sins could be visited upon us. We know that, as honorable and sensible as we, our friends and our colleagues try to be, it could happen to us.

Now you would be absolutely justified in saying to me right now

Excuse me, mister big shot anchor man, but what the hell do you expect me to do about it? If I go to my boss and talk about television as a weapon, and why don't you take *Current Affair* or *Hard Copy* or *Inside Edition* off the air next week and let me put on a tell-it-like-it-is documentary about race relations—I *know* they're gonna put me on the unemployment line, and I'll be *lucky* if they don't put me on the funny farm.

Well, none of us is immune to self-preservation and opportunities for advancement. I'm not asking you for the kind of courage that risks your job, much less your whole career.

Ed Murrow had that kind of courage, and took that kind of risk several times. But you and I, reaching deep down inside ourselves, are unlikely to muster that kind of courage often, if ever.

But there are specific things we can do. They won't cost us our jobs. But they will make a difference—a start. A warning shot that the battle is about to be joined.

Number one: Make a little noise. At least question (though protest would be better) when something, anything incompatible with your journalistic conscience is proposed. When it comes to ethics and the practice of journalism, silence is a killer.

No, you won't always be heeded or heard. And yes, even to question may be a risk. But it is a wee, small risk, and a tiny price to pay to be worthy of the name "American journalist." To be a journalist is to ask questions. All the time. Even of the people we work for.

Number two: In any showdown between quality and substance on the one hand, and sleaze and glitz on the other, go with quality and substance. You know the difference. Every one of us in this room knows the difference because we've been there. We've all gone Hollywood. We've all succumbed to the Hollywoodization of news because we were afraid not to. We trivialize important subjects. We put videotape through a cuisinart trying to come up with high-speed, MTV-style cross-cuts. And just to cover our asses, we give the best slots to gossip and prurience.

We can say "No more." We can fight the fear that leads to Showbizzification. *Act* on your knowledge. You know that serious news—local and regional, national and international—doesn't have to be dull, not for one second. People *will* watch serious news, well-written and well-produced. The proof, it's all around, but I'll give you two examples. Look at *Sunday Morning* and *Nightline*. No glitz, no gossip. Just compelling information. You can produce your own *Nightline* or *Sunday Morning*. All that's required of you is determination and thought, taste and imagination. That's what Tom Bettag and Ted Koppel, that's what Linda Mason, Missie Rennie, Charles Kuralt, and their teams bring to work.

Number three: Try harder to get and keep minorities on the air *and* in off-camera, decision-making jobs. Try, and be determined to succeed.

I know that there are market survey researchers who will bring you confusing numbers and tell you they add up to one thing: your audience wants to see Ken and Barbie, and your audience *doesn't* want to see African-Americans, or Arab-Americans, or Latinos, or Asian-Americans, or gays or lesbians, or older Americans or Americans with disabilities. So we give our audience plenty of Ken and Barbie, and we make the minorities we have hired so *uncomfortable* that they hold back on the perspective, the experience, the intelligence, the talent that they could have offered to make us wiser and stronger.

Those market researchers, with their surveys and focus groups, are playing games with you and me and with this entire country. We actually pay them money to fool us. Money that I submit to you could be better spent on news coverage. Their so-called samples of opinion are no more accurate or reliable than my grandmother's big toe was when it came to predicting the weather. Your own knowledge of news and human nature, your own idealism and professionalism will guide you more surely than any market researcher ever will. But the market researchers will keep getting away with their games so long as you and I and the people we work for, let them.

If we change the voice and the face of broadcasting, honestly and fairly, on the basis of excellence and ethics, talent and intelligence, we can shatter false and cheap notions about news. We can *prove* that our audience wants electronic journalism that is ethical, responsible, and of high quality, and that is as diverse, as different, as dynamic as America itself.

There is another thing we all can do. A difference we can make. One word: *More.*

Let's do more to think more. Let's bring all the brilliance and imagination this industry has to bear. *That's* what Ed Murrow was talking about. Let's phase out fear. If we've got an idea, let's not hide it out of fear. The fear of doing things differently, the fear that says, "They can't fire you if they don't know you're there." That fear runs rampant through the corridors of broadcasting today.

The people we work for are more fearful than we are. Fear leads them to depend on thoughtless, lifeless numbers to tell them what fear convinces them are facts: American audiences won't put up with news from other countries. Americans won't put up with economic news. Americans won't put up with serious, substantive news of any kind.

Bull-feathers. We've gone on too long believing this nonsense. We've bought the lie that information is bad for news. We are told, and we are afraid to disbelieve, that people want to be entertained. And we have gone so far down the info-tainment route that we'll be a long time getting back to where we started.

But as long as the people we work for believe this kind of nonsense, the less inclined we have been to prove them wrong. We go about our days, going along to get along. The fear factor freezes us.

The greatest shortage on every beat, in every newsroom in America, is courage.

I believe, as Ed Murrow did, that the vast majority of the owners and executives and managers we work for are good people, responsible citizens, and patriotic Americans. I believe that the vast majority of the people in this room also fit that description. We all know what's at stake. We know that our beloved United States of America depends on the decisions we make in our newsrooms every day.

In the end, Murrow could not bring himself to believe that the battle about which he spoke so eloquently could be won. He left the electronic journalism he helped to create believing that most, if not all, was already lost, that electronic news in America was doomed to be completely and forever overwhelmed by commercialism and entertainment values.

About that, I believe Murrow was wrong. What is happening to us and our chosen field of work does not have to continue happening. The battle is dark and odds-against. But it is not irreversible, not—not yet. To prevent it from being so requires courage.

A few, just a few, good men and women with courage—the courage to practice the idealism that attracted most of us to the craft in the first place—can make a decisive difference. We need a few good men and women . . . with the courage of their convictions, to turn it around. We can be those men and women. If the people in this room tonight simply agreed, starting tomorrow, to turn it around, we would turn it around. All we need is courage.

I don't have to tell you. You already know. But it is important for me to say it to you anyway. I haven't always had that courage.

I said earlier that to talk about Ed Murrow before you tonight was humbling. And perhaps that's true most of all in this respect: it is humbling to realize how little courage I have, compared to

Murrow who had so much, and how many opportunities I have
already wasted.

But tomorrow is a new day. We toil and are happy in this craft,
because of the way Edward R. Murrow brought it into being. We
can be worthy of him. We can share his courage. Or, we can
continue to work in complacency and fear.

Let us remember the words that inspired Murrow himself at
the end of a famous broadcast:

Men at some time are masters of their fates; The fault, dear Brutus, is not
in our stars, But in ourselves. . . .

VALUES DESERVING OUR ATTENTION[1]
William A. Hilliard[2]

"Is the press too mean?" American newspaper editors, under
attack for the ethics and emphasis of their publications, indulged
in something of a "group worry session" on this subject at the
annual convention of the American Society of Newspaper Editors, held in Washington, D.C., on April 13, 1994. According to
William Glaberson, writing in the *New York Times* (April 14, 1994):

Editors from hundreds of the country's biggest newspapers have clearly been stung by criticism from the public and even some journalists,
contending that news columns have degenerated into "gotcha" efforts to
embarrass public figures.

The American Society of Newspaper Editors is an influential
organization whose 920 members determine the editorial and
news policies of most of the country's major newspapers.

The keynote address at the opening general session of the
convention was delivered by the society's president, William A.
Hilliard, editor of the Portland *Oregonian*. Warning of a "cancer of
mean spiritedness festering in the journalistic gut today," Hilliard
asked his audience of 800 Society members whether they had
after all become captives of the desire to draw attention to themselves. Hilliard called for cultural diversity, greater civility, and an
end to First Amendment abuses.

----

[1]Keynote address to the national convention of the American Society of Newspaper Editors held in Washington, D.C., April 13, 1994.
[2]For biographical note, see Appendix.

William A. Hilliard's speech: I hope all of you agree that a man can do worse than be remembered for his consistency and perseverance. If you agree with that premise, you won't be disappointed if I stick to what I know best and care about most.

I have composed my remarks around three points. I want you to remember them whenever you think about what it takes to run a good newspaper. And I want to express these points as values that need to be accommodated when newspaper managers make decisions: news decisions, editorial decisions, and people decisions.

These are the values I believe are most deserving of that accommodation:

Cultural diversity. Assurance that the people newspapers hire and promote mirror the community's cultural demographics.

Civility. It seems to me there is a cancer of mean-spiritedness festering in the journalistic gut today. It troubles me. It troubles thoughtful readers. I think it should trouble you.

And last, *First Amendment abuses* of our profession's most vulnerable and least protected practitioners: high school, college, and university newspaper staffs.

First, the issue of cultural diversity.

Our profession took giant strides toward cultural diversity when professors in our schools of communication and journalism stopped telling people of color, especially young blacks, as one professor told me: that big newspapers wouldn't hire them. We took an additional step forward when ASNE [American Society of Newspaper Editors] announced publicly that by the year 2000, its member newspapers' staffs would reflect the percentage of minorities in the population.

But cultural diversity is more than just race or color. Cultural diversity in American newspapers means that all components of our buildings will accommodate the wheelchairs, guide dogs, and unique accouterments of our employees with disabilities.

It means that white reporters and photographers don't dress down when they visit tribal officials in Native American communities.

And it means that our employees' sexual orientations are irrelevant to who gets hired, who gets fired, who gets the "good" assignments, and who gets promoted. We will have achieved true diversity when the differences among us don't make any difference.

But we are not there yet. And, in my view, a newspaper that

does not look like a cross-section of the community it serves will not, and cannot, serve that community as it wants and deserves to be served.

No newspaper can claim immunity from a role in helping to build and maintain the cultural collaboratives that comprise rich and successful societies. And a successful society's greatest virtues, the wellsprings of its greatness, are tolerance, respect, and unyielding commitments to common values.

And such are the values of great newspapers.

What would most of the newspapers in our large cities look like if they had circulation wards and the readership had say in the newspaper's racial, ethnic, gender, and age mix? Would they look different? Probably.

And what if ASNE itself chose arbitrarily to forfeit some of the rich diversity it has? What if our membership excluded newspapers from, say, Wisconsin, Michigan, Illinois, Indiana, Ohio, and Iowa?

Would ASNE represent newspaper America? Of course not. Would we be poorer for our omission? Of course we would. Would newspaper editors in those states hold ASNE in much regard? I doubt it.

Without those editors, important regional values and perspectives would be missing from key ASNE policy discussions and decisions, much less from our college basketball coverage. And if those editors' principles and perspectives were not sought out and valued by ASNE, then ASNE would be of no value to them.

So it is with minority elements among our constituent readers.

Any newspaper editor still in denial about our nation's cultural evolution may, sometime in the next century, be part of a displaced institution when people of color comprise the majority in America.

To those few who are threatened by that prospect, let me remind them that this is not a case of winners and losers. No one has to be disenfranchised when we accommodate and nourish cultural diversity everywhere—in our newsrooms, in our communities and in our nation.

The Oregonian did not fire a white male reporter to make room for me. And I was not promoted at the expense of more competent or deserving colleagues. Nobody lost because I succeeded.

On the contrary, I want to believe that, over the years, scores of young people of color have looked at me and said, "It can happen."

With that responsibility in mind, I have tried to make sure that when any prospect applies for work at *The Oregonian,* that person's only cause for anxiety should be: Am I good enough? Not, am I man enough? Or white enough? Or young enough? Not, can I cut it as a black reporter? Or a lesbian reporter? Or a disabled reporter? Just, can I cut it as a reporter? That is all that counts.

In 1978, ASNE set a goal. We gave ourselves 22 years to make our news and editorial rooms reflect America's racial makeup. It is projected that by the year 2000, 30 percent of our news and editorial staffs must be people of color, one out of every three, if we are to meet this goal.

That was 16 years ago. We have less than six years in which to reach our goal. We are only one-third of the way there. The first one-third was somewhat easy. The last one-third will be even more difficult. But nobody said it would be easy.

On civility. According to my *Webster,* civility is courtesy. It is "a polite act or expression." Civility implies maturity and respect for other people and other opinions, or at least calm restraint in the fact of contentiousness.

It follows that incivility is a discourtesy, an impolite act or expression, a lack of maturity, a lack of respect for other people and other opinions, and the inability to exercise restraint.

Not too long ago, James J. Kilpatrick, one of my favorites, wrote about President Clinton's nomination of Ruth Bader Ginsburg for the Supreme Court. I frankly do not know why Kilpatrick felt compelled to write, and I quote: ". . . Given his repeated vows before the gods of diversity and multiculturalism, Clinton could not have nominated a white male to the court."

To my ear, Kilpatrick's choice of words "gods of diversity and multiculturalism" deliberately holds in cold contempt sincere comments to end discrimination in this country. Kilpatrick is not a frequent offender, although in my view, he missed an opportunity to give young writers a lesson in cool persuasion and civility.

Many of you read the op-ed piece by Thomas R. Roeser, a conservative activist and founder of the Republican Assembly of Illinois. In the piece, Roeser wrote about President Eisenhower's "tragic judgment" in abandoning Berlin instead of capturing the city at the close of World War II. Years later, in 1953, the first year of the Eisenhower presidency, the Berlin judgment came back to haunt the new president.

Wrote Roeser: "TV news features it endlessly. Ike's approval numbers plummet. The partisan advantage is clear."

But, according to Roeser, the feeding frenzy failed to bring down the president, thanks to bipartisan support from Congress. "Frankly," Roeser observed, and I quote, "we had better men then." "In contrast," he continued, "if our decadent age of sensationalistic incivility, whoever can manipulate media facts and put them to political use can cause reputations to fall like dominos."

Continuing from the Roeser piece, and again I quote:

It crested with Watergate—where opportunism on all sides caused Richard Nixon, a successful foreign policy president, to fall. Bill Safire and others vowed to get even. Watergate-era rules maimed the administrations of Jimmy Carter, Ronald Reagan, and George Bush . . . and now, Bill Clinton,

concluded the Illinois conservative.

If Roeser is right, and I think to a great extent he is, American politics seem destined to be awash in blood feuds that rank retribution above common decency, above accountability, and above the salvation of the republic.

The question then becomes: are American newspapers independent, objective chroniclers of events? Or is our future mortgaged to grotesque one-upmanship where news stories begin and end with an empty headline?

There may or may not be perfect parallels in the 1950s and the 1990s. The 1950s were different times, and to some perhaps better times.

But I think we misjudge our readers' capacity to tolerate the media's sometimes manic and ill-tempered self-indulgence.

I do not believe American newspaper readers have an infinite capacity to tolerate incivility. And I believe that the newspaper executive who expects infinite indulgence does so at his or her peril.

I want to commence the last of my remarks with a question. When is the First Amendment kid stuff?

I think the answer is never.

I am certain, however, that every one in this audience, at one time or another, defended his or her or someone else's right to free speech protection under the First Amendment.

In our business, the quickest way to rally the troops is to challenge free speech. Nothing is as righteous and heroic as an embattled newspaper editor exercising and defending his or her sacred duty to resist being told what he or she can print and what he or she can't.

Well, there is a need to rally the troops when the local college or university suspends the campus newspaper for offending some ivy-covered moral protocol, almost always ill-defined. There is a tendency for most of us to report the incident as news and too often to forego an editorial opinion.

It is my view that it was not the intent of our founding fathers that the First Amendment be held in abeyance through one's adolescence. If the American newspaper establishment fails to defend free speech for high school and college journalists, how can we claim it for ourselves?

Can we be credible models and leaders in our profession and condone censorship at the same time?

ASNE has, in my view, done some important work in this emotionally charged and not altogether rational journalistic area. We have urged hometown, mainstream newspaper editors to get involved in hands-on, community-level workshops for high school journalism advisers. We have urged managers to send professional staffers to meet and talk with campus newspaper staffs.

Last year we published and distributed *How to Rescue High School Journalism* to editors of every daily newspaper in the country and to high school journalism teachers. These are meaningful steps, but are they enough?

I believe ASNE needs to step into the campus journalism censorship fray every time a meritorious opportunity arises. I cannot conceive of an ASNE-member newspaper not intervening in this most fundamental constitutional issue.

Because I am an individual who has suffered personally from the indignities of discrimination, I am extremely sensitive to the feelings of those around me, so these values have a special meaning for me.

I believe the daily newspaper is indispensable to the survival of a free society. It can show best the need to celebrate one's ethnicity and its benefits to a multicultural society: the achievements of women, black Americans, Native Americans, Hispanics, and Asians.

In doing so, we must be careful to move more toward a unified America, without divisions along racial, economic and cultural lines.

ARTS AND THE HUMANITIES

BEYOND THE CULTURE WARS[1]
SHELDON HACKNEY[2]

Over that past decade there has been an increase in the attention paid to racial, ethnic, religious, and sexual hostility in this country. Educators, civil libertarians, and religious leaders, among others have sought ways to reduce social friction. On several university campuses attempts to regulate or prohibit "hate speech" proved offensive because such regulations also tend to curb the constitutional guarantee of freedom of speech. Even groups that strongly deplore "hate speech" generally oppose such restrictions on the First Amendment. In almost every case where laws on politically incorrect speech reached the courts, they were struck down.

Inevitably, the government has become involved in the controversy. In 1991 Lynne V. Cheney, at the time the head of the National Endowment of the Humanities, which controls $180 million in federal grants for research and cultural institutions, spoke out strongly against political correctness. (See *Representative Speeches 1991–1992,* pp. 116–126.)

On November 10, 1993, Sheldon Hackney, Cheney's successor at the National Endowment, made his first major speech, a nationally broadcast address to the National Press Club in Washington, D.C.

Hackney, while President of the University of Pennsylvania had become embroiled in several widely publicized campus skirmishes in the cultural war. As a result he was able to bring to the subject of his address a personal knowledge of the complexities and controversy that seem always to accompany the issue of political correctness.

Hackney delivered his speech at a Newsmaker Luncheon in the National Press Club ballroom at 1:00 P.M. to an audience of 122 members of the club, reporters, and communication profes-

[1]Delivered to the National Press Club, Washington, D.C., at 1 P.M., Monday, November 10, 1993.
[2]For biographical note, see Appendix.

sionals. The speech was carried of C-SPAN, National Public Radio, and the international network.

Hackney's call for a "national conversation"—rather than the posturing, slogans, and epithets that pass for debate on pluralism and racial diversity—attracted much favorable comment, especially among educators.

Sheldon Hackney's speech: What we think about ourselves, what we see as admirable behavior, what we think it means to be human, what we recognize as the human condition, what we learn from human experience and human thought, what we accept as the purpose of life, what we define as a just society, what we decide we owe to each other, what we understand as the way the world works, are not simply matters of idle curiosity but fundamental determinants of our existence. The humanities matter. They are important to everyone.

They are so important that the federal government needs to foster their development and insure their broad availability. That is the genius of the vision of Senator Claiborne Pell and Senator Jacob Javits and Senator Edward Kennedy and President Lyndon Johnson and the other founders of the National Endowment for the Humanities in 1965. And it has been the inspiration of the nurturers of that vision in the succeeding twenty-eight years. What we *think* determines what we *do.* And what we think (even about the values we hold dear) will be enormously improved if it is informed by knowledge and disciplined thought by the study of history and philosophy and literature and religion.

That is what Maya Angelou had in mind in her inaugural poem last January when she rephrased George Santayana: "History, despite its wrenching pain, / Cannot be unlived, but if faced/ With courage, need not be lived again." The same theme was struck by President Clinton in his dedication of the United States Holocaust Memorial Museum in April. After enumerating some of the evil forces loose in the world that threaten civilization with brutality just as the Nazis once did, the President exhorted us all to be vigilant against the falsifiers of history. "With them we must all compete for the interpretation and the preservation of history, of what we know and how we should behave."

I begin with these powerful sentiments because I believe that I am joining a distinguished tradition at the NEH at a particularly critical juncture in the nation's history when the benefits of the humanities are especially important. Let me explain.

Last week (November 3, 1993) Mark Shields in his newspaper column reminded us of the current cynicism of the American public, or more precisely, the lack of confidence that the public has in the national government to handle our domestic problems adequately. One can think of a lot of reasons for the public to be in an anxious mood these days. But as Mr. Shields points out, the decline in public confidence began more than two decades ago, sometime in the 1960s.

My own understanding of this worrisome phenomenon is helped by realizing that it is not simply the national government that has slipped in the estimation of the American public, but that public confidence in all American institutions has declined. I used to take a smidgeon of perverse pleasure as a university president in the fact that universities ranked higher in the public's estimation than our chief tormentors, the congress and the press. But the grim truth is that levels of confidence in the institutions of American life rise and fall together, and the secular trend line for more than the last two decades has been down.

Just before the election (October 31, 1993 in the *Washington Post*), Kevin Phillips wrote about voter hostility towards elites of all kinds, about popular opposition to NAFTA as being a matter of suspicious locals versus arrogant globals who are out of touch with mainstream America, and about ethnic and racial tensions throughout the country. The off-year elections confirmed this diagnosis of anger and volatility in the public mood.

Why the cynicism? Why the insecurity? Why the alienation? The short answer is that the new geopolitical forces of the still evolving "new world order," and the newly visible economic forces of the global marketplace are battering a society whose bonds of social cohesion have been loosening for a quarter of a century or more. This is not the place to try to explain in detail the fundamental economic, demographic and social forces that have an atomizing effect on society, but they are real and they have been acting over a long period of time. In addition, the basic confidence and optimism thought to be embedded in American national character were dealt severe blows in the early 1970s by the loss of the war in Vietnam, the disgrace of the presidency in the Watergate scandal, and the economic shock of the Arab oil embargo which was perhaps the first painful message that our economy was vulnerable to developments and decisions in the world economy over which we had no control.

Into this condition of attenuated solidarity "the politics of difference" have introduced another level of fragmentation. During the turbulent decade of the 1960s, almost all the values and verities of middle-class life were challenged by the counterculture, leaving the domain of values a contested territory. The cultural consensus of the 1950s was destroyed in the process, and we have not yet fully developed a new consensus.

In addition, the successful civil rights movement provided a paradigm of progress through protest. Movements on behalf of other groups that had been excluded from full participation in American life (women, gays and lesbians, the handicapped, Native Americans, Latinos, and to some extent Asian Americans) adopted that paradigm.

Then, the collapse of the Soviet system, while lifting our spirits in hopes for the spread of human freedom, has also unleashed pent up ancient animosities. Around the globe we see conflict and violence sowing misery along the fault lines of race, religion, language, and ethnicity—just the sorts of divisions being brought to our attention by the politics of difference and by the increasing cultural diversity of our population. As the insecurities of a rapidly changing world are luring Americans and others into clutching and reasserting their parochial identities, Americans must wonder if Bosnia and Azerbaijan are previews of our future.

Several weeks ago (October 17, 1993) The *New York Times* published a feature article by William Grimes entitled "Have a #%!&$! Day" about the rising tide of incivility engulfing the country. From Howard Stern to Beavis and Butthead, we are assaulted daily by countless acts of public rudeness. Among the cultural roots of this phenomenon, Mr. Grimes focuses on cultural diversity. "New Yorkers have never been terribly civil," he quotes a professor of the humanities at Cooper Union as saying, "but it never had an ideological edge, which it now has." Mr. Grimes goes on to quote the same professor approvingly in his critique of the "new tribalism." "If we have fundamentally different values and assumptions, there's no reason to believe we can transcend them in the political arena. . . . Multiculturalism argues that persuasion is irrelevant."

Small wonder that reasonable voices have lately been saying that we have been paying too much attention to our differences, and not enough attention to the things that hold us together. From the other direction, however, we continue to hear assertions of what Charles Taylor refers to as "the politics of recognition," the notion that there are still disadvantaged groups in

America whose members will never feel equal or really part of America until their group is recognized in some way as being legitimate and equal. There is truth in both of these positions.

We find ourselves caught in a dilemma. All of our legal rights are universal in nature and apply equally to all citizens as individuals. Yet, we know that racial, ethnic, gender, and religious discrimination exists, and that group identities are real factors in our lives. Ethnic politics has been a staple on the American political scene for more than a hundred years and is still very much present in our system. The dilemma is that our legal rights are for individuals, but our politics are for groups.

That this is more than an academic argument is clear if one recalls the hand-to-hand combat of school board battles involving such issues as bilingual education or Afrocentric curricula, the dispute over the literary canon at the college level, or the court decisions seeking to remedy past patterns of discrimination in voting rights cases by requiring redistricting or changes in the form of local government so as to guarantee the minority community representation on the legislative body. In each of these cases, and others you can probably think of, public authorities are being asked to confer some sort of official status on a particular cultural group. Large parts of the public sense that this form of particularism is a problem in a system based on universal values of individual rights. Simply saying that everyone must respect everyone else's ethnic identity therefore does not solve the problem.

Yet, a solution must be found if we are to recapture a confident sense of shared values that will let us then deal with divisive public policy issues with a common goal in mind. What is needed in our country is nothing short of a national conversation about this difficult and troubling dilemma. All of our people, left, right and center, have a responsibility to examine and discuss what unites us as a country, about what we share as common American values in a nation comprised of so many divergent groups and beliefs. For too long we have let that which divides us capture the headlines. Current public debate is little more than posturing. Bombarded by slogans and epithets, points and counterpoints, our thoughts are polarized in the rapid-fire exchange of sound bites. In this kind of argument, one is either right or wrong, for them or against them, a winner or a loser.

Real answers are the casualties of such drive-by debates. In this kind of discussion, there is no room for complexity and ambiguity. There is no room in the middle. Only the opposite poles are given voice. This may be good entertainment, but it is a disservice to the American people. It only reinforces lines of division and does not build toward agreement. I want to change the rules of engagement for this national conversation.

This is to be a national conversation open to all Americans. A conversation in which all voices need to be heard and in which we must grapple seriously with the meaning of American pluralism. It is a conversation that is desperately needed, and I believe the National Endowment for the Humanities can stimulate and facilitate the discussion. The NEH will not bring answers, but we will bring questions.

To be sure, the NEH has other important tasks. As the single most important source of support for the humanities in American life, receiving approximately 9,000 applications per year and dispensing $150 million in about 2,000 grants, we have a major role to play in assisting in the creation of new knowledge, translating knowledge in the humanities into educational experiences both formal and informal, and in extending the reach of humanities programs to embrace many more Americans so that they may benefit from the transforming power of the humanities in their everyday lives.

We will continue to support individual scholars both in the academy and outside; we will continue to bring high school and college teachers together on university campuses for summer seminars that refresh and reinvigorate them; we will continue to support programs in museums and libraries and archives where our cultural heritage is preserved, used for public programs, and made available for study; we will continue to fund excellent programs through the mass media, such as Ken Burns' documentary on the Civil War and Henry Hampton's series on the Great Depression; and we will work with renewed enthusiasm with state humanities councils to enlist more Americans in humanities activities, be it reading and discussion groups or chautauqua or communities recording and telling their own story, connecting individuals and groups with the broader context of human experience so that they become the subjects of history rather than its objects.

With some of our time and energy, however, and a little bit of our money, we will conduct a national conversation. I have been pleased to discover that numerous programs sponsored by state humanities councils have already started people talking to each other about who we are as a nation and what holds us together.

The projects have taken many forms: small town residents and farmers gathering under chautauqua tents in North Dakota or Wyoming exploring American democracy and the ideas of Thomas Jefferson; citizens in Florida meeting to explore "The Search for the Common Good." Californians reading and discussing serious essays on the topic of "Longing for Community: Dream or Nightmare"; or hundreds of Iowans meeting to explore religious pluralism in a program called "Faith and Politics: American Pluralism, Can We Live Together?"

I am encouraging the Federation of State Humanities Councils and the individual state councils to intensify their pursuit of the theme and to explore it in programs of their own devising. I will set aside a modest but significant amount of money for an endowment-wide initiative that can respond to competitive proposals from around the country—from state councils, from libraries, museums and archives, from schools, colleges and universities, from centers and institutes.

I am also delightfully aware that a number of scholars from various disciplines and many different points of view have been thinking and writing about the subject of this national conversation over the past two or three years. The MacArthur Foundation has agreed to be an early partner in this enterprise by bringing together a group of these already engaged scholars to talk to each other. Out of that small discussion, and others that are already going on at the local level, we will gain some insights into different aspects of the subject, into how to phrase the questions productively, into what sorts of materials stimulate the most fruitful discussions, and into the range of possible answers. I imagine that, after some experience, we will be able to conduct this conversation through mass media formats. This is an exciting undertaking for the NEH and for the country.

My own notion of the meaning of American pluralism is still evolving, and in any case is certainly not prescriptive. Yet it might help for me to sketch some elements of it here. My answer has as its preface a belief that there is an American identity that is different from the identities of any one of the ethnic groups that comprise the American population, that is inclusive of all of them, and that is available to everyone who is American. It is an identity that has been shaped by the buffeting and melding of individuals and groups in North America over the last three hundred years.

I believe that the most important thing that we share as Americans is a belief in our political system, in the values that are enshrined in the Constitution, and in the open democratic system for determining who makes and enforces the laws, and that the laws should be consistent with those principles.

Further, in the land of opportunity, we believe in equal economic opportunity for individuals. We know that we do not provide perfect equality of opportunity, but it is an ideal that we hold dear, and we have historically provided enough opportunity to keep individual hope alive, and to maintain faith in the ideal.

We also have a history that belongs to all Americans, whenever their ancestors happened to have migrated to these shores. That history is a proud one, but it has some dark spots, and we must come to terms with those imperfections as well as the glories. I am a white southern male, but I claim as part of my own story the experiences of Italians and Irish and Jews coming into America through Ellis Island in the late nineteenth and early twentieth century, and the experiences of African Americans who lived in the south with my ancestors and saw it from their own point of view, or more recently the experiences of South Asians and Latinos. My story should be theirs as well. And we all possess together the national story, the resultant of many different vectors, the story of our being able to find solutions, to rise to historical challenges, and find ways to transform particular interests into the national interest.

Beyond these fundamental building blocks, there are certain precepts that might help us as we go through the discussion of what it means to be American. The traditional way of handling cultural differences has been to think about a public sphere and a private sphere. In the public sphere only universalistic rules are legitimate and only individual rights are legally protected. In the private sphere, we can give voice and form to our birthright identities without being any less American. This distinction still goes a long way in sorting out the conflicts between the universal and the particular.

Indeed, if there is no distinction between the public and the private, all values would be up for political adjudication, and that is not a system I find very attractive. One of the factors causing the current sense of urgency about this subject is the feeling that the public or political sphere has been encroaching on the private sphere. "Let your culture be your politics," the cultural radicals of the 1960s chanted. "All politics are personal, and all personal relationships are political," assert some contemporary activists. Where in all of this are the ordinary virtues that we ought to be able to expect from each other? Perhaps they can emerge from the conversation.

It helps also to realize that all ethnic groups have permeable boundaries, and that the meaning of any particular identity will change over time. What it felt like to be a white southerner in 1865 is different from what it felt like in 1950 and it is different again today. What it means to be a Jew in America is different today from what it was in 1940. History has a way of changing who we think we are.

The subject is elusive, but it is very important. If the conversation works well, we will stake out some common ground. And by doing that we will make it possible to celebrate more fully the variations among us that play against each other and reinforce each other to produce a dynamic national identity. As President Clinton said in a different context at the dedication of the Holocaust Memorial Museum, "We must find in our diversity our common humanity. We must reaffirm that common humanity, even in the darkest and deepest of our own disagreements."

In that spirit, I am looking forward to this conversation among the American people. In that spirit, I challenge you to help focus the attention of the American people on this quest for the meaning of *E Pluribus Unum*.

A SENSE OF PROPORTION[1]
David McCullough[2]

Arts Advocacy Day, an annual spring event in Washington, D.C., brings together arts leaders from across the country to meet with their Congressional representatives and urge greater support for the arts. The event also gives representatives of national, state, and community arts organizations a chance to meet with the more than 250 members of the bipartisan Congressional Arts Caucus to examine the range of government programs affecting the arts.

Since 1988 the Nancy Hanks Lecture on Arts and Public Poli-

[1]Delivered as the Nancy Hanks Lecture on the Arts and Public Policy at the Kennedy Center for the Performing Arts in Washington, D.C., on April 11, 1994.
[2]For biographical note, see Appendix.

cy, which is sponsored by the American Council for the Arts, has been an important part of Arts Advocacy Day. The lecture memorializes Nancy Hanks (1927–1983) who served as chairperson of the National Endowment for the Arts from 1969 to 1977.

The 1994 Nancy Hanks lecturer was David McCullough, winner of the 1993 Pulitzer Prize for his biography *Truman*. He delivered the address at the Kennedy Center for the Arts in Washington, D.C., on the evening of April 17, 1994.

David McCullough's speech: This is a great honor to be the Nancy Hanks Lecturer on the Arts and Public Policy, to have the opportunity to speak to you.

Art and history, culture and history, must not be seen as separate, any more than science and history. Dividers are imposed too often. We have the history of art over here, the history of science over there, the history of medicine, the history of music made separate, with walls between, as if music isn't medicine. Plain history, too often, winds up with only politics and wars.

But it is all part of human experience. To leave painting and song out of the story, theater, architecture, poetry, is to leave out too much of life, too much that matters above all.

Creativity, innovation, invention are impossible without imagination and without risk. This was true in times past. It is true today. Yet we do too little in educating our children to encourage and reward imagination and the willingness to take risks.

"How many things can you think of to do with a brick?"

It's a question I like to ask students in writing courses. "Take out a piece of paper, make a list. There's no right or wrong answer. Use your imagination." It's wonderful to see how liberating many find that.

History is about who we were. In the arts we show who we are. History is about time. Art transcends time. "Who's statue is that, there in the park, with the pigeon on his hat?" How many politicians have strutted their stuff here down the years—hundreds, thousands—confident they were taking their place in history? How few are remembered at all.

But Gershwin lives. Every time everywhere his music is played, Gershwin lives. Whitman and Willa Cather, Thomas Eakins, Louis Sullivan, Martha Graham, Langston Hughes speak to us still, touch our lives. Take away our art, our music, the best of our buildings, take away Mark Twain and Julia Ward Howe and Woodie Guthrie and Scott Joplin and who are we? Take from this our capital city Daniel Chester French's Lincoln or that greatest of the city's works of abstract art, the Washington Monument by Robert Mills, take away the great collections of the Library of Congress, and how then would we feel?

Culture might be defined as what matters to a society. And certainly a good measure of what matters is how we spend our money.

Nearly everywhere in the country libraries are shortening their hours, laying off staff, putting a freeze on book purchases, or closing their doors. The explanation always is that there's not enough money.

Yet in all the years of the Great Depression, not one library is known to have closed its doors anywhere in all the country. Not one. And in the worst of times when our material abundance individually and as a nation was nothing like what it is today.

In Massachusetts, where I live, twenty libraries have closed in the last three years alone. In California since 1980 more than half the public school libraries have closed. Libraries in Los Angeles are open now only a few days a week. This in California, golden California.

The Library of Congress, too, has lately cut back its services, closing the main reading room plus six other reading rooms on Sundays, a severe blow to anyone wishing to use the Library on weekends.

As a personal note I might add that it was on a weekend at the Library of Congress in the early '60s that I happened to see a collection of newly acquired, rare old photographs taken in Johnstown, Pennsylvania, soon after the calamitous flood of 1889. Photographs that led me to write my first book, that led me to writing history as I had never anticipated I would. So I am particularly sympathetic to those with full-time jobs who can only make use of the Library on weekends.

How do we spend our money? For all public libraries nationwide: $4.3 billion a year, which is considerably less than we spend on potato chips or sneakers. Less than we spend on our lawns or for cellular phones. Last year, we spent $7.5 billion on our lawns, $9 billion on cellular phones.

Have we changed so much in our regard for libraries since the Great Depression? Not to judge by the demand for library services. Library use, even with the cutbacks, is up substantially. What is not up is our willingness to pay the price, or more specifically to vote the taxes to pay the price for a measure of civilization that has long been standard to our way of life and that so many benefit from in ways beyond anything determinable by cost-accounting.

Still more serious, even more shameful, is what is happening to programs in the arts in our schools. And it is this especially that I want to talk about.

All across the country arts programs in the schools are being cut or eliminated altogether, and it's a disgrace. We are cheating our children!

"We hold these truths to be self-evident." We teach them from history books that all men are created equal, that they are endowed by their Creator with certain inalienable rights, that among these are Life, Liberty, and the pursuit of happiness. But how will they have any idea of happiness, of all that Thomas Jefferson had in mind when he used that word, if they are shut off from art and architecture and music and theater and dance and literature, if they are denied that part of life, that vital center, if they have only a limited chance at the experience of self-expression, or no chance at all?

There are new figures for what's to be spent by the federal government on the arts. And for the first time there is a specific allotment for art and music in the schools. For fiscal 1995 it's to be $75,000,000. Federally funded cultural programs including money for the National Endowment for the Humanities, the National Endowment for the Arts, and education in the arts comes to approximately $600,000,000, while the overall figure, the grand total, which includes money for the Smithsonian, museums, art galleries, and the like is $882,000,000. And what's that? It's a pitance is what it is.

$882,000,000 is one sixth-hundredth of one percent of the federal budget.

We need to recover a Jeffersonian sense of proportion. Jefferson, whose passion for education exceeded that of any of our political leaders, worked out his own guide "to the faculties of the mind," as he called it, in his classification system for his library. This was the private collection of 6,500 books assembled over fifty years that Jefferson sold to the government at half its value to create a new congressional library after the British burned the capitol during the War of 1812. It took eleven wagons to haul the books here. And what a picture that must have made as they left Monticello and started through the countryside.

There were three main categories and he gave them equal importance.

First was *memory,* by which he meant history: history civil, history ecclesiastical, natural history, history ancient and modern.

Second was *reason,* which included philosophy, the law, and mathematics.

The third category, titled *imagination,* was the fine arts. And on this lovely spring evening in the city he helped design, I would like to mention that within fine arts, along with painting, sculpture, architecture, music, poetry, drama, oratory, and criticism, he included gardening.

Three parts equally weighted, and history and the arts are two of the three: history, philosophy, and the fine arts.

I grew up in Pittsburgh, Pennsylvania. I was number three in a family of four sons. My father worked with his father in a family-owned electrical supply business, McCullough Electric, now run by my brother George.

I began public school in kindergarten in 1938, about the time when the National Gallery was being built here. The building, along with a surpassing collection of old masters, were a gift from the late Andrew Mellon of Pittsburgh, about whom I knew nothing, of course, but whose generosity to his country I've come to appreciate more and more. The paintings alone were the largest gift of any individual to any government.

Like McCullough Electric, the Linden Avenue School is still in business, a fine two-story, yellow brick building about mid-way between Point Breeze and Squirrel Hill, if you know Pittsburgh. To me then, its marble halls and great sweeping double stairway to the second floor were grand in the extreme. When I returned last year for the school's 90th anniversary celebration, I was delighted to find that those marble halls and sweeping stairs are in fact just as grand as I remembered.

We had music at Linden School, lots of music, and Miss Polichio, our music teacher, was perfectly beautiful. For quite a while I was in love with Miss Polichio. We had music several times a week in a room reserved for music. We played tamborines, woodblocks, and the triangle. (I thought myself something of a woodblock virtuoso.) We sang, learning by heart most of Stephen Foster, who came from Pittsburgh. There was a school orchestra. My oldest brother played the violin in the school orchestra.

There was an auditorium with a stage and real pull curtains and we were all in plays, the whole way along. There was an art room and an art teacher, Miss Bridgewater, and the day she took her chalk and with a few fast strokes demonstrated two point perspective on the black board, is one I've never forgotten. She had performed pure magic right before our eyes. I had to be able to do that. I had to learn how. I began drawing and painting and I'm still at it at every possible chance. (One of the particular pleasures of painting is you don't have to work with words.)

By now these were the World War II years, when the steel mills were going at capacity and at night the sky pulsed red from the flames of the blast furnaces.

There was a library at school, with books on every wall except for where the windows faced the street. It is still that way. The first morning we were declared sufficiently advanced to go to the library—a very great step in the upward march at Linden—we were told we could each go to the shelves and choose any book we wished. What a moment! I remember especially one called *Ben and Me* written and illustrated by Robert Lawson. It was about a mouse who lived in Ben Franklin's hat and who consequently had much to report.

When my oldest brother, Hax, went to Peabody High School, he both played the violin in the Peabody Symphony orchestra and stole the show in a Peabody production of *Arsenic and Old Lace*. He was Teddy Brewster, the one who thought he was Theodore Roosevelt and was kept busy down in the cellar—down in "Panama"—digging the canal and burying the supposed yellow fever victims. It was the most marvelous stage production I had ever seen and my first realization of there ever having been anyone like Theodore Roosevelt or a place like Panama.

"How do you pick the subjects for your books?" I'm asked. "Whatever made you decide on Theodore Roosevelt? The Panama Canal?"

There's no telling, I suppose, when the seed of an idea takes hold. But on the first day I went to the Carnegie Library—in Pittsburgh this means *the* Carnegie Library, the mother church as it were—and with my new, first library card took out a book, I was perhaps eleven years old. It was *A Tree Grows in Brooklyn*. About that same time, as I remember, our wonderful science teacher at Linden School, Miss Schmeltz, had arranged an exhibit of bridges of all kinds. They were made of match sticks and I can see them still, lined up along the window sills, flooded with sunlight.

At a party, long afterward, when I told her what I was working on, a Washington socialite boomed loud enough for everyone to hear, "Who in the world would ever want to read a book about the Brooklyn Bridge?"

August Wilson, whose best-known plays are set in Pittsburgh, has described how, in boyhood, the Carnegie Library became his preferred classroom, where he read Ralph Ellison, Richard Wright, and Langston Hughes. "Just the idea black people would write books," he has said. "I wanted my book up there, too."

Art, music, science, history, putting on plays, it was all part of school and childhood and I loved school, almost every day. Nor was there ever a thought that the arts were frills. Or that everyone had to stay stuck in the same interests, at school or at home.

Brother Hax had his music; George, engineering; I had my painting; brother Jim, astronomy. We were not rich, certainly not by Pittsburgh standards. I suppose we could be described as comfortable. Except for engineering, my father had no interest in any of these other pursuits. Neither my father nor my mother played a musical instrument, or, as far as I know, ever painted a picture or had a part in a play. When Hax tuned the radio to the Metropolitan Opera on winter Saturday afternoons, the volume cranked up full throttle, it about drove my father crazy. "Who's getting murdered now," he'd call out. And while my father and mother willingly paid for paints and music lessons, concert tickets, and the like, and mother welcomed such activity, it was really at school that we got the bug, got the chance. And I say this because I think it so important to understand that it is not just children who are economically deprived who benefit from school libraries, from arts programs, from community commitment to the arts for children. And to argue for support of the arts on that basis primarily is to miss the point. All boats rise with the incoming tide.

What I didn't know then was how exceptional the arts program was throughout the Pittsburgh school system; indeed how exceptional it had been for years. And many of the results were exceptional, too, as we now know.

A who's who of those in the arts who attended the public schools of Pittsburgh is strong testimony to just how the whole country benefits from that kind of education: Andy Warhol, Earl Hines, Erroll Garner, Mary Lou Williams, August Wilson, Rachael Carson, composer Henry Mancini.

From Peabody High School alone came Malcolm Cowley, Gene Kelly, Billy Eckstine, Fritz Weaver, novelist John Edgar Wideman.

Gene Kelly, the son of a sales executive, was a football and baseball star at Peabody. He excelled in gymnastics, played the violin and banjo, edited the school paper, wrote poetry, and was praised on his report card for his "vivid imagination."

Erroll Garner, a mill worker's son, played the tuba in the Westinghouse High School band. Henry Mancini, whose father was a steel worker, started on the piccolo at age eight, by twelve turned to the piano. The 1942 Aliquippa High School yearbook says of him: "a true music lover, collects records, plays in the band, and has even composed several beautiful selections. He wishes to continue his study of music and to have an orchestra of his own some day."

I thought I could also include Martha Graham, who was born in Pittsburgh, but damn, she moved away at age 3.

Willa Cather once taught high school English in Pittsburgh. "So vivid was her personality," remembered a student, "so unforgettable her method of making us see the picture (as she read aloud), that even yet I hear her voice. . . ."

Selma Burke lived, worked, and taught in Pittsburgh through the 1960s and 70s, founding her own art center for children. She is a sculptor and one of the country's most respected black artists and teachers. If you have a dime with you, you own one of her works. She did the sculpted profile of Franklin Roosevelt.

And then there was Carolyn D. Patterson, a name you don't know. She was the principal of Linden School and a force, unforgettable, tall, severe-looking. A woman who brooked no nonsense whatsoever. My friend Richard Ketchum, the historian, who also went to Linden, remembers her looking at least six foot eight. Just the sound of her approaching steps could freeze you cold in your chair. She wore stout, black, lace-up shoes with thick high heels hard enough to drive a ten-penny nail. And down those marble halls she would come, making her rounds.

"Boys and girls," she would say, "Remember always you are a reflection on your parents." I'm not sure any of us knew what that meant exactly, except that we'd better tow the line. Yet, I think deep down inside we knew she was right: that our education mattered, that we mattered, each of us, and that we had potential beyond anything we might imagine.

Miss Patterson, I now appreciate, ran an outstanding school. She was dedicated, far-seeing. A pioneer. She helped found the country's first educational television station. Pittsburgh's WQED, the beginning of public television, and the station that would introduce to Pittsburgh and ultimately to the entire country, Fred

Rogers, "Mister Rogers," who in his years on the air has touched and influenced the lives of more children than any teacher who ever lived. The longest running national program in the history of public television, *Mister Rogers' Neighborhood,* broadcast still from WQED, reaches more than 8,000,000 households on some 318 public stations.

I feel I had a huge advantage growing up in Pittsburgh, *because* I grew up in Pittsburgh. For along with the schools, besides all the programs in art and music, went the Carnegie Library, the Carnegie Museums, and Carnegie Music Hall, all in one great complex in the Oakland section of town, close by Carnegie-Mellon University and the University of Pittsburgh, and, in those days, Forbes Field. I can hardly overstress the importance of this: that art, science, music, literature, history, the world of books, were joined, all together, to be taken as parts of the same whole, all under one roof. There were school trips to the Carnegie Museum of Natural History, free Saturday morning art classes at the Carnegie Museum of Art.

Or you could go on your own in perfect safety, "down" to the library or museums by bus or streetcar, though the streetcars were preferable. They were more fun. Annie Dillard, who grew up in my neighborhood, has described them as "orange, clangy, beloved things—loud, jerky, and old." That they were.

The looming stone exterior of the Carnegie then was black as coal, from the smoke in the air, and a lot inside seemed gloomy and boring. But not the dinosaurs, or the big scale model of the Parthenon, presented as it looked in its prime. There were some paintings in the permanent collection that I fed on, Edward Hopper's *Cape Cod Afternoon,* for example. And year after year, the great Associated American Artists exhibition came to the Carnegie Museum of Art, with paintings by Andrew Wyeth, Burchfield, Benton, Raphael Soyer, Grant Wood, Horace Pippin, Georgia O'Keeffe, Joe Jones, Walt Kuhn, Reginald Marsh. There was something about those Reginald Marsh girls that was beginning to interest me.

I remember also coming into one of the galleries and seeing at the far end, bigger than life, John Stuart Curry's painting of John Brown, his arms flung out, great beard flying in the wind, a cyclone roaring out of the background. How could anyone not want to know about that man, the story there?

The Kaufmann family, owners of Kaufmann's Department Store and staunch supporters of the arts, brought a string of eminent artists to Pittsburgh to paint the city, then staged an exhibition of their work. Something that ought to be done again and not only in Pittsburgh. The Kaufmann family also sponsored exhibitions of the work of school children and believe me to go downtown with your family to see one of your own paintings hanging in Kaufmann's window, *that* was something!

Private benefactors like the Kaufmann's should get all the credit they deserve. And so should the many corporations that support the arts.

What is so important to understand about education in the arts, is that there especially you learn by doing. Think of the lesson in that.

You learn to play the piano by playing the piano. You learn to paint by painting. It's not just a way to learn; it's the only way.

"She knew that the only way to learn to write was to write, and she set us to writing," remembered a student of Willa Cather.

Especially in the arts you learn how very much can be learned from a teacher, and that a great teacher is a true God-send, an opener of doors, giver of gifts, a star to steer by. Especially in the arts, you learn to bring out what is unique in you, to express yourself, your feelings, and to experience the incomparable, high-octain lift of that. But you learn about working with others, too, of being part of something larger than yourself, as anyone knows who has ever played in an orchestra, ever taken part in a theatrical production.

And—*and*—maybe it's in the arts above all that we learn most directly, discover for ourselves most immediately in the doing, that the reward *is* the doing, that the payoff for the effort is the effort.

"I want to show the children that art is not money," Selma Burke has said. "It's a life."

Selma Burke is in her 94th year.

You can see beauty and creation without ever drawing a line—if you just look . . . You can see the beauty of creation in an apple. To many people it's just an ordinary red object. But if you take a bite into it, you transform it. Now you see the white solid juicy inside. If you bite deeper you get to the core and you see the black seeds from which the apple came. Then, if you take that seed and lay it down on paper—it's almost magic! That such a big red apple could come from that seed. It's the fascinating process of creation. The art teacher has to find a simple way to teach that.

I'm hard on my students—to get them to see how important that apple is.

To see that—right in your hand—you have the beauty of creation.

"Do all you can—and then some," she would tell her students. "Do all you can—and then some."

Coaching his young son Andrew, talking of the world around them, N. C. Wyeth would say, "You must be like a sponge. Sponge it up. Soak it up."

Andrew Wyeth describes how, at 15, he learned anatomy:

He got me a skeleton. Had it there and had me draw it from every angle. Every bone. And I did that for about a winter and towards spring he said, "Now you've drawn this enough. Now . . . . I want to see how much you can remember." So he took the skeleton away. "Now I want you to draw that figure at all angles—what you remember.

Learning to appreciate the miracle of creation . . . learning to observe and remember . . . learning to see beneath surface appearances to the essential: and yet some deride education in the arts as frivolous, irrelevant.

But listen please to one more teacher. Ann Marshall has been teaching the visual arts at Peabody High School for 20 years and is herself a graduate of Peabody:

You can teach all of life with art. You learn the lessons of life. You learn that you are unique and that what you make is unique. You learn self-worth. You learn to make decisions, to make mistakes. You learn to take risks. You learn that sometimes what you think are big mistakes can turn into big successes.

Yes, but we must be practical, argue the nay-sayers. Alright, let's be practical.

Consider that in Pittsburgh the new Andy Warhol Museum, scheduled to open next month, will bring an estimated 200,000 people to the city this year. With more than 3,500 pieces in its collection, it will be the largest art gallery in the world devoted to one person. Andy Warhol, the son of a coal miner, excelled in the free Saturday art classes at the Carnegie Museum.

Or on a national level, consider the astonishing transformation of Chrysler Corporation. In less than three years Chrysler went from being the "basket case" of the American automobile industry to "leading the resurgence" of the American automobile industry. Chrysler is suddenly the most profitable car maker in the country. And the reason? Above all? Design. Inspired design. The "alchemy of design," as *The New York Times* reported. If there are heroes to the story they are Chrysler's vice president in charge of design, Tom Gale, and his extraordinary young staff. And yes, Gale remembers being inspired first by a fourth grade art teacher. Designer Michael Santoro remembers looking down from a seventh floor window at New York City's High School of Art and Design, and studying the cars waiting at the red light. "You look out the window and all the cars look the same," he told a reporter for the *Times*. "I said, 'If I ever get the chance, my car's going to look different . . .'"

How do you appraise the "practical" value of a program like the Saturday art classes at Carnegie Museum or a school like New York's High School of Art and Design? How do you calculate the return on such public dollars as it takes to educate an Andy Warhol or a Tom Gale or Michael Santoro?

The nation needs artists and designers to work in the automobile industry, in advertising, publishing, fashion, interior design, television, the movies. And musicians and singers and dancers and actors for all the so-called entertainment industry. And teachers. And teachers to teach teachers. Teachers, teachers, teachers for all the arts and not just for those who will perform but for all who will learn to care and enjoy the arts all their lives. Surely that is obvious.

Talent doesn't just happen. Training, craft, experience can't be summoned willy-nilly out of nowhere as needed. It has to be developed, brought out, brought along with education. And the process has to begin early. The earlier the better.

"Would the gentleman be opposed to federal funding to assist in educating school children in the arts and music?" asked Representative Sidney Yates of Illinois of Representative Philip Crane, also of Illinois, in an exchange on the floor of Congress last summer.

"To educating school children, making art a part of the curriculum?" asked Crane.

"As the arts Endowment does," affirmed Yates.

"It should not be doing that," said Crane.

"Is the gentleman opposed to federal funding of such institutions as the Lincoln Memorial?" asked Yates.

"National statues, basically, I would not have a problem with that," replied Crane.

In Pittsburgh now the prospect is shadowed. The number of teachers in the visual arts has been cut. Music programs have been cut. Two high schools have no music program at all. Saturday art classes at the Carnegie Museum continue, but where in years past thousands enrolled, the number now is about a hundred.

Instead of a separate budget for the arts in the schools, there is a large overall allotment for "support services" which includes the arts but a lot else besides, general equipment for example. And how the money is spent is left to the principal of each school. Instead of $800 being spent, say, for musical instruments, it buys a new office typewriter.

Pittsburgh, according to a former director of art education in the public schools is "slowly, but surely decimating its art programs."

The arts, as Fred Rogers says, give children ways to say who they are, how they feel, to say whether they are happy or sad or angry, and without hurting anyone.

The late Margaret McFarlan, professor of child development at the University of Pittsburgh and an inspiration for three generations of specialists in child studies, including Fred Rogers, liked to say:

We don't teach children. We just give them who we are. And they catch that. Attitudes are caught, not taught. If you love something in front of a child, the child will catch that.

So what is our attitude to be here in America? What do we love? What do we want our children to see that we love?

And who will be the leaders with both the spirit and courage of a Theodore Roosevelt, who loved the poetry of Edward Arlington Robinson and on hearing that Robinson was in financial straits, found him a job in the Treasury, then sent him a note saying, "Think poetry first, Treasury second."

I am an optimist, by nature and from reading history. I am also of that generation raised on the belief that we Americans can do anything we set our hearts and minds to. I still believe that.

A new set of national standards for education in the arts has been drawn up and approved by Secretary of Education Richard Riley. The standards are voluntary and national in name only, but a step in the right direction.

We should be grateful for what's being done for the arts here in Washington by people like Jim Wolfensohn, like Sidney Yates in the House, Claiborne Pell, Jim Jeffords, and Alan Simpson in the Senate. Jane Alexander is magnificent. But we mustn't count on government only. Congress is always slow catching up with what the country wants. The energy, the commitment, the determination must come from us. That's how the system works. And money, too, that has to come from us.

We must be "the public policy" on the arts.

If we want libraries open again, if we want a generous, exciting, creative education for our children, if we want a culture that counts for something, it's up to us. We must get busy and make it happen: "Do all we can, and then some."

WRITING FOR THE READER[1]
EUGENE L. ROBERTS, JR.[2]

An important feature of intellectual activity on most college and university campuses are talks given by visiting lecturers. At many institutions, lectureships are endowed as a memorial to the accomplishments or contributions of a distinguished graduate or professor.

One such endowed lecture series is the Red Smith Lectureship in Journalism at the University of Notre Dame. Established in 1983, the lecture honors Red Smith, a 1927 graduate of Notre Dame who went on to achieve renown as a sportswriter, and to receive the 1976 Pulitzer Prize for distinguished commentary.

Since the first lecture in 1984, given by James Reston, the goal of the lectures has remained constant. Professor Robert Schmuhl described it as follows:

At a time when so many people working in print journalism are preoccupied with the bottom line, the Red Smith Lectureship—in its own obsessive way—celebrates the written word. The guidelines of the Lectureship are clear and unchanging: foster good writing and recognize high journalistic standards.

The 1993 Red Smith Lecturer was Eugene L. Roberts, Jr., who had served for 18 years as executive editor of *The Philadelphia Inquirer*. During that time, *The Inquirer* won seventeen Pulitzer Prizes and over 150 other national awards. Roberts himself won several honors, and shortly after delivering the 1993 Red Smith Lecture, he received the National Press Club's Fourth Estate Award for his accomplishments in journalism.

Professor Robert Schmuhl introduced Roberts. At the conclusion of the lecture, Roberts answered questions from the audience.

Eugene L. Roberts speech: Let me say with unbecoming immodesty that I have sound credentials for attesting to the writing magic of Red Smith: One, I have no interest in golf. Two, I've never played a single hole. Three, I plan to depart this life with my record intact.

[1]Delivered at the University of Notre Dame, Notre Dame, Indiana, 1993.
[2]For biographical note, see Appendix.

In the Red Smith era I searched the sports pages for baseball stories. My eyes raced to Red's columns to see if he were writing about my favorite sport; but Smith was a shameless seducer. If he had me for ten seconds, he had me to the finish—even on his golf stories. To me, golf emerged from his typewriter not as news from a game but as word from a remote and exotic world—like Tibet, like Xanadu. I saw the sweating players. I felt the tension in the crowd. I was transported, dammit, to the last place I ever wanted to be—the middle of a golf course.

Take, for example, the 1964 match in Houston between Sam Snead and Ben Hogan:

Snead was disconsolate because his long irons got him in trouble four times, but he scrambled sensationally. The seventh hole, for example, is a dogleg to the left around a thicket of tall trees. Along the left side behind the woods five traps yawn, one behind the other from turn to green.

Hogan hit an iron to the knee of the dogleg and had an open shot to the green. Sam tried to clear the trees with a wood, hit a pine, and his ball bounced back toward the tee. It wasn't humanly possible to get home from there, but somehow he whistled his second shot through the trees to the edge of the green beyond the last trap.

"You dodged a bullet there," said Fred Corcoran after Sam got down in two and halved the hole with a four.

"If I'da cleared the trees and drove the green," Sam said, "it woulda been a great tee shot."

"But I was lousy," he said at the end.

"No, you weren't," a man told him. I'm so glad I was able to see this match. I'll remember it along with the War Admiral-Seabiscuit match race, Graziano-Zale, and Don Larsen's perfect game."

How do you resist a charmer who writes like that? To this very moment I couldn't pick a long iron from a line-up of clubs, but for the length of that column, I enjoyed golf. That, of course, is what the finest writing is all about: putting the reader on the scene, making him see. Red Smith seems to have been born knowing this. For ordinary mortals the elementary truths of good writing come harder. It took a blind man to make *me* see.

I've told this story before, but it seems appropriate for to-night's occasion. My first newspaper job was with the *Goldsboro News-Argus*, which is the leading newspaper in Wayne County, North Carolina. It then had a circulation of 9,000. I wrote its farm column, "Rambling in Rural Wayne." I wrote about the first farmer of the season to transplant tobacco plants from the seed bed to the field; about the season's first cotton blossom; of picnic tables sagging at family reunions under the weight of banana sandwiches, banana pudding, chicken pastry, sage sausage, fried chicken and collard greens. I wrote of hail storms and drought. I once wrote about a sweet potato that looked like General Charles de Gaulle.

The editor of the paper was Henry Belk, then in his sixties and sightless. This was in the 'fifties, but he wore battered fedora hats like newsmen wore in the movies in the 'thirties and 'forties, when he could still see. He was tall; no, towering. There were no ready-made canes to fit his six-foot, seven-inch form, so he tapped with a stretch cane specially made for him out of aluminum. He cared passionately about the paper, and it was read to him word for word over the years by a succession of high school students. In the mornings, his wife, Lucille, once a journalist herself, read him the newspaper published in the state capital, *The Raleigh News and Observer.* He was awesomely informed. Most days, at the office, he would call out from his cubicle and say things such as, "On page 17 of *The News and Observer* in column three, halfway down the fold, there is a three-inch story about Goldsboro under an 18-point head." Then, he would demand, "Why didn't we have it?"

Mr. Belk was nothing if not demanding. Often when he heard my footfall in the morning he would summon me to his cubicle and criticize the "Rambling in Rural Wayne" column I had written the day before. On too many days, alas, my writing was insufficiently descriptive. "You aren't making me see," Mr. Belk would say. "Make me see." In an effort to force me to be graphic and vivid, he made me end every column with a paragraph labeled "Today's Prettiest Sight." Let me tell you: It's tough to go into a pool room in your hometown for an end-of-the-work-day beer known as the guy who writes "Today's Prettiest Sight"; but I persevered.

It took me years to appreciate it, but there is no better admonition to the writer than "make me see." There is no truer blueprint for successful writing than making your readers see. It is the essence of great writing. There are, be assured, many ways to make your reader see, and Red Smith, I am convinced, knew them all.

Mostly, the best way is simple, but vivid, description. Smith was in the press box for the unprecedented World Series game in 1972 when Reggie Jackson knocked three home runs in a row. "For the third time," Smith wrote, "Reggie hit the first pitch but this one didn't take the shortest distance between two points. Straight out from the plate the ball streaked, not toward the neighborly stands in right but on a soaring arc toward the unoccupied bleachers in dead center, where the seats are blacked out to give batters a background. Up the white speck climbed, dwindling, diminishing, until it settled at least halfway up those empty stands, probably 450 feet away."

Sometimes making the reader see involves cutting to the heart of things, as when Red called Reggie "this Hamlet in double knits," or when he said in memorializing Babe Ruth: "The man was a boy, simple, artless, genuine and unabashed. This explains his rapport with children whom he met as intellectual equals." To craftsmen such as Smith, the right words are to writing as the right tools are to carpentry. Notice that he didn't use a hammer on occasions that called for a sharp chisel.

A few years ago there was a great movement in the newspaper business toward explanatory journalism. Explain things to the reader so that he will understand, we editors implored. We even created awards for explanatory journalism. We were like coaxing parents who cheer and applaud when training their children to go to the potty. Of course, old foxes such as Red Smith knew all along that sometimes you can't make the reader see unless you explain things so well that he—or she—can't possibly miss the meaning. One of the finest examples of explanatory writing (of journalism, if you will) that I've ever read was a Red Smith column in 1981, just months before he died but ahead of the explanatory journalism movement. It was a brilliant lecture on what extraordinary progress had transpired in the mile race in track. Smith summed up the whole history of the sport in about eight hundred readable words. You can find it on page 194 of a remarkable book called *The Red Smith Reader*. This, in part, is what he wrote:

> It doesn't seem possible that twenty-seven years have passed since Roger Bannister broke what has been nicknamed the 'four-minute-barrier,' yet it was May 6, 1954, when he did the deed.
>
> Since man dropped out of a tree and took off with a saber-toothed tiger on his heels, no pedestrian had traveled 5,280 feet in four minutes. In 1864 one Charles Lawes of Great Britain had gone the distance in 4 minutes, 56 seconds, and 90 years later Sweden's Gunder Haag had lowered the record to 4:01.4.
>
> May 6, 1954, five days after Determine won the Kentucky Derby, was gray and drizzly at Oxford but Bannister knew that if he waited for ideal weather in that blessed plot, that earth, that realm, that England, hardening of the arteries could set in first. So he ran, and the stopwatches read 3:59.4.

In years following, scores ran the mile in under four minutes. In the two weeks before Smith wrote this column, the record changed hands three times. And Smith concluded his column this way:

Much more interesting than the numbers is the mental attitude involved. It doesn't make sense that scores of milers since 1954 have been faster than all the milers who preceded them in human history. It is obvious now that the barrier was psychological rather than physical.

For a millennium or two, nobody ran a mile in four minutes for the excellent reason that it was impossible. . . . Then Roger Bannister showed that it was not impossible, and it was like divine revelation. Suddenly it got to be like this:

Jesse Abramson, covering a Boston track meet for the *New York Herald Tribune,* was in a taxi with a colleague and they were discussing runners and their times. The cabbie spoke up:

"Anything that starts with four," he said, "is slow."

One of the many important benefits of fine writing on a newspaper is that it often begets more fine writing. It is no accident, I think, that two of the finest writers in all journalism history were to be found on the *New York Herald Tribune* at the same time: Red Smith, who covered sports events; Homer Bigart, who covered wars. The same newsroom climate that nourished one, attracted the other. Each looked well-scrubbed. Homer stuttered; Red was modest. Both were slow, painstaking writers. Each emitted an earnestness that allowed him to pick almost anyone's pockets for a scrap of news. Each made readers see.

There were, of course, some important differences between the two. Smith liked hyperbole. Bigart favored astringent understatement. Smith labored, if necessary, to avoid "I" or "we" in his copy. Bigart was comfortable with either word if it helped put the reader on the scene. But Red and Homer were as one in making liberal use of simple, vivid, straightforward description. "Generally," Homer wrote from a battlefield in Italy in 1943, "there is no mistaking the dead—their strange contorted posture leaves no room for doubt. But this soldier, his steel helmet tilted over his face, seemed merely resting in the field. We did not know until we came within a few yards and saw a gray hand hanging limply from a sleeve." Later, Bigart transferred from the European theater of war to the Pacific. He wrote the last combat dispatch of World War II. It was datelined: "In a B-29 over Japan, Aug. 15, 1945." This is the opening paragraph of that memorable story: "The radio tells us that the war is over, but from where I sit it looks suspiciously like a rumor. A few minutes ago—at 1:32 A.M.—we firebombed Kumagaya, a small industrial city behind Tokyo near the northern edge of the Kanto Plain. Peace was not official for the Japanese either, for they shot right back at us."

I think Homer and Red would have approved of the way you have arranged academics here at Notre Dame, placing journalism and American Studies together in the same department. It is a natural. It combines writing instruction with something worth writing about. Of course, American Studies is more than a mere subject. It cultivates a vision, a way of looking at America's people—us. It makes you see.

Some thirty years ago, a young writer graduated from Yale University with a Ph.D. in American Studies and made his way onto the staff of the *Herald Tribune* in New York, as Homer and Red had done before him. His name was, and is, Tom Wolfe. Not for him, the straightforward description of a Smith or a Bigart. He layered adjectives and nouns into sentences like "Kandy Colored, Tangerine Flake, Streamline Baby." He strung letters, asterisks and exclamation marks together in an effort to create sound effects on the printed page. He used techniques of fiction, such as foreshadowing, to heighten suspense and increase tension and readership. He tried to crawl into the skins of his subjects. He recreated scenes, events and episodes. He called all of this New Journalism.

He raised the blood pressure of a not inconsiderable number of journalism historians and professors of writing who pointed out that journalists, for decades, had been writing non-fiction that read like short stories and novellas—John Reed's *Ten Days That Shook the World* and John Hersey's *Hiroshima*, for example. Other critics ignored the early writers and accused Wolfe and his followers of—in the name of readability—writing things that they couldn't possibly have known about the moods and thoughts of their subjects. In the furor, not nearly enough attention was paid to how Wolfe was transferring American Studies from the classroom to the newsroom so effectively it would become a permanent part of what today we might call "journalistic vision."

When you peered past Wolfe's layered nouns and the snap-crackle-and-pop sound effects, there was this wonderful American Studies way of looking at things. He told us about a California subculture, the custom car crazies. He made us see Puerto Rican New York in a different light. How? He spun the story of a Puerto Rican troubadour and folk-hero who sold a million records by singing in Spanish of his loneliness and how he wouldn't trade his Puerto Rico, señor, for ten thousand New Yorks. We saw Appalachian America differently after he took us to the race track with Junior Johnson, who was then king of stock-car races.

Yes, there are many ways to make the reader see. Wolfe, Bigart and Smith showed us and re-showed us. Wolfe is alive and

well. Red Smith and Homer Bigart are not; but by making readers see, they are remembered, and they ought to be remembered
as long as good writing is taught in our colleges and universities.
They were giants. Most of us, even when we write vividly, will
make our contribution by making our readers see: for a minute,
an hour, a day. I can cite only one instance in which I am reasonably sure I made an indelible impression.

I learned of it in the Vietnam War when I was a correspondent for The *New York Times*. It was 1968 during the Tet Offensive, more than a decade after I left the *Goldsboro News-Argus*. I
heard vague reports of trouble in Hué, the capital city of Annam's
puppet emperors during the French colonial era. I made my way
there by truck and helicopter and found that the Marines were
surrounded and held only two blocks of the city. The Viet Cong
and the North Vietnamese forces held on to the rest. Each day
after the Marines were reinforced by fresh units, they re-took two
or three blocks of the city, only to lose most of it again during the
night to enemy troops who infiltrated into houses during the
darkness.

It took about ten days for the Marines to get ten blocks or so
from their headquarters compound. When they did, they found
several American advisors who had been hiding under a house
since the night the enemy overran the city. They had little water,
even less food, and were hanging on by their nerve ends when the
Marines broke through.

The Marines took the survivors to the headquarters compound and, to give them a sense of security, put them in the safest
place they could find—a bunker dug deep into the center of the
compound. I heard about the survivors and went to interview
them. I snaked over some sandbags and entered a tunnel. I
crawled a bit, rounded a bend and dimly made out some human
forms.

"My name is Gene Roberts," I said. "I'm with The *New York
Times*. I've come to get your story."

Out of the darkness came a voice, and it said: "Hey, did you
ever write the 'Rambling in Rural Wayne' column for the *Goldsboro News-Argus*?"

Henry Belk, my old editor, would not have been surprised.
"Of course that reader remembered you," he would have said.
"You made him see."

INTERNATIONAL POLICY DECISIONS

PREPARING FOR OUR GREATEST CHALLENGE[1]
JAMES H. BILLINGTON[2]

One of the most appropriate commencement addresses in 1993–1994 was given to the graduates of the Edmund A. Walsh School of Foreign Service at Georgetown University by Dr. James H. Billington, a graduate of Princeton and Oxford, a Rhodes Scholar, former professor of history at Harvard and Princeton, current Librarian of Congress, and acknowledged expert on Russia. In addition to inviting him to deliver the commencement address at the school of Foreign Service, Georgetown conferred an honorary Doctor of Humane Letters on Dr. Billington.

The topic of Dr. Billington's address was the question of how the United States, despite its huge investment in international studies over the past half-century, has failed to predict most of the major overseas crises the country had faced in recent years: Vietnam, Iran, Iraq, Poland, Russia, and Yugoslavia.

Billington delivered his address to 353 graduates and approximately 2000 guests at 10:00 A.M. on May 30, 1993, on the Healy Lawn on the Georgetown University main campus.

James H. Billington's speech: Those of you going through the rite of passage from academia to the broader international world might normally expect the designated nerd who has been thrust on you as graduation speaker to praise the value of the academic enterprise and the special importance of what you have learned here for what you will be doing out there.

But I am going to be a bit abnormal today and suggest instead that there are serious deficiencies in our academic study of the world and that whatever you are taking from here is a lot less important than what you need to bring back, which I hope may be

[1]Delivered at the commencement ceremony of the Edmund A. Walsh School of Foreign Service, Georgetown University, Washington, D.C., held on the Healy Lawn at 10:00 A.M., May 29, 1993.

[2]For biographical note, see Appendix.

something deep or new, that will come from embracing more of the world's otherness than you may have yet done.

Why has the greatest investment any nation has ever made in international study, which is what America has done in the last half century, failed so utterly to help America predict—or even allow for the possibility of—any of the great overseas crises this nation has faced in the last quarter century: Vietnam, Iran, Iraq, and now Yugoslavia? Why have we failed equally to anticipate or even allow for the possibility of the great positive breakthroughs in Poland and Russia? Why, closer to home, did our massive academic-media complex fail to anticipate, and still finds itself largely unable to understand, the rise in this same quarter century of new political movements on either the right in North America or the left in South America?

The answer, I am afraid, lies not just in continued provincialism or self-centered materialism in our general culture but also in the dominance within academia of the behavioral social sciences. Their often excessive general laws rather than specific people, tidy models rather than messy historical reality, and their belief that it does not count unless it can be counted, have often left otherwise educated people with no sense of the overwhelming, driving power in real life of cultural and psychological factors and of the great forces of ethnicity, nationalism, and religion that bind people together and drive them to forms of actions that elude our radar screens of predictability and that cannot be programmed on our computers.

With the end of the Cold War, we have moved from the correlation of forces to the balance of trade, but we are still counting things rather than studying people. The new reign of economics like the old reign of strategic studies leaves us tone deaf to all the ways other people tell us who they are and what they want to become: in their art, their music, their language, and their religion. We impose on them our present-day generalities without ever listening to the unique sounds of their yesterdays which may provide the themes for their tomorrow.

If you cannot learn to listen to people when they are whispering their prayers, you may have to deal with them later when they are howling in their battle cries. The only person I know of who predicted the rise of Khomeini was the one banker in Teheran who had spent more time in mosques than at cocktail parties.

I had the good fortune to be in Moscow in August, 1991 in the middle of the final great drama of the Cold War. The failure of the attempted putsch led to the rapid collapse of the most powerful secular ideology, land empire, and political machine of the twentieth century. It was a classical case of something that was not foreseen and can never be understood by our generalized, behaviorist forms of analysis: political Kremlinology focused on personalities, macroeconomic analysis focused on programs and interest groups, or historical analogies focused on past revolutions. Least of all, can it be explained by that great intellectual sacred cow of strategic studies: the correlation of forces.

During the fateful 48 hours when the outcome was uncertain, no more than 150 armed military professionals at the core of the motley resistance in and around the Russian White House faced the largest armed force in the world at the very heart of the empire—all of whose major structures were controlled by the putschists. The forces that turned the tide and opened the way to a new future were not the kind that Realpolitik takes seriously, yet it was possible to feel them working at the time and to get an early sense, even amidst all the fear and chaos, of what was going to happen.

Subliminally, one felt the ultimate outcome was assured before sunset on the first day by the indelible contrast people drew between the only two clear pictures they had in their minds amidst all the confusion: that of a confident, white-haired Yeltsin smiling atop a tank with a firm but unthreatening fist upraised versus that of the putsch leader Yanaev with his hands shaking and his eyes shifting during his televised press conference. The face and hands were the only parts of the human body presented in the flesh and left uncovered by metal coverings in Russian icons; and, just as the face and hands conveyed the spiritual essence of a figure in the pictorial theology of the East, it conveyed to ordinary Russians that day the essence of who was good and would ultimately win in what became, from the beginning, a spiritual contest of an almost medieval and epic sort.

Crucial to the subsequent moral struggle to dissuade the military from attacking on the second day, after it had become clear that a mere show of force would not be sufficient, was the role of a group that, as far as I know, has never appeared on anybody's correlation of forces totally off our strategic radar screen: old, religious women. "I am here," one of those women standing beside me that second night said, "because although we always kept praying, we were also among those who kept silent all those years." They refused to go home even when it was suggested by the men in charge when an attack was expected. They went instead to remonstrate with the potential attackers. In so doing, they changed the nature of the face-off between the crowd and soldiers in the tanks on the one side and the pony-tailed students on the barricades on the other, which might have become at any moment a macho contest between two groups of young men bound to fight into a radically different and pacifying face-off in which the young men in the tanks were in effect being scolded by their mothers—as indeed Yazov, the army commander-in-chief, was being scolded by his wife.

The funeral of the three young men who were killed that night seemed to revalidate the half-forgotten core Judeo-Christian concept of the redemptive value of innocent suffering. The whole country experienced an emotional breakpoint when the funeral cortege passed the White House and Yeltsin came out, went up to the parents of the boys, and simply said: "Forgive me, your president, that I was unable to defend and save your sons." There was hardly a dry eye as all Russia watched on their newly liberated television. The totalitarian value system which diffused the very concept of moral responsibility was being replaced, not just by a new freedom, but by an unprecedented acceptance of individual responsibility at the top for something that was not his fault. "Forgive me" is what Russian Orthodox believers say to whomever is standing beside them before they take communion. It is what that other Boris, Boris Godunov, said to the Russian people with his last breath in the greatest of all Russian operas about an earlier Russian time of troubles.

What has been going on since August 1991 in Russia was once again predicted better by creative artists than by social scientists. Andrei Siniavsky, still writing anonymously as terminal stagnation descended over the Soviet system in the late 1960s, prophesied then that it would all end through what he called "peristaltic metamorphoses in the entrails of God." The bowels are indeed extruding into a newly free society—vulgarity, venality, and corruption; but all of this is also fertilizing a new civil society that is growing rapidly from the bottom up and from the periphery in this hitherto top-down, overcentralized autocracy.

And it is happening in the entrails of *God*. Parishes are multiplying in the Orthodox and other churches more rapidly than priests can be found to handle them. The loss of a religious vocabulary in Western public discourse makes it hard for us to realize that evil has been transcended by repentance without revenge in post-Communist Russia; that innocent suffering in past gulags has been given redemptive value; and that the amazingly non-violent breakthrough of August 1991, which occurred on the Feast of the Transfiguration, was indeed a "miracle" through which ordinary people rediscovered a moral dimension to their lives.

The key question now for the future of Russia can probably be stated better in the language of classical drama than of computerized scenarios: Will the catharsis that Russia is going through of its Communist past ultimately prove to be a violent nationalistic one that involves internal purges and external enemies or a deeper, moral catharsis within individuals involving the rebirth of conscience and the transcending of violence?

In the long run, I believe it will be the latter, but in the short run, there is a very real risk of the former, which would probably produce a kind of Russian fascism that could turn much of the territory of the former Soviet Union into a nuclear Yugoslavia. I hail the most prominent alumnus of the Georgetown School of Foreign Service, our President, for committing America to become involved despite all the problems at home and for making clear in his speeches that he understands the deeper cultural and spiritual dimension of the drama.

I believe that you, newly credentialed graduates, could make both individually and collectively the same kind of difference in the valleys where you will be working that President Clinton made at the summit in Vancouver with his timely and forceful support of the Russian reformers. You can overcome our creeping intellectual provincialism by nurturing and sustaining a life-long passion for some key aspect of the world's otherness—and why not by committing yourself to bringing back periodically to this unique school that has given you so much the new insights and practical wisdom that can come only when experience is combined with reflection. Just as the church needs lay leaders, this school needs and deserves more alumni participation in its ongoing work.

There are all manner of seminars, reunions, teleconferences, temporary exchanges, mentoring relationships, cultural events, and communal projects that could creatively punctuate your professional lives and maybe help realize the full promise of the intercultural center here at Georgetown.

I am impressed by the fact that half of your class has studied abroad, that a third has won honors, and that you represent 41 states and many foreign countries. I hope you appreciate the privilege of being part of America's oldest and largest school of international service—a place where roots go deeper spiritually and chronologically than the behaviorist-oriented creations of more recent times, a place with an extraordinarily dedicated dean and staff. What impresses me most of all is my sense that you are a pretty motivated lot, that you are not yet downwardly mobile and have not picked up the illusion that you know it all—or even as much as you want to find out.

Perhaps you can help us prepare for what may well be the greatest challenge of the early twenty-first century: the multi-faceted coming encounter with the awakening cultures of Asia. Your school has once again been a pioneer with the establishment of a Center for Muslim-Christian Understanding. I hope that many of you will reach out and embrace the otherness not just of the many faces of Islam but of the even more ancient, elusive, complex, and linguistically inaccessible cultures of East and South Asia. Nothing pains me more as Librarian than to see how piti-fully few Americans even use the incomparable collections we have on all these cultures.

Adventure of understanding can be pursued in books and libraries and should, of course, not leave out the natural and social sciences but rather reunify them with the humanities. But understanding the world requires a special life-long effort for us Americans who are generally a little too pleased with ourselves to come to grips with the uniqueness of others. This effort is also needed if we are to sustain the American dream at home. With new immigrants from Asia and Latin America being increasingly added to our older immigrants from Europe and Africa, America has become the first nation in the world to accommodate substan-tial populations from every continent in the world. But America is a country that has historically renewed itself with a continuing immigration of ideas as well as people, and there may be things we can all learn from the ways that post-Confucian East Asia has built relatively crime-free and productive industrial cities, the way that East Africa has kept the village as a mediating entity between family and state, or even the way the seemingly familiar but little studied small countries of Europe like Switzerland and Holland have often been able to integrate technology with the environment in ways that enhances both. I have often wondered what might have happened if anyone had ever acted on the advice I was once asked to relay to a president before a summit by the head of a Buddhist monastery in Kyoto: to breathe together in unison for 11 minutes before saying anything at all. Could this be a missing element in conflict resolution?

One of the great benefits of the deep life-long study of a foreign culture is, paradoxically, a deeper understanding of one-self and one's own country. Those who appreciate America the most are often either the new immigrants or those who have just arrived back after a long time abroad. Only they can fully under-stand how unique our country is, how important so much of what we have is, not just for ourselves but for others.

America grows stronger by constantly rediscovering and shar-ing its own legacy of freedom even as we import the ideas, absorb the achievements, and increasingly celebrate the aspirations of others. Our pluralistic country can be a model as well as a leader in the development in peace of a pluralist world.

For America, like this historic university in its capital, was built on spiritual aspiration even more than material achievement. It is the search for Faulkner's bear, Melville's whale, and Citizen Kane's Rosebud. And it is the hope that buds of all colors will blossom in a land that values its technicolor as much as its technol-ogy.

But America may not thrive—or even ultimately survive—in a crowded and competitive world if people who have been as favored as you sink into apathy and decide just to grasp for goods, rather than to grope for goodness. In Shakespeare's *Troilus and Cressida,* the old Ulysses reminded the spoiled Achilles, who had done well earlier with the Agamemnon all-stars but had since taken to sulking in his tent and resting on past laurels, that:

Time hath, my lord, a wallet at his back,
Wherein he puts alms for Oblivion,
a great-siz'd monster of ingratitudes.
. . . For Time is like a fashionable host
That slightly shakes his parting guest by th'hand,
And with his arms outstretch'd as he would fly
Grasps in the comer.
. . . O, let not virtue seek
Remuneration for the thing it was;
For beauty, wit,
High birth, vigour of bone, desert in service,
Love, friendship, charity, are subjects all
To envious and calumniating Time.
One touch of nature makes the whole world kin,
That all with one consent praise new-born gawds,
Though they are made and moulded of things past, . . .

EDUCATION FOR NATIONAL SECURITY[1]
SOL M. LINOWITZ[2]

The National Security Education Program was created by an act of Congress and signed into law in 1991 by President Bush. Its purpose was simple: to encourage students to study, and schools to focus on, non-Western languages and cultures that are important to America's future. The program created a trust fund to support graduate fellowships for students willing to serve in government after their studies ended; scholarships for undergraduates to study in foreign countries; and the establishment of language and cultural programs at universities.

On Monday, May 9, 1994, representatives from higher education, government, and the private sector convened at the very first Board Meeting of the National Security Education Program. One purpose of the meeting was to announce the names of the first group of graduates and undergraduates to study overseas. The students represented all 50 states and over 100 colleges and universities. The graduate students would study 47 different languages in 57 countries; the undergraduates were to study 34 languages in 48 different countries.

The principal speaker at the Board meeting was Sol M. Linowitz, a former ambassador to the Organization of American States who had been instrumental in the negotiations of Panama Canal Treaty and the Camp David Accords. Senator David Boren of Oklahoma, who had introduced the National Security Education Act and was instrumental in the establishment of the NSEP, described Ambassador Linowitz in his introductory remarks as "one of the wisest people in the country."

Sol M. Linowitz's speech: I am very pleased to be here and to have the opportunity to say a few words about NSEP. It takes real presumptuousness for me to undertake to talk with you about the area of your own responsibility and concern. I am presuming to do so only because I am so persuaded of the importance and the promise of your mission, and I'd like to tell you why.

[1]Delivered to the National Security Education Program luncheon, Washington, D.C., May 9, 1994.

[2]For biographical note, see Appendix.

At the outset, I want to pay my respects to the man who is entitled to our lasting gratitude for his leadership in the enactment of NSEP, Senator David Boren. Senator Boren is a friend of mine and I know him to be man of commitment and dedication who has clearly perceived the importance of reaching out to the other people of this earth, of coming to know them and their cultures, if we are to live together peacefully in today's world. We are all deeply in his debt for his independence, foresight and wisdom. As President of the University of Oklahoma later this year, he will be changing not his focus, priorities, commitments or involvements—just his geography and work place—and we wish him well with his university responsibilities.

I think that to get a real sense of what NSEP really means, it has to be seen against the backdrop of the kind of world and the kind of time in which we live.

For we are living at a difficult, anxious, uncertain time in world history, a time which has been called both the Age of Anxiety and the Age of Science and Technology. Both are accurate, for indeed one feeds upon the other. As our scientific and technological competence has increased, so have our fear and anxiety.

It is also a fateful time. In the past, men have warred over frontiers. They have come into conflict over ideologies. They have fought to better their daily lives. Today, however, each crisis overlaps the other and we find ourselves at an upheaval that touches every phase of our existence.

Just think what has happened in the past few years.

The collapse of the Soviet Bloc has fundamentally and irreversibly transformed international relations for our time.

The most significant military and ideological adversary of the United States has ceased to exist. The central principle U.S. foreign policy for the last half century, the Cold War, is over, and the foundation of our international alliances, military strategies, and defense budgets has been swept away.

Regional wars that involved the super-powers—Angola, Cambodia, Central America—are all winding down. At the same time, and as the war in the Persian Gulf and the fighting in the former Yugoslavia and Armenia have made all too clear, loss of super-power influence, combined with the deadly proliferation of armaments, could lead to more rather than less armed conflict in the world.

Economic competition is displacing military conflict as the main arena of international rivalry. According to recent polls, most Americans now consider Japan, not the former Soviet Union or Russia, to be our main adversary.

From Argentina to Poland, authoritarian politics and centralized economies have been discredited; and the value of free elections and open markets has been strongly affirmed.

The handling of the Persian Gulf crisis suggested that we may be entering a new era of multilateral cooperation. But we can't yet be sure whether a new world order will truly emerge, or whether we will regress to a fragmented world of regional power balances and conflicts.

Whatever happens, we have not had to confront such breathtaking global changes since the end of World War II.

Against this backdrop it is important to recognize some hard facts:

First, the people of this world are no longer thousands of miles away, but just down the runway. Whether we like it or not the world is pressing in upon us; and we simply can't isolate ourselves or stop the world and try to get off. For better or worse, we are all in this together.

This means that problems, misunderstandings, confrontations involving countries we have never seen or people we have never met can suddenly and dramatically impinge upon our own lives and drastically affect our future and the future of our children.

Second, we are living in an instantaneous world where the world is as close to us as our TV sets, where we are all part of a global society in which there is no longer such a thing as separate areas of concern or a clear division between domestic and foreign. A world in which peace is truly indivisible; in which what happens in places like Somalia, Bosnia, Russia, China is in the truest sense happening to us. Our lives—our futures—are now inextricably intertwined with those of the rest of the people in this world.

Third, in such a world national security is inseparable from global insecurity. We cannot hope to be safe and secure if the world is unsafe and insecure.

What do we mean when we use the word secure? What does the word security mean when we talk of the National Security Education Program? Let me give you my own view. I start with the fact that security in the world in which we live depends on far more than military weapons or economic strength. Security, real security, also depends on the kind of relationships we have with other people and other countries—where we are able to understand them and relate to them and work with them toward a more stable, peaceful world.

We will not find security for ourselves if we are estranged from the other people of this world and alienated from them and their cultures. We will not find peace for ourselves and our children by continuing to ignore other people and by arrogantly insisting that the rest of the world must learn from us what we are willing to teach, and must speak to us only in our tongue.

In short, we will not be secure if we do not build bridges of security—bridges of understanding and cooperation and empathy to the other people on this earth. And that, I believe, is what NSEP is all about.

In Mexico City there stands the statue of Benito Juarez. On it are the words: "Respect the rights of others in peace." Respect for the rights of others underlies the whole concept of NSEP. It means treating others with dignity; respecting their right to fulfill their own destiny in their own way; learning their culture and their language.

The Chinese write the word crisis by combining the symbol for the word danger with the symbol for the word opportunity. In these times of crisis, we have been confronted with both dangers and opportunities, and we have failed to seize the opportunities to increase our understanding of the other human beings on this earth.

How bad is the situation? In introducing NSEP legislation, Senator Boren presented some deeply disquieting facts. Let me remind you of a few: Last year over 350,000 college undergraduates came to America from other countries. At the same time, only about 50,000 American students went to study at the undergraduate level in the rest of the world; and, if you exclude Great Britain, France and Germany, only 4,000 or 5,000 American students studied abroad.

In the year 2000, the European community will require fluency in two foreign languages for all high school graduates. Japan now requires that all of their students study at least two years of English before graduating from high school. (By way of contrast, three-tenths of one percent of Americans study Japanese.)

At this moment when we should be trying to learn all we can about the rest of the world, only 8 percent of our college students are studying any foreign language and over 80 percent of all the universities in this country do not require a foreign language for an undergraduate degree.

I submit to you that we simply can't live with those numbers if we expect to build the kind of future we say we want.

For in the future as never before in our history we will need men and women who are at home in the world, who are people of perspective and breadth with a far better understanding of the world than has ever been required before. We will need men and women who understand where we have been and where we are going, who knows about the kind of world in which we live and the future we should be trying to achieve. We will need men and women able to communicate with one another and with other people and other places; people who know how to transmit and stimulate ideas; people who recognize that things human and humane are even more important than the computer, the test tube, the IBM or even the Xerox machine. We will need people who understand that know-why is even more important than know-how, people who will see our problems as part of total human experience and who will be able to understand something of what yesterday teaches us about today and tomorrow.

In short, we will need people of vision who will be able to help us find effective solutions to the problems besetting the world by coming to know and understand the people who make up that world. I strongly believe that NSEP can do much to move us in that direction and I wish you Godspeed on your mission.

AMERICAN MILITARY LEADERSHIP[1]
COLIN L. POWELL[2]

The retirement of General Colin L. Powell as Chairman of the Joint Chiefs of Staff in September, 1993, was the occasion for several celebratory events and widespread political speculations. The *Washington Post* observed (September 30, 1993):

If General Colin Powell is planning to fade away, it may be the only fade in history preceded by drumrolls, fireworks, trumpet fanfares, orchestral overtures and the steady thunder of artillery salutes.

The political speculation centered on Powell's party prefer-

[1] Delivered to the National Press Club, Washington, D.C., in the club ballroom at 1:00 P.M., September 28, 1993.
[2] For biographical note, see Appendix.

ence and political aspirations, neither of which he had ever disclosed. The *Chicago Tribune* noted:

> In a country that reveres its military leaders but rarely elects them, he is often compared to Dwight D. Eisenhower. He admires Eisenhower, Grant, and Washington, all three generals who became president. No one is sure whether Powell is a Republican or Democrat, a mystery that only adds to his allure. (September 30, 1993)

A *U.S. News and World Report* poll taken shortly before Powell's retirement showed that Americans had a more favorable view of him than they had of President Clinton, Ross Perot, and Senate Republican leader Bob Dole.

The public's obvious esteem for Powell was based on his record of accomplishments and on his character. The son of a seamstress and a shipping clerk, both Jamaican immigrants, and raised in a New York City ghetto, he joined the army as an officer through the Reserve Officer Training Corps at the City College of New York. In 35 years he rose through various levels of military command to the position of National Security Advisor to President Ronald Reagan and then became chairman of the Joint Chiefs of Staff.

His personality was evidently a factor in his success. "Low key, direct, and with a common touch, Powell earned the respect and admiration of both the military and the public," reported the Gannet News Service (September 28, 1993). Reuter (September 29, 1993) described him as "an engaging, popular man who knows politics as well as the battlefield."

The most highly publicized event surrounding his retirement was his last speech as the Joint Chiefs of Staff chairman, which he gave at the National Press Club's Newsmaker Luncheon in Washington, D.C., on Tuesday, Wednesday, September 28, 1993, the day before the official resignation ceremony. The event attracted 500 club members, reporters, and media professionals. The speech was carried on CNN, C-SPAN, and National Public Radio and received wide coverage in most major newspapers in the country.

In his introduction, National Press Club President Clayton Boyce described Powell as "the only man who could win either the Democratic or Republican presidential nomination without ever setting foot in New Hampshire."

Colin L. Powell's speech: Thank you very much for that kind introduction, and let me say that we will not be discussing politics. And

I am, once again, delighted to be back at the National Press Club. And before beginning my talk on the role of the military and some of the things we have been doing in recent months and years, let me take this final opportunity perhaps to express my appreciation to the members of the press for the relationship that I've enjoyed with you over the last six years. It's been tough, and you've ripped me apart a lot, but I think I've managed to survive it. But there's still two days left to go.

We haven't always agreed on every issue that's come along during my four years as chairmanship and my two years as national security advisor. When you have agreed with me, I've been amazed at your brilliance. When you've disagreed with me, I have been dismayed by your ignorance. But it has always been for the single purpose of making sure that the American people got the best information. We always had the same mission: to keep the American people informed and to do it in an adversarial way, where the government tries to put out a point of view and it's the purpose of a free and aggressive press to attack and to come at us and to make sure that we were always on the mark, that we were serving the American people.

And so I thank you for the relationship that we've had over the last several years. And I think the people who have benefited from it the most are the people that we treasure the most: the American people. And I once again express my appreciation to you for that relationship.

It's a pleasure for me to be here for my third appearance. My first appearance was five years ago, and it was a final appearance in a sense, because it was the last major speech I gave as national security advisor to President Reagan. It was in the fall of 1988 when we were within a few months of the end of the Reagan-Bush administration. I realized the other day that by coincidence this, of course, is my last major speech as chairman of the Joint Chiefs of Staff. It is a coincidence, but, of course, if I ever appear here again giving a last major speech in some capacity, by then it will become a tradition. Who knows what might happen?

But five years ago when I was here, the theme of my speech was to talk about what the Reagan presidency had been about with respect to foreign policy. It was a proud record, and we could take credit for a number of things. I talked about the historic summit meetings that had been held between President Reagan and President Gorbachev, and I talked at some length about the historic results that had flowed from those meetings. I suggested conservatively five years ago that we might be entering a fundamentally new era in our relationship with the Soviet Union.

I also noted a number of other things that were happening in the world. The cease-fire in that terrible, eight-year old Iran-Iraq war. The Soviet withdrawal from Afghanistan was underway. The flourishing of democracy under Mrs. Aquino in Manila. I touched on the INF treaty, a marvelous treaty that had been concluded which for the first time would begin the process of destroying nuclear weapons and not building them anymore. And I noted at that time that we were on the verge of perhaps having a mandate to begin work on a CFE treaty, conventional forces in Europe, where we could do with conventional forces what we were doing with nuclear weapons, start at disassemble the huge armies that had been created during the course of the cold war.

I also shared some disappointments. I noted that Panama was still under the heel of General Manuel Noriega, and noted that in due course, something would have to be done about that. The world, as I would report to President Reagan a few months later on his last day in office, was relatively quiet. There was a feeling of hope. There was a feeling of anticipation. Yes, there was smoldering and bubbling, but overall, the world seemed quiet and very hopeful. Little did I know, nor did anyone else here at that time know what really was in front of us, what was in store for us for the five years between that appearance and my appearance today.

Yes, it was quiet for a while, and then the lid blew. Eleven months after I spoke here as national security adviser, President Bush appointed me to be chairman of the Joint Chiefs of Staff on the 1st of October, 1989. In the first ninety days, the Berlin Wall fell. My old friend, Manuel Noriega, was dealt with. Mrs. Aquino got in trouble, and American armed forces very surgically and precisely came to her assistance one night in December of 1989. The Warsaw Pact started to crumble. Russian Jews were finally being allowed to emigrate in significant numbers. We saw a free government arise in Hungary. Honecker was out in East Germany, Ceausescu out in Romania. We invaded Panama, as I noted, and in that particular operation, we allowed an elected president to assume office.

And after those first ninety days, things really began to pick up. Total collapse of the Warsaw Pact. The freeing of Eastern Europe and the rise of democratic institutions and nations and movements around the world. The reunification of Germany, something we thought might take years, suddenly burst upon the world stage in a matter of months. Then we saw the end of communism, the end of communism as a political system, the end of communism as an economic system, the end of communism, more importantly, as a value system, the end of communism as something for people to believe in. We watch now patiently months ahead for those few remaining aging starlets in Havana and Pyongyang and one or two other places to catch up with history and realize that their time is past. And we defeated communism by the strength of our economy, our political system, our value system, our military forces, but ultimately it was a contest between ideas. And the idea of communism failed. We saw the end of the Soviet Union, and Mr. Gorbachev, that great reformer, who did so much, was replaced by a great revolutionary by the name of Boris Yeltsin, who we watch on the stage in Moscow today, pushing that revolution forward.

Gorbachev, however, unlike old Soviet leaders, did not disappear and go into oblivion. I discover that, among other things, he has become an environmentalist, and he is setting up his office at a United States Army base, in the Presidio in San Francisco. Is this a great world or what?

CFE that we talked about in 1988 actually became a treaty, and the armies that once glowered at each other in Europe began to fall back and shrink. Elsewhere in the world, we saw Nelson Mandela freed to join South Africa's turbulent political process. We saw elections in Namibia and Angola. Even in Cambodia, we saw in our newspapers this week how that U.N. operation has achieved a brilliant success and the U.N. was able to turn Cambodia back over to its people. In our hemisphere, we saw the end of conflict in El Salvador and Nicaragua. The democratically-elected civilian president in South Korea completed the transition from military rule.

We have marveled at the emergence of the United Nations, assuming responsibilities dreamed of by its founders but only now realizable. There will be difficulties ahead, but we shouldn't allow these U.N. difficulties to overshadow the immensity of this development. Old enemies becoming new friends and partners. Old alliances, such as NATO, adapting to new roles and realities. Shortly after I became chairman in 1989 and early '90, there was much debate about NATO. "Whither NATO?" was the question that all the Europe think tanks were talking about. Now, in 1993, it's not "Whither NATO?"; it's "How can I get in? Where do I find an application card? How can I join this solid alliance?"

In the aftermath of the Gulf War, our hostages in Lebanon were released. The major aggressor in the region, Iraq, was neutralized and made irrelevant, even though Saddam Hussein and the Iraqi regime is still very annoying. And the Middle East peace process re-energized, leading ultimately to the historic ceremony that we all saw just a few weeks ago, where President Clinton presided on the White House lawn over the signing of those agreements between Prime Minister Rabin and Chairman Arafat, where they shook hands in that memorable picture on an agreement to recognize each other.

Chairman Arafat, who was also a guest here, wasn't even wearing his trademark pistol that day, but he was turned out in a smartly-tailored uniform, and a little while later, that afternoon or the next day, he was asked by an inquisitive reporter why he wore a uniform. And he remarked, "Why not? Chairman Powell wears a uniform." So even in my declining days I find myself a fashion role model.

But who—if I had come to this audience three months ago and told you that on Friday, the 24th of September, 1993, the two lead stories combined on the front page of the *New York Times* would be the Israeli Knesset approving an agreement to recognize the PLO and right underneath it the South African Parliament agreeing to integrate blacks into the political process— amazing times, historic times, unprecedented times.

And the United States' armed forces have been incredibly busy dealing with these historic events. Panama—but that's not all. We rescued United States' embassies in Liberia and Somalia. We had to send troops, regretfully, to Los Angeles, to deal with a riot that shocked us, and we sent our troops to rescue our fellow Americans in south Florida after a terrible hurricane. We rescued Haitians at sea and ran a camp for them at Guantanamo while working for a restoration of their democracy, a restoration that we hope is almost at hand. We undertook humanitarian operations on a scale never seen before in Bosnia and Bangladesh, in Guam and Somalia, in northern Iraq, in Russia, and a dozen other places.

And of course, the highlight of all of these activities of the last four years can best be characterized as Desert Storm and Norm. Saddam Hussein reminded us, in case we needed any reminding, that there was still evil in the world, and President Bush and

Secretary Cheney sent 541,000 Americans 8,000 miles to join a massive coalition to deal with this particular brand of evil. Led by General Schwarzkopf, whose performance, brilliant performance, electrified a nation and a world. Those troops under his command did well and made America proud of its armed forces again in a way that we had not seen since VJ and VE days back in 1945.

We were engulfed in parades. It got so bad that by July I was getting calls from commanders saying, "Chairman, we've got to stop the parades. The troops are getting tired of parades. Their feet are getting flat, they are getting fat from all of this food that they get at these parade parties. When can we go back to training?" I said, "Not till the American people have had their fill." Those parades bonded us again—people's Army, Navy, Air Force, Marine Corps, Coast Guard—bonded us again with the American people in a way that bridged the estrangement of the post-Korea and post-Vietnam periods. We included in those parades our Vietnam veterans and our Korean buddies, and shared with them so that they finally had the parades that they didn't get before. GI Joe and GI Jane again became terms of endearment and not derision.

Almost 30 times in the past four years our armed forces have been called on to fight wars, to restore and preserve peace, to relieve pain, to provide hope, to deter aggression, to show the flag, to back up diplomacy, to show the American will, to stand watch quietly in places like Korea, to reassure friends and to sober enemies. In every instance they've gone about their job with a competency and with a spirit too rarely seen in our country: proud, patriotic, selfless, drug-free, the best and brightest of American youth. And the American people responded. Perhaps that's why now as an institution we are polled as perhaps one of the most highly regarded institutions in the nation.

Now, ladies and gentlemen, I won't bother comparing the polling data on the American armed forces with any groups that might perhaps be represented in this room today. Of this record of accomplishment on the part of the armed forces, I am enormously proud, and I am, of course, enormously proud to have been a member of this group.

And yet, for all that has happened in these five years, it is probably only a foretaste of the revolutionary events that are just ahead. History seems to be taking two paths. On one path, some nations are moving forward to new democratic futures with hope for their people. President Yeltsin and what he's doing in Russia is a good example. The other path, however, is a little more confused, a little more dangerous. Some have yet to step on other paths, but others have taken this second path and have returned to 1914 to fight out old hatreds and grudges that had been put on hold by the superpower cold war pause button.

So we enter a time of hope and promise and a time still of great danger and uncertainty. It will take all of our best wisdom to navigate through these troubled times. It will take American leadership. The debates that we're seeing now about unilateralism or multilateralism or isolationism and interventionism and the other "isms" are somewhat silly and they miss the point. The point is that history and destiny have made America the leader of the world that would be free. And the world that would be free is looking to us for inspiration. The world that would be free trusts America, trusts our values, trusts our people, trusts what we stand for.

We must play that role in whatever form it presents itself. It means political leadership. It means diplomatic leadership. It means economic leadership. And it means leadership of all kinds backed up by a strong military. This isn't to say we will go everywhere and do everything or be the world's policemen. We will have to make choices, and there will be limits. But we cannot step back away from this position of leadership. Where we can make a difference, we must try to make that difference. And so I expect our armed forces to be busier in the days ahead than they have been in the nice static garrison days of the cold war.

In this torrent of history over the past four years, I have had two primary goals as chairman. The first one was to make sure that we accomplished successfully every operational mission assigned to us by the secretary of defense and the president and the American people. Second, to begin the process of restructuring and downsizing all of our armed forces in response to this new changed environment, the absence of the cold war and to do it in a way that preserved the capability and the quality of our armed forces. No demobilization, no breaking apart this superb aggregation of young men and women.

Others will make the final evaluation, but I feel pretty good about both of these goals. The more difficult of the two was the downsizing and restructuring. The first thing we did a few years ago was to drop the cold war as a planning assumption. In the absence of a Soviet Union, in the absence of an empire of communism to orchestrate all of this, cold war was over. World War III was unthinkable. We no longer had to be prepared to fight everywhere in the world at once against an empire. And the new strategic assumption which was adopted by President Bush and Secretary Cheney in 1990 was to concentrate on fighting two regional conflicts that might emerge. Why two? Because you don't want to be so occupied with one that you don't have a capacity to handle another one and thereby tempt another one. It's as simple as that.

I'm pleased that President Clinton and Secretary Aspin have now built on that rather simple strategic principle and we are allowed to move forward with our restructuring of the armed forces. We used first the concept of the base force to control our descent from our cold war highs. President Clinton has now approved Secretary Aspin's bottom-up review force, which allows us to go down even lower, but a controlled descent. I am not concerned about the name of the force or the name of the process. I am driven of a need to preserve for future presidents, for future secretaries, for future chairmen, for future generations a force capable of executing any future strategy of successfully dealing with a future crisis, a crisis that nobody today can predict, but most assuredly will arrive at 2:00 one morning some time in the future. And I am confident, hopeful, my prayer is there'll be a force ready to deal with that crisis when it comes.

What we had to do to avoid this rapid demobilization was to begin it in a sensible, prudent manner. We decided to go down about 25 percent, and now we have accelerated that to go down even further. This hasn't been an easy process. It's been one of the most difficult management challenges ever presented to the Department of Defense. Six hundred thousand to seven hundred thousand troops are in the process of being discharged. We've cut the size of the Army and the Navy and the Air Force 40 percent, 25 percent of the Marine Corps. We've eliminated or will eliminate in the course of the next several years 70 percent of the nuclear weapons that were in our inventory when I became chairman just four years ago. That'll be done shortly after the turn of the century.

Hundreds of hardware programs have been cut. Hundreds of bases being closed. Reserves and civilian employees being reduced by the hundreds of thousands. In the last several years alone, 200,000 troops have been brought home with their families from Europe, a major contraction of the defense industry. So the armed forces, ladies and gentlemen, are paying and will continue to pay a peace dividend. But we have also seen that the peace dividend has temporarily hurt the economy. That will sort itself out in time as our free economic system and the conversion practices of the Department of Defense allow the economy to move into this new direction and away from too much of a reliance on defense spending.

And through it all, the force remains ready. The force remains of extremely high quality with high morale, ready to perform missions and performing difficult missions around the world today. In some ways, the force of today is even better than a few years ago. We have gone a long way toward operating as a team, rather than just four separate services. You saw that in Desert Storm, where we all came together under a single commander, General Schwarzkopf, and service preferences and parochial considerations was secondary to the needs of the team.

But we learned a lot about ourselves in Desert Storm. We found that we had to make improvements. And we've been hard at work for the last two years making those improvements. We worked hard then to come up with a joint doctrine for all services, joint procedures for all services. We don't want to unify the services, however. Some critics of mine have suggested that in the roles and missions work I've done I didn't go far enough with respect to merging the activities of the services. Some people would even take it to the extreme, and I'm rather critical of these views. I'm not interested in creating the Aeroflot model in the armed forces of the United States.

We need each and every one of our services. They bring forward from the past proud traditions. I have yet to find a combat capability in any of those four services we did not have a need for at some time over the last four years. So we could do better. We can get rid of redundancy, but let's not get rid of complementarity where it serves the nation's purpose.

We have to remember also that we're warriors. We're not a church picnic group. We're warriors. And I want every Air Force fighter pilot to go into the sky believing he's the best fighter pilot in the world, he's a top gun alongside his Navy counterpart. I want them to believe each one is better than the other. I want an American Marine infantryman to believe there is no infantryman better on the face of the earth. And I want an Army American infantryman to be sure that that Marine is wrong because he's better than he is. That kind of competition serves our interests well. It gives you the kind of proud force that we have now. But when it's time to do a mission, when it's time to go to war, all of that gets set aside and there has to be one team going to war. On any one crisis, one service might get the game ball, but it takes the team to win.

Tomorrow in Norfolk, Virginia, or later this week in Norfolk, Virginia, probably Friday, we're going to take this one step forward when we re-designate the United States Atlantic Command with a new mission. Traditionally, all of our forces in overseas theaters worked for a single commander. Thus, everybody in Europe worked for General Shalikashvili. Everybody in the Pacific works for Admiral Larson. But here in the United States the services maintain control over the operational training of units here in the United States. So that the Army had principal responsibility for large unit training of Army units; similarly with the other services.

What we are going to do with this Atlantic Command, we're going to give the Atlantic Command the operational control of all of the available, deployable active forces here in the United States, and the responsibility of that command will be to train them as joint teams, train them so that when the whistle blows and a General Schwarzkopf needs troops in the future or a General Thurman needs troops in Panama, what they will receive are forces that have been trained jointly by a single commander whose headquarters is in Norfolk. No more pickup games. You're going to get forces ready to go to combat right away. And since it is no longer just a Navy command with a focus on the Russian navy—no longer a problem—the commander of our Atlantic Command may be a Naval officer or an Army officer or a Marine officer or an Air Force officer. From now on, best person gets the job; no longer service-oriented.

So we're going to be doing more and more things like that. We are starting to send Navy instructor pilots to Air Force schools and Air Force instructor pilots to Navy schools so we can ultimately integrate the training of all of our pilots. We have done quite a bit in terms of integrating our strategic forces. We're going into the common development of aircraft components. More will follow as this team concept really becomes imbedded within the Department of Defense.

And I want to give great credit to my colleagues on the Joint Chiefs of Staff—brilliant military leaders, dedicated military leaders—for their efforts to bring this about. They are not what you all refer to all the time as the "Pentagon brass," a term I absolutely detest. And if you're going to give me a gift as a result of this luncheon, do not give me some cheap mug. What I want you to do is go back to your computers and get rid of the term "Pentagon brass." Is that too much to ask? Probably, but I make the case anyway. We have some of the most distinguished leaders in the Armed Forces of the United States, and that's what you ought to call them, and not "the Pentagon brass." But, alas, I know I dream.

You see how proud I am of this force. One of the questions that is always on everybody's mind is how and when do we use that force, what are the circumstances under which you commit the Armed Forces of the United States? And I am usually characterized in this debate as the reluctant warrior and someone who always seeks decisive results. I'm guilty. I'm guilty. Because the fact of the matter is that one of the most important decisions that a president has to make is to commit the Armed Forces of the United States in combat. And the single most important job, the legal job, of the chairman of the Joint Chiefs of Staff and the other members of the Joint Chiefs of Staff have is to advise the president and the secretary of defense on issues relating to the commitment of those armed forces.

This is not an abstract intellectual exercise. It is nothing less than sending young American sons and daughters off to a foreign land to fight other sons and daughters, perhaps to kill them and to be killed. And sometimes it does end tragically, as we saw again this past weekend in Somalia, where we lost three of our youngsters in that terrible tragedy with the helicopter. But it's what they are trained to do. They're warriors. That's why we have armed forces. But it is never a decision to be taken lightly. We are not committing mercenaries. We are committing sons and daughters.

And committing forces of the United States also means that you're committing the will and the strength of the American people. We must go into battle with the support and understanding of the American people. Frequently a president has to make a quick decision and to go into battle before he really knows what the American people might think about his action. But in due course the American people will indicate their support of a particular decision, and that decision should always be made, in my view, with a clear purpose in mind. And if it isn't possible to come up with a clear purpose, if the situation, as is too often the case, is murky, then you should understand its murkiness and know that, as you go into this, you have to find the clarity that you will eventually need.

Reluctance to use military force is an American military tradition. I can trace it back from Washington to Grant to Eisenhower. Since war is ultimately a political act, not a military act, give political tools the opportunity to work first. Military power can back up political tools and make them credible. We saw that in the cold war, which we prevailed in without firing a shot. And it is the responsibility of military leaders to ensure that political leaders have an analysis of all the options: the good, the bad, the popular, the unpopular, the fashionable, the unfashionable. And only then, when the candid advice of the military leaders are provided to our political leaders, can they then make proper decisions, make that political decision that the Constitution only gives them the right to do, and then we, the military leaders, execute.

And my view is we should always execute for decisive results. Decisive doesn't mean overwhelming. Decisive means decisive. It means committing the force needed to achieve the political objective. If the political objective is very, very limited, very circumscribed, the force should still be decisive in order to achieve that limited objective. The Philippines is one of my favorite examples. On the first of December, I think it was, 1989, late at night we got a call for help from the Philippine government. Rebellion was underway. "We want you to come bomb a Philippine air base" where Philippine planes were taking off to attack Mrs. Aquino.

We examined it quickly. We made some judgments and decided that in this case we didn't need to apply overwhelming force. We thought that just sending some F-4 fighters with great young Air Force pilots aboard buzzing the airfield would be enough to keep those planes on the ground without us having to kill a single person. Precise application of military force for a very limited objective. And we made it all up within about two hours, and the mission was over in two hours. And the instructions we gave to the pilots were very simple and clear: go over the airfield and demonstrate extreme hostile intent. They did. Mission completed.

My philosophy in all this is rather simple: match political expectations to military means in a wholly realistic way. Don't slide in, don't mislead yourself. This isn't some syndrome I'm suffering from. It comes from 35 years of experience. As a first lieutenant, I saw what doing otherwise was: results were in the Bay of Pigs, President Kennedy. As a major and a captain and a lieutenant colonel, I saw what doing otherwise produced in Vietnam. And in Beirut as a major general in 1983, I saw what doing otherwise can result in.

In the case of places like Somalia where the mission was nice and clear cut when we went in, but it's becoming a little more difficult now. We will have to continue our calculus of political objectives, means applied to that objective, and sort them out. But because things get difficult, you don't cut and run. You work the problem and try to find a correct solution.

I'm pleased that the philosophy I've just espoused has seen favor with the two presidents and the two secretaries of defense that I have worked for in the past four years. We've learned our lesson I think. At the end of the day, though, strategy and force structure and matters such as I have been talking about kind of go by the wayside. At the end of the day, all of our plans, the missions we have in mind, rest on the shoulder of the individual GI, be he a soldier, a sailor, an airman, a Marine, or Coast Guardsman, he or she is at the heart and soul of our armed forces: cold, tired, frightened, away from home, a soldier of the nation willing to go anywhere, to do anything, to sacrifice whatever is required for the mission. Hundreds of thousands of such wonderful young men and women, trained and bonded together, make up the armed forces of the United States. They are a treasure. And they count on us, all of us here today, for leadership, for support, and for caring for them.

I am so very proud to have been one of them for the past 35 years, and for the last four years to have represented them. It all ends for me on Thursday. I've been a soldier all my life. I've never wanted to be anything else. I have loved every single minute of it, and I thank the nation for having given me the opportunity to serve in the proud armed forces of the United States.

Thank you.

APPENDIX

BIOGRAPHICAL NOTES

ARAFAT, YASIR (PSEUDONYM OF MOHAMMED ABED AR'OUF ARAFAT). (1923–   ). Born, Jerusalem; member of League of Palestinian Students, 1944, president 1952–1956; formed Al Fatah movement, 1956; president of executive committee, Palestine National Liberation Movement, 1968–   , president, 1973–   .

BILLINGTON, JAMES H. (1929–   ). Born, Bryn Mawr, Pennsylvania; B.A., Princeton University, 1950; Ph.D., Oxford University, Rhodes Scholar, 1953; Litt. D., Lafayette College, 1981; University of Pittsburgh, 1988; L.H.D., LeMoyne College, 1982; Rhode Island College, 1982; Catholic University of America, 1983; New York University, 1987; Furman University, 1986; 1st lieutenant, U.S. Army, 1953–56; instructor, Harvard University, 1957–58; fellow, Russian Research Center, 1958–59, assistant professor, 1958–61; associate professor, Princeton University, 1962–64, professor, 1964–73; director, Woodrow Wilson International Center for Scholars, 1973–87; Librarian of Congress, Library of Congress, 1987–   ; visiting research professor, Inst. History of Academic Sciences of USSR in Moscow, 1966–67, University of Helsinki, 1960–61; Ecole des Hautes Etudes en Sciences Sociales, 1985, 1988; scholar-in-residence, Aspen Institute for Humanistic Studies, 1974, 1975, 1977; distinguished visitor, Japan Foundation, 1976; chairman, Board of Foreign Scholarships, 1971–73; member, 1973–76; vice-chairman, Atlantic Council's Working Group on the Successor Generation, 1982–86; trustee, St. Alban's School, 1979–82; director, American Association for the Advancement of Slavic Studies, 1968–71; special consultant on East-West matters, Chase Manhattan Bank, 1971–73; guest commentator for CBS on Nixon-Brezhnev summit meetings, 1972, 1973; member, American Academy of Arts and Sciences, Phi Beta Kappa, American Philosophical Society; McCosh Faculty fellow Princeton University, Guggenheim fellow, 1960–61; Fulbright research professorship, University of Helsinki, 1960–61; decorated, Chevalier Order and Arts and Letters of France; author, *Mikhailovsky and Russian Populism*, 1958, *The Icon and the Axe, an Interpretive History of Russian Culture*, 1966, *Fire in the Minds of Men: Origins of the Revolutionary Faith*, 1980; contributor to books and journals; member of the advisory board, *Foreign Affairs, Theology Today*, 1974–84; script writer and host, Humanities Film Forum, 1973.

BRADLEY, BILL (WILLIAM M.) (1943–   ). Born, Crystal City, Missouri; B.A., Princeton University, 1965; M.A., Oxford University, 1968 (Rhodes Scholar, 1965–68); United States Air Force Reserve, 1967–78; player, New York Knickerbockers professional basketball team, 1967–77; United

States Senator, New Jersey, 1979–   ; member, Finance Committee, Energy Committee, Special Committee on Aging, Select Committee on Intelligence; member, National Advertising Council on Rights of the Child; author, *Life on the Run,* 1976, *The Fair Tax,* 1984.

CLINTON, HILLARY RODHAM (1947–   ). Born, Chicago, Illinois; B.A., Wellesley College, 1969; J.D., Yale University, 1973; attorney, Children's Defense Fund, 1973–74; legal counsel, Carnegie Council on Children, 1973–74; assistant professor of law, University of Arkansas, 1974–77; partner, Rose Law Firm, Little Rock, 1977–   ; lecturer, Law School, University of Arkansas—Little Rock, 1979–80; board of directors, Children's Defense Fund, New World Foundation, Arkansas Advocate for Children and Families; Arkansas Woman of the Year, 1984, Arkansas Young Mother of the Year, 1984, Outstanding Layman of the Year, Phi Delta Kappa, 1984; author, *Handbook on Legal Rights for Arkansas Women.*

CLINTON, BILL (WILLIAM JEFFERSON) (1946–   ). Born, Hope, Arkansas; B.S., Georgetown University, 1968; Rhodes Scholar, Oxford University, 1968–70; J.D., Yale University, 1973; professor, University of Arkansas Law School, 1973–76; Attorney General of Arkansas, 1977–79; Governor of Arkansas, 1979–81, 1983–92; counsel, Wright, Lindsey, & Jennings, Little Rock, 1981–82; president of the United States, 1993–   ; chairman, Education Commission of the States, 1986–87; chairman, Democratic Leadership Council, 1990–91.

COLSON, CHARLES WENDELL (1931–   ). Born, Boston, Massachusetts; A.B., Brown University, 1953; J.D., George Washington University, 1959; L.L.D. (Honorary), Wheaton College, 1982, Houghton College, 1983, Eastern College, 1983, Anderson College, 1984, Taylor University, 1985, Geneva College, 1987, John Brown University, 1988, Ashbury College, 1989, Le Tourneau University, 1990, Palm Beach Atlantic College, 1989; USMCR, captain, Korea; assistant to assistant secretary of the Navy, 1955–56; administrative assistant to Senator Leverett Saltonstall U.S. Senate, 1956–61; private practice, Washington, 1961–69; special counsel to president of U.S., 1969–72; partner, Colson & Shapiro, Washington, 1973–74; associate, Fellowship House, Washington, 1975–76; Prison Fellowship, 1976–   ; member, Order of Coif, Beta Theta Pi; awards, Religious Heritage award, Freedom Foundation, 1977, Abe Lincoln award, Southern Baptist Convention, 1984, Poverello award, University of Steubenville, 1986, Distinguished Service award, Salvation Army, 1990, Humanitarian award, Southern Baptist Convention, 1991, Domino's Pizza award, the Templeton Prize for Progress in Religion, 1993; author, *Born Again,* 1975; *Life Sentence,* 1979; *Crime and the Responsible Community,* 1980; *Loving God,* 1983; *Who Speaks for God,* 1985; *Kingdoms in Conflict,* 1987; *Against the Night,* 1989; *The God of Stones and Spiders* (with Jack Eckerd); *Why America Doesn't Work,* 1991; *The Body,* 1992.

GORE, ALBERT JR. (1948–   ). Born, Washington, D.C.; B.A., Harvard University, 1969; postgraduate work, Graduate School of Religion, Vanderbilt University, 1971–72, Law School, 1974–76; U.S. Army, 1969–71,

Vietnam; investigative reporter, editorial writer *The Tennessean,* 1971–76; member 95th–98th Congress from Tennessee, 1977–1985; U.S. senator from Tennessee, 1985–93; homebuilder and land developer Tanglewood Home Builders Company, 1971–76; livestock and tobacco farmer, from 1973; Vice President of U.S., 1993–   ; author, *Earth in the Balance: Ecology and the Human Spirit,* 1992.

HACKNEY, FRANCIS SHELDON (1933–   ). Born, Birmingham, Alabama; B.A., Vanderbilt University, 1955; M.A., 1963; Ph.D., 1966 Yale University; USNR, 1956–61; member of the faculty, Princeton University, 1965–75; associate professor, history, 1969–72; professor and provost, 1972–75; president, Tulane University, New Orleans, 1975–80; professor of history, University of Pennsylvania, Philadelphia, 1981–   ; chairman, National Endowment for the Humanities, Washington, 1993; Board of directors, Carnegie Foundation for Advancement in Teaching, 1976–84, 86–   ; Educational Testing Service, 1977–83; American Council on Education, 1977–78, 91–   ; member of American Philosophy Society; American History Association; Southern History Association; Organization of American Historians; recipient Charles S. Sydnor award, Southern History Association 1970; Bevridge prize, American History Association, 1970; author, *Populism to Progressivism in Alabama,* 1969; editor, *Populism: The Critical Issues,* 1971; *Understanding the American Experience* (with others), 1973.

HILLIARD, WILLIAM ARTHUR (1927–   ). Born, Chicago; B.A., Pacific University, 1952; Oregonian Publishing Company, 1952–   ; vice-president, American Society of Newspaper Editors, 1992–1993, president, 1993–1994; U.S. Navy, 1945–1946; Anti-Defamation League Torch of Liberty award, University of Oregon Public Service award, Amos E. Voorhies award, 1991.

LINOWITZ, SOL MYRON (1913–   ). Born, Trenton, New Jersey; A.B., Hamilton College, 1935; J.D., Cornell University, 1938; honorary degrees from 23 colleges and universities; admitted to New York bar, 1938; assistant general counsel OPA, 1942–44; partner in Sutherland, Linowitz & Williams, 1946–58; Harris, Beach, Keating, Wilcox & Linowitz, 1958–66; senior partner, Coudert Brothers, 1969–   ; member of boards of numerous corporations; USNR, 1944–46; ambassador to OAS, 1966–69; chairman, National Urban Coalition, 1970–   ; member, Phi Beta Kappa, Phi Kappa Phi, Delta Sigma Rho, Order of Coif; author, *This Troubled Urban World;* contributor, professional journals.

MCCULLOUGH, DAVID (1933–   ). Born, Pittsburgh, Pennsylvania; B.A., Yale University, 1955; honorary degrees from several colleges and universities; writer, editor, Time Inc. 1956–1961; author of *The Great Bridge,* 1972, *The Path Between the Seas,* 1977, *The Johnstown Flood,* 1978, *Mornings on Horseback,* 1981; *Brave Companions,* 1991, *Truman,* 1992 (winner of Pulitzer Prize for biography, 1993), freelance author and contributing editor to various journals and magazines.

MENEILLY, ROBERT H. (1925–   ). Born, Pittsburgh, Pennsylvania; A.B., Monmouth College, 1945, Pittsburgh Theological Seminary, 1947; D.D., Monmouth College, 1956, L.L.D., College of Emporia, 1975; Senior pastor, The Village Presbyterian Church, Prairie Village, Kansas, 1947–   ; Junior Chamber of Commerce Man of the Year; Silver Beaver Scout award; Johnson County, Kansas, Citizen of the Year award; Salvation Army Booth award; Citation by National Conference of Christians and Jews; author, *Happiness Is*, 1980.

MOSELEY-BRAUN, CAROL E. (1947–   ). Born, Chicago, Illinois; B.A., University of Illinois, Chicago, 1969; J.D., University of Chicago, 1972; law clerk, 1970–71; associate, Davis, Miner, and Barnhill, 1972; assistant attorney, United States Department of Justice of Illinois, 1973–1977; Illinois state representative, 1977–1992; Cook County recorder of deeds/registrar of titles; United States Senate, 1993–   ; recipient of several public service, legislative official, and education awards.

PERES, SHIMON (1923–   ). Born in Poland; emigrated to Palestine, 1934; head of Israel Naval Service, 1948; deputy director of Ministry of Defense, 1952–1953, Director General, 1953–1959; member, Knesset, 1959–   ; holder of several government ministries, 1969–   ; prime minister of Israel, 1984–1986; author, *The Next Step*, 1965, *David's Sling*, 1970, *Tomorrow is Now*, 1978, *From These Men*, 1979.

POWELL, COLIN LUTHER (1937–   ). Born, New York, New York; B.S., City University of New York, 1958; M.B.A., George Washington University, 1971; commissioned 2nd lieutenant U.S. Army, 1958; advanced through grades to general, 1989; commander, 2nd Brigade, 101st Airborne Division, 1976–77; executive assistant to secretary Department of Energy, 1979; senior military assistant to secretary Department of Defense, 1979–81; assistant division commander 4th Infantry Division, Department of Defense, Ft. Carson, Colorado, 1981–83; military assistant to Secretary of Defense, 1983–86; U.S. V Corps, Europe 1986–87; deputy assistant to the president for national security affairs, The White House, Washington, 1987; assistant to President for national security affairs, Washington, 1987–89; commander-in-chief, Forces Command, Ft. McPherson, Georgia, 1989–   ; chairman Joint Chiefs of Staff, The Pentagon, Washington 1989–93; Decorated, Legion of Merit, Bronze Star, Air Medal, Purple Heart; recipient, Medal of Freedom.

RABIN, YITZHAK (1922–   ). Born in Jerusalem; Kadoorie Agricultural School, Kfar Tabor, and Staff College, England; holder of several posts in the Israel military, 1943–1968; ambassador to the United States, 1968–1973; member, Knesset, 1974–   ; prime minister of Israel, 1974–1977, 1992–   ; recipient of several honorary degrees; author, *The Rabin Memoirs*, 1979.

RATHER, DAN (1931–   ). Born, Wharton, Texas; B.A., Sam Houston State College, 1953; instructor of journalism, Sam Houston State College for 1 year; later worked for U.P.I. and *Houston Chronicle;* with CBS; joined staff of radio, Station KTRH (CBS affiliate), Houston, as newswriter, reporter, and later, as news director; became director of news and public affairs with CBS Houston TV affiliate, KHOU-TV, in the late 1950's; became White House correspondent, 1964; overseas bureaus, including chief of London bureau, 1965–66; worked in Vietnam then returned to White House position, fall, 1966; anchorman-correspondent, "CBS Reports," 1974–75; co-editor "60 Minutes," CBS-TV, 1975–81; anchorman Dan Rather Reporting CBS Radio Network, 1977–   ; Midwest desk CBS news coverage of national election night returns, 1972–88; anchorman, managing editor "CBS Evening News with Dan Rather," 1981–   ; recipient, 115 Emmy awards; Distinguished Achievement for Broadcasting award, University of Southern California Journalism Alumni Association; author, *The Palace Guard* (with Gary Gates), 1974; *The Camera Never Blinks* (with Mickey Herskowitz), 1977; memoirs, *I Remember* (with Peter Wyden), 1991.

RENO, JANET (1938–   ). Born, Miami, Florida; A. B. Cornell University, 1960; LL.B. Harvard University, 1963; associate, Brigham and Brigham, 1963–1967; partner, Lewis and Reno, 1967–1971; staff director, Florida House of Representatives, 1971–1972; Florida state attorney, 1978–1993; U.S. Attorney General, Department of Justice, 1993–   .

ROBERTS, EUGENE LESLIE, JR. (1932–   ). Born, Goldsboro, North Carolina; AA Mars Hill Jr. College, 1950–52; BA University of North Carolina, 1952–54; postgrad, Harvard University, 1961–62; LLD (hon.), Colby College, 1989. Local government reporter Goldsboro News Argus, North Carolina, 1956–58; maritime reporter, Norfolk, Virginian-Pilot, Virginia, 1958–59; Raleigh News & Observer, 1959–61, Sunday editor, 1962–63; labor writer, Detroit Free Press, 1963–64, city editor, 1964–65; chief So. correspondent New York Times, 1965–67; war correspondent New York Times, 1969–72; executive editor, vice president Philadelphia Inquirer and Philadelphia Newspapers, Inc., 1972–80, executive editor, senior vice president, 1980–86, executive editor, president, 1986–   ; member Pulitzer Prize Board, Columbia University, New York, 1982–89, chairman, 1989–90; chairman American committee International Press Institute., 1987–   ; chairman national advisory board UPI, Washington, 1986–   ; board visitors school Journalism, University of Maryland, 1983–   , School of Journalism Pennsylvania State University, 1983–89; chairman board visitors School of Journalism, University of North Carolina, 1989–   , Knight Center for Specialized Journalism, University of Maryland, 1987–   ; board visitors University of Michigan Journalist-in-residence Program; board governors Columbia University Seminar and News Media on Society, Graduate School of Journalism. Author (with Jack Nelson) *The Censors and the Schools*, 1963; editor (with David R. Jones) *Assignment America*, 1973. Recipient William Allen White award, University of Kansas. 1985, John Peter Zenger award for Freedom of the Press, University of Arizona, 1987, Distinguishing Contributions to Journalism award National Free Press Foundation, 1989, Elijah Parish Lovejoy award for Freedom of the Press, 1989, Distinguishing Achievement in Journalism award University of Southern California, 1989; Nieman fellow,   , 1961–

62. Member American Society of Newspaper Editors, Society of Professional Journalists, First Amendment Coalition (executive board).

SIMON, PAUL (1928–   ). Born, Eugene, Oregon; student, University of Oregon, 1945–46; student, Dana College, 1946–48; LL.D., Dana college, 1965; D. Litt., McKendree College, 1965; D.C.L., Greenville College, 1968; LL.D., Concordia College, 1986, Lincoln College, 1969, Loyola University, 1969, Valparaiso University, 1976; publisher, *Troy (Illinois) Tribune*, 1948–66; member, Illinois House of Representatives, 1955–63, Illinois Senate, 1963–69; lieutenant governor of Illinois, 1969–73; professor of public affairs, Sangamon State University, Springfield, 1973; member, 94th–98th Congresses from 24th District of Illinois; United States Senator from Illinois, 1985–   ; U.S. presidential candidate, 1987–88; board of directors, Dana College, McKendree college; member, Lutheran Human Relations Association, NAACP, Urban League; fellow, John F. Kennedy Institute of Politics, Harvard, 1973; recipient, American Political Science Association award, 1957; named Best Legislator 7 times; author, *Lovejoy: Martyr to Freedom*, 1964; *Lincoln's Preparation for Greatness*, 1966; *A Hungry World*, 1966; *Protestant-Catholic Marriages Can Succeed* (with Jeanne Hurley Simon), 1967; *You Want to Change the World? So Change It*, 1971; *The Glass House, The Politics of Hunger* (with Jeanne Hurley Simon), 1973; *Politics and Morality in the Nation's Capitol*, 1984; *Beginnings*, 1986; *Let's Put America Back to Work*, 1986; *Winners and Losers*, 1989; *Advice and Consent*, 1992; contributor, articles to periodicals.

CUMULATIVE SPEAKER INDEX

1990–1994

A cumulative author index to the volumes of *Representative American Speeches* for the years 1937–1938 through 1959–1960 appears in the 1959–1960 volume, for the years 1960–1961 through 1969–1970 in the 1969–1970 volume, for the years 1970–1971 through 1979–1980 in the 1979–1980 volume, and for the years 1980–1981 through 1989–1990 in the 1989–1990 volume.

INDEX TO VOLUME 66 (1994)
BY SUBJECT

AFRO-AMERICAN CHILDREN
Conduct of Life
If the child is safe. M.W. Edelman. From *The Measure of Our Success*. **66:1**

ALIEN LABOR
Mary Poppins speaks out. M. Beck. *Newsweek* F. 22, '93. **66:1**

ANIMAL SACRIFICE
A chicken on every altar? Supreme Court Santería case. B. Cohn and D.A. Kaplan *Newsweek* N. 9, '92. **66:4**

ART, CHINESE
Chinese art today: no U-turn. J.L. Cohen. *Art News* F. '92. **66:3**

ART AND STATE
China
Chinese art today: no U-turn. J.L. Cohen. *Art News* F. '92. **66:3**
United States
A sense of proportion. D. MacCullough. Speech delivered Ap. 11, '94. **66:6**

BILINGUAL EDUCATION
United States
Bilingual education. *CQ Researcher* Ag. 13, '93. **66:2**
English in a multicultural America. D. Baron. *Social Policy* Spring '91. **66:2**
Student leader a reflection of bilingual model. L. Davis. *Phoenix Gazette* D. 20, '93. **66:2**

BILINGUALISM
The battle over preserving the English language. G. Imhoff and G. Bikales. *USA Today* (periodical) Ja. '87. **66**
English plus: statement of purpose. *Epic Events* F. '89. **66:2**
Language debates in the United States. J.B. Draper and M. Jimenez. *Epic Events* F. '90. **66:2**

Legislating assimilation: the English-only movement. M.R. Halton. *Christian Century* N. 29, '89. **66:2**

Official English might sound good, but it could translate into school trouble. J. Crawford. *American School Board Journal* Mr. '89. **66:2**

One nation . . . indivisible? S.I. Hayakawa. From The Washington Institute for Values in Public Policy. **66:2**

Pro-con: should English be our official language? L. Eskin. *Scholastic Update* My. 6, '88. **66:2**

A story of two children. A. Shanker. *New York Times* D. 26, '93. **66:2**

Towards a united America. Brochure from U.S. English '93. **66:2**

Arizona

Against English only. R. Rodriguez. *Hispanic* Ap. 18, '90. **66:2**

White supremacy or apple pie? K.L. Adams. *Arizona English Bulletin* Winter '92. **66:2**

Florida

English vs Spanish in south Florida. *CQ Researcher* Ag. 13, '93. **66:2**

BLACK FAMILY

Endangered family. M. Ingrassia. *Newsweek* Ag. 30, '93. **66:1**

BOOKS AND READING

Foreign Languages

"The Babel myth": the English-only movement and its implications for libraries. I. Betancourt. *Wilson Library Bulletin* F. '92. **66:2**

BRANCH DAVIDIANS (CULT)

How David Koresh got all those guns. G. Witkin. *U.S. News & World Report* Je. 7, '93. **66:4**

CHILD PSYCHOLOGY

An emotional moonscape: trauma in children. D. Gelman. *Newsweek* My. 17, '93. **66:4**

The meaning of poverty in the world of children. J. Garbarino. *American Behavioral Scientist* Ja./F. '92. **66:1**

CHILD REARING

United States

If the child is safe. M.W. Edelman. From *The Measure of Our Success*. **66:1**

CHILD WELFARE

United States

Government can't buy you love: the best children's program is to put parents first. W.F. Horn. *Policy Review* Spring '93. **66:1**

How community violence affects children, parents, and practitioners. C. Barfield. *Public Welfare* Fall '92. **66:1**

Official English might sound good, but it could translate into school trouble. J. Crawford. *American School Board Journal* Mr. '89. **66:2**

Official English or English only. J.C. Stalker. *English Journal* Mr. '88. **66:2**

One nation . . . Indiviible? S.I. Hayakawa. From The Washington Institute for Values in Public Policy. **66:2**

Towards a united America. Brochure from U.S. English '93. **66:2**
Arizona

Against English only. R. Rodriguez. *Hispanic* Ap. 18, '90. **66:2**

White supremacy or apple pie? K.L. Adams. *Arizona English Bulletin* Winter '92. **66:2**

Florida

English vs Spanish in south Florida. *CQ Researcher* Ag. 13, '93. **66:2**
Court Rulings

Bilingual education. *CQ Researcher* Ag. 13, '93. **66:2**

English-only labels OK, court rules. H. Chiang. *San Francisco Chronicle* D. 10, '93. **66:2**

A story of two children. A. Shanker. *New York Times* D. 26, '93. **66:2**

Workplace language rules. W.E. Lissy. *Supervision* Ap. '93. **66:2**
Military

American military leadership. C. Powell. Speech delivered S. 28, '93. **66:6**
Minorities
Public Opinion

Beyond the cultural wars. S. Hackney. Speech delivered N. 10, '93. **66:6**

If the child is safe. M.W. Edelman. From *The Measure of Our Success*. **66:1**

Language politics and American identity. J. Citrin. *Public Interest* Spring '90. **66:2**

Language debates in the United States. J.B. Draper and M. Jimenez. *Epic Events* F. '90. **66:2**

Official English or English only. J.C. Stalker. *English Journal* Mr. '88. **66:2**

Towards a united America. Brochure from U.S. English '93. **66:2**
Popular Culture

Old news is good news. B. Moyers. *New Perspectives Quarterly* Fall '92. **66:5**

The role of the media in shaping public policy. C. Green. From *The Great Society and Its Legacy: Twenty Years of U.S. Policy*. **66:5**
Religion

The social adaptation of marginal religious movements in America. C.L. Harper and B.F. Le Beau. *Sociology of Religion* Summer '93. **66:4**

UNITED STATES. BUREAU OF ALCOHOL, TOBACCO AND FIREARMS

About

A botched mission in Waco, Texas. J. Popkin and J. Thornton. *U.S. News and World Report* Mr. 15, '93. **66:4**

Tripped up by lies. H.G. Chua-Eoan. *Time* O. 11, '93. **66:4**

UNITED STATES. CONGRESS. SENATE. COMMITTEE ON FOREIGN RELATIONS

U.S. and Chinese policies toward occupied Tibet. From the United States Senate Committee on Foreign Relations. Jl. 28, '92. **66:3**

UNITED STATES. CONGRESS. SENATE. COMMITTEE ON THE JUDICIARY
About

The Clarence Thomas hearings. W. Boot. *Columbia Journalism Review* Ja./F. '92.

UNITED STATES. CONSTITUTION
Amendments

The battle over preserving the English language. G. Imhoff and G. Bikales. *USA Today* (Periodical) Ja. '87. **66:2**

UNITED STATES. FEDERAL BUREAU OF INVESTIGATION
About

The Waco blame game. J. Taylor. *New York* My. 3, '93. **66:4**

UNITED STATES. FEDERAL COMMUNICATIONS COMMISSION
About

Shaping a new media policy. L. Bogart. *The Nation* Jl. 12, '93. **66:4**

UNITED STATES. SUPREME COURT
About

A chicken on every altar. B. Cohn and D.A. Kaplan. *Newsweek* N. 9, '92. **66:4**
Nominees

The Clarence Thomas hearings. W. Boot. *Columbia Journalism Review* Ja./F. '92. **66:5**

WACO (TEX.) CULT SIEGE, 1993

A botched mission in Waco, Texas. J. Popkin and J. Thornton. *U.S. News and World Report* Mr. 15, '93. **66:4**

Eager for the end. J.M. Wall. *Christian Century* My. 5, '93. **66:4**

The last revelation from Waco. I. Solotaroff. *Esquire* Jl. '93. **66:4**

Reflections after Waco: millennialists and the state. M. Barkun. *Christian Century* Je. 2, '93. **66:4**

Tripped up by lies. H.G. Chua-Eoan. *Time* O. 11, '93. **66:4**

The Waco blame game. J. Taylor. *New York* My. 3, '93. **66:4**

Waco revisited. A. Cockburn. *The Nation* O. 18, '93. **66:4**
Children

Children of a lesser god. S.S. Gregory. *Time* My. 17, '93. **66:4**

Children of the cult. G. Carroll. *Newsweek* My. 17, '93. **66:4**

WASHINGTON HEIGHTS (NEW YORK)
Covering the cops. J. Katz. *Columbia Journalism Review* Ja./F. '93. **66:5**